TAXATION OF BILATERAL INVESTMENTS

TAXATION OF BILATERAL INVESTMENTS

Tax Treaties after BEPS

CARLO GARBARINO

*Angelo Sraffa Department of Legal Studies, Bocconi University, Italy and
Senior Fellow of the Melbourne Law School, 2018–19*

Cheltenham, UK • Northampton, MA, USA

Published by
Edward Elgar Publishing Limited
The Lypiatts
15 Lansdown Road
Cheltenham
Glos GL50 2JA
UK

Edward Elgar Publishing, Inc.
William Pratt House
9 Dewey Court
Northampton
Massachusetts 01060
USA

A catalogue record for this book
is available from the British Library

Library of Congress Control Number: 2018967526

This book is available electronically in the **Elgar**online
Law subject collection
DOI 10.4337/9781788976893

ISBN 978 1 78897 688 6 (cased)
ISBN 978 1 78897 689 3 (eBook)

Typeset by Columns Design XML Ltd, Reading

Printed and bound in Great Britain by TJ International Ltd, Padstow, Cornwall

CONTENTS

EXTENDED CONTENTS

ABBREVIATIONS

ACT	Advance Corporation Tax
APA	Advance Pricing Agreements
BEPS	Base Erosion Profit Sharing
CFA	Committee on Fiscal Affairs
CIV	Collective Investment Vehicle
Commentary	Commentary to Model Tax Convention on Income and on Capital (OECD 2017)
CS	Contracting State
CSs	Contracting States
EIG	European Interest Group
FTC	Foreign Tax Credit
LOB	Limitation of Benefits
MAP	Mutual Agreement Procedure
MFN	Most-favoured Nation
MLI	Multilateral Instrument
Model	Model Tax Convention on Income and on Capital (OECD 2017)
PE	Permanent Establishment
PEs	Permanent Establishments
RC	Residence-country
RCs	Residence-countries
REIT	Real Estate Investment Trust
SC	Source-country
SCs	Source-countries
TIEA	Model Tax Information Exchange Agreement
TP	Transfer pricing
VCLT	Vienna Convention on the Law of Treaties

TABLE OF CASES

ARGENTINA

AUSTRALIA

AUSTRIA

BELGIUM

BRAZIL

CANADA

CZECH REPUBLIC

DENMARK

FINLAND

FRANCE

GERMANY

GREECE

INDIA

INDONESIA

ISRAEL

ITALY

JAPAN

LUXEMBOURG

MALAYSIA

MEXICO

THE NETHERLANDS

NEW ZEALAND

NORWAY

POLAND

PORTUGAL

RUSSIA

SINGAPORE

SOUTH AFRICA

SOUTH KOREA

SPAIN

SWEDEN

SWITZERLAND

THAILAND

TURKEY

UNITED KINGDOM

UNITED STATES OF AMERICA

ZIMBABWE

TABLE OF LEGISLATION

INTERNATIONAL LEGLISLATION

EU LEGISLATION

NATIONAL LEGISLATION

USA

INTRODUCTION

In recent years the focus of corporate tax departments has changed from mere **0.01**
tax compliance to aggressive tax planning. Corporate tax departments are
increasingly viewed as profit centres to obtain the most advantageous tax
position, through techniques which include, in addition to tax sheltering,
tax-enhanced financing structures and tax-efficient reorganizations.

These corporate practices can be loosely labelled as 'aggressive tax strategies' **0.02**
and are now compounded with a new phenomenon which has taken even
broader dimensions and that in 2013 has been denominated by the OECD as
'base erosion and profit shifting' (BEPS).[1] The OECD and G20 countries
adopted in July 2013 a 15-point Action Plan to address BEPS (hereinafter the
'BEPS Project') with the aim to create consensus-based international tax rules.
In 2014–15 the OECD has issued 15 reports in the context of the overall
BEPS project.[2] In 2016 a Multilateral Instrument[3] (hereinafter the 'MLI') has
been issued and in 2017 the Commentary to the *OECD Model Tax Convention
on Income and on Capital* (hereinafter respectively the 'Commentary', and the
'Model'[4]) have been released.

The changes advocated by the BEPS project to the OECD Model Tax **0.03**
Convention to become directly binding require amendments to, or renegotia-
tions of, thousands of bilateral treaties currently in existence. This creates a
real issue in terms of timing because such process of renegotiation is time-
consuming and uncertain. To address this problem the MLI is ultimately
aimed at implementing the BEPS treaty-related measures and amending
bilateral tax treaties.[5]

---

1   OECD (2015), Measuring and Monitoring BEPS, Action 11 – 2015 Final Report, OECD Publishing,
    Paris.http://dx.doi.org/10.1787/9789264241343-en.
2   OECD (2013), Action Plan on Base Erosion and Profit Shifting, OECD Publishing, Paris, http://
    dx.doi.org/10.1787/9789264202719-en; OECD (2014), 'Part 1 of a report to G20 Development Working
    Group on the impact of BEPS in low income countries', OECD, Paris, www.oecd.org/tax/part-1-of-report-
    tog20-dwg-on-the-impact-of-beps-in-low-income-countries.pdf.
3   OECD (2015), Developing a Multilateral Instrument to Modify Bilateral Tax Treaties, Action 15 – 2015
    Final Report, OECD Publishing, Paris.http://dx.doi.org/10.1787/9789264241688-en.
4   OECD, 2017 Update to the OECD Model Tax Convention (adopted by OECD Council on 21 November
    2017), http://www.oecd.org/tax/treaties/2017-update-model-tax-concention.pdf (accessed 8 August 2018).
5   Austry, Stephane et al., 'The Proposed OECD Multilateral Instrument Amending Tax Treaties', (2016) 61
    Brit. Tax Rev., 454; Streinz, Rudolf, 'Multilateral Instrument and EU Competence Special Issue: The

0.04 The BEPS measures are expected to become applicable via changes to bilateral tax treaties (now facilitated by the MLI) or through changes in domestic laws and with support from internationally agreed guidance.[6] The BEPS proposed policies affect the sharing of information and propose models for national tax policies. In respect to *sharing of information* Actions 12, 5 and 13 were released respectively on mandatory disclosure, harmful tax competition, and transfer price documentation.[7] These proposals are connected to measures on the Common Reporting Standard ('CbCR'), and Tax Information Exchange Agreements. This is a broader trend about information sharing that is not directly addressed by the BEPS project. In respect to *BEPS models for national*

OECD Base Erosion and Profit Shifting Action Plan and European Union Law', (2015) 60 *Brit. Tax Rev.*, 429; Zalasinski, Adam, 'Conclusion of the BEPS Multilateral Instrument and Distribution of Competences between the EU and Its Member States Special Issue: The OECD Base Erosion and Profit Shifting Action Plan and European Union Law', (2015) 60 *Brit. Tax Rev.*, 444; Broekhuijsen, Dirk and Vording, Henk, 'The Multilateral Tax Instrument: How to Avoid a Stalemate on Distributional Issues', (2016) 60 *Brit. Tax Rev.*, 39; Becerra, José Antonio, 'A Practical Approach to Determine the Influence of the OECD Multilateral Instrument on North American Tax Treaty Networks', (2017) 71 *Bull. Intl. Taxn.*; Nikolakakis, Angelo et al., 'Some Reflections on the Proposed Revisions to the OECD Model and Commentaries, and on the Multilateral Instrument, with Respect to Fiscally Transparent Entities – Part 1', (2017) 71 *Bull. Intl. Taxn.* 9; García Antón, R., 'Untangling the Role of Reservations in the OECD Multilateral Instrument: The OECD Legal Hybrids', (2017) 71 *Bull. Intl. Taxn.* 10; Hattingh, Johann, 'The Multilateral Instrument from a Legal Perspective: What May Be the Challenges?', (2017) 71 *Bull. Intl. Taxn.*, 77; Bosman, Alexander, 'General Aspects of the Multilateral Instrument' (2017) 45 *Intertax*, 642–659; Bravo, Nathalie, 'The Multilateral Tax Instrument and Its Relationship with Tax Treaties', (2016) 8 *World Tax J.*, 279; Hattingh, Johann, 'The Impact of the BEPS Multilateral Instrument on International Tax Policies', (2018) 72 *Bull. Intl. Taxn.*

6   Brauner, Yariv, 'BEPS: An Interim Evaluation' (2014) 6 *World Tax J.*, 10; Eccleston, Richard and Smith, Helen, 'The G20, BEPS and the Future of International Tax Governance', in *Global Tax Governance: What is Wrong with it and how to fix it*, Diestsch, Peter and Rixen, Thomas, (eds), (ECPR Press 2016), pp. 175; Baker, Philip. 'Is There a Cure for BEPS?', (2013) 58 *Brit. Tax Rev.* 605; Avi-Yonah, Reuven S., and Haiyan Xu. 'Evaluating BEPS.' (2017) *Erasmus L. Rev.* 10: Avi-Yonah, Reuven S., and Haiyan Xu. 'Global Taxation after the Crisis: Why BEPS and MAATM Are Inadequate Responses, and What Can Be Done About It', University of Michigan Public Law Research Paper No. 494, (2016) available at: https://papers.ssrn.com/sol3/papers.cfm?abstract_id=2716124; Grinberg, Itai, 'Breaking Beps: The New International Tax Diplomacy', (2015) *Georgetown University Law Center*, 1137; Brauner, Yariv, 'What the BEPS', (2014) 16 *Fla. Tax Rev.* 55; Cooper, Graeme and Stewart, Miranda, 'The Road Home? Finalizing and Implementing the BEPS Agenda', (2015) 69 *Bull. Intl. Taxn.*, 311; Shay, Stephen E., and Christians, Allison, 'Assessing BEPS: Origins, Standards, and Responses.', General Report, in 102A *Cahiers de Droit Fiscal International: Assessing BEPS: Origins, Standards, and Responses* 17 (Int'l Fiscal Ass'n 2017); Brauner, Yariv. 'Assessing BEPS: Origins, Standards, and Responses–The United States Report for the 2017 Annual IFA Congress, Rio De Janeiro, Brazil.' (2017); Vann, Richard J. 'Policy Forum: The Policy Underpinnings of the BEPS Project-Preserving the International Corporate Income Tax?' (2014) 62 *Can. Tax J.*, 433–41; Dourado, Ana Paula, 'The Base Erosion and Profit Shifting (BEPS) Initiative under Analysis' (2015) 43 *Intertax*, 2; Christians, Allison, 'BEPS and the New International Tax Order', *Brigham Young University Law Review*, Forthcoming, pp. 1604; Brooks, Kim. 'What's up: BEPS and the New International Tax Order' (2017) Jotwell: J. Things We Like, 1.

7   OECD (2015), Mandatory Disclosure Rules, Action 12 – 2015 Final Report, OECD Publishing, Paris.http://dx.doi.org/10.1787/9789264241442-en; OECD (2015), Countering Harmful Tax Practices More Effectively, Taking into Account Transparency and Substance, Action 5 – 2015 Final Report, OECD Publishing, Paris. http://dx.doi.org/10.1787/9789264241190-en; OECD (2015), Transfer Pricing Documentation and Country-by-Country Reporting, Action 13 – 2015 Final Report, OECD Publishing, Paris.http://dx.doi.org/10.1787/9789264241480-en.

tax policies, the main policies proposals addressed to national legislators are: Cfc rules (Action 3),[8] limitations to the deduction of interest (Action 4),[9] policies for hybrid mismatches (Action 2),[10] and transfer pricing (Action 8–10).[11]

The BEPS Project in Action 1 also addressed the tax problems of the digital **0.05** economy and concluded that the digital economy cannot be ring fenced as it is increasingly the economy itself.[12] As both the challenges and the potential options raise systemic issues regarding the existing framework for the taxation of cross-border activities that go beyond the issues of the digital economy, OECD and G20 countries have agreed to monitor developments and analyse data that will become available over time. As a result Action 1 produced a broad overview of the BEPS issues within the digital economy.

Changes to the treaty Model are a longstanding prerogative of the OECD and **0.06** the proposed BEPS treaty measures are to become eventually binding in bilateral treaties and may have an effect on BEPS in respect of double-exemption achieved through treaties. The Commentary 2017 Update primarily comprises changes to the OECD Model Tax Convention (the OECD Model) that were approved as part of the BEPS Package in Actions 2, 6, 7 and 14. These changes include changes to:

- the Title and Preamble of the OECD Model, as well as to its Introduction, and related Commentary changes contained in Action 6 (Preventing the Granting of Treaty Benefits in Inappropriate Circumstances);
- the section of the Commentary on Art. 1 on 'Improper use of the Convention' (draft proposals for these optional provisions were included in Action 6);
- Artt. 3 and 4, and related Commentary changes, concerning the treaty residence of pension funds;
- paragraph 2 of Art. 3 and related changes to the Commentary on Artt. 3 and 25 (Action 14 called for the development of these changes);
- paragraph 3 of Art. 4 (the tie-breaker rule for determining the treaty

8 OECD (2015), Designing Effective Controlled Foreign Company Rules, Action 3 – 2015 Final Report, OECD Publishing, Paris.http://dx.doi.org/10.1787/9789264241152-en.
9 OECD (2015), Limiting Base Erosion Involving Interest Deductions and Other Financial Payments, Action 4 – 2015 Final Report, OECD Publishing, Paris. http://dx.doi.org/10.1787/9789264241176-en.
10 OECD (2015), Developing a Multilateral Instrument to Modify Bilateral Tax Treaties, Action 15 – 2015 Final Report, OECD Publishing, Paris.http://dx.doi.org/10.1787/9789264241688-en.
11 OECD (2015), Aligning Transfer Pricing Outcomes with Value Creation, Actions 8–10 – 2015 Final Reports, OECD Publishing, Paris.http://dx.doi.org/10.1787/9789264241244-en.
12 OECD (2015), Addressing the Tax Challenges of the Digital Economy, Action 1 – 2015 Final Report, OECD Publishing, Paris.http://dx.doi.org/10.1787/9789264241046-en.

residence of dual-resident persons other than individuals) and related Commentary changes (these changes appear in Action 6);

- Art. 5 and its Commentary, resulting from Action 7;
- subparagraph 2 a) of Art. 10, and related changes to the Commentary introducing a minimum holding period to access the 5 per cent rate applicable to dividends, and related Commentary changes, as a result of Action 6;
- paragraph 4 of Art. 13, addressing transactions that seek to circumvent the application of that provision, and related Commentary changes, as a result of Action 6;
- Artt. 23 A and 23 B and related changes to the Commentary on Artt. 10, 11, 21, and 23 A and 23 B addressing issues relating to the relief of double taxation;
- Art. 25 and the Commentary on Artt. 2, 7, 9 and 2, as a result of Action 14.

0.07 The 2017 Update also replaced paragraph 17 of the Commentary on Art. 10 with a paragraph containing an alternative provision that would deny the benefit of the lower rate provided in Art. 10(2) a) to certain collective investment vehicles; that alternative provision was contained in Action 6. The 2017 Update also added a new paragraph 2 to Art. 1 (the transparent entity provision) and related Commentary changes and a new paragraph 3 to Art. 1 (the 'saving clause') and related Commentary changes, as a result of Action 2. Finally the 2017 Update added a new Art. 29 (Entitlement to Benefits) and related Commentary, which includes in the Model a limitation-on-benefits (LOB) rule (simplified and detailed versions), an anti-abuse rule for permanent establishments situated in third states, and a principal purposes test (PPT) rule as a result of Action 6. Other changes to the Model and Commentary were made not directly in relation to the BEPS Project.

0.08 This book focuses on tax treaty issues induced by the BEPS Project because the main direct impact of that project is on tax treaties, through the 2017 OECD Model/Commentary and also focuses on the main features of the 2016 MLI. The book mainly focuses on the changes to Model/Commentary because it is too early to assess with exactitude the impact of the MLI on individual bilateral treaties. Moreover, the provisions of the MLI essentially overlap with the actual changes of the Model/Commentary 2017, which therefore, at the current stage, are a proxy of the eventual impact of the MLI.

0.09 So the book describes the Model/Commentary 2017 discussing changes with respect to the past, from the perspective of the *country of destination of the investment*. This perspective reveals important aspects of the BEPS impact on tax treaties, and notably that there are now new limitations (i) to the avoidance of the permanent establishment status, and (ii) to the access to the benefits of a bilateral treaty, in addition to a general ban to double treaty exemption. In essence the book looks at three main dimensions for a resident of a Contracting State of doing business in the other Contracting State (hereinafter 'CS').

Over time the majority of states have concluded thousands of treaties that **0.10** densely interconnect them. The involvement of the OECD is not in the traditional form of delegation of powers to states, because the OECD limits itself to the creation of soft law and standards for actual treaty-making.

In bilateral tax treaties each self-interested state confers benefits to another **0.11** state in a tax treaty because it extracts from that specific treaty benefits that are superior to those it would extract without resorting to such a treaty (cooperation based on reciprocity). Tax treaties can be modeled as coordination games in which both states' dominant strategy is to make the same choice (neither of the two states has a dominant strategy). In a bilateral tax treaty there are two Contracting States (hereinafter 'CSs'). Each CS can act, depending on the situation, either as the treaty residence-country (hereinafter 'RC') or as the treaty source-country (hereinafter 'SC'). So for example in the treaty between France and Japan, in a certain transaction France is the RC and Japan is the SC, while in other transactions in which Japan is the RC France is the SC. So tax treaties are bilateral and are based on reciprocity and regulate the tax aspects of bilateral investments.

Because tax treaties are strictly bilateral, the benefits of a treaty between A and **0.12** B are not extended by either A or B to third countries, while the lack of a multilateral dispute settlement and enforcement can be attributed to the fact that tax treaties are incomplete contracts that refer dispute settlement to the national judicial systems or to a bilateral non-binding dispute settlement (MAP).

So the book, within tax regulation of bilateral investments, looks at the tests **0.13** that an investor resident for treaty purposes in the RC must consider when doing business in the SC. These tests are the following: first, the tests required for doing business through PE (Chapter 1); second, the new set of requirements that need to be met to have full entitlement to the tax treaty (Chapter 2); third, the basic rules for doing business through a corporate vehicle, once the entitlement requirements have been met (Chapter 3). The book concludes with the discussion of tax treaty dispute settlement and enforcement by looking at the mutual agreement procedure, transfer price allocations in tax treaties, and tax treaties and information (Chapter 4).

1

DOING BUSINESS THROUGH A PERMANENT ESTABLISHMENT (PE)

The perspective of the country of destination of the investment reveals **1.01** important aspects of the BEPS impact on tax treaties, and notably that there are now new limitations to the avoidance of the PE status. Before 2017 one of the planning techniques was in fact for non-resident investors to carry out activities in the SC to avoid the so called 'PE status', avoiding the payment of taxes in the SC.

This chapter focuses on the new aspects of operating through a PE in the SC, **1.02** by looking at the tax PE threshold, the tests to determine the existence of PE, and by discussing BEPS changes in respect to preparatory/auxiliary activities, the anti-fragmentation rule, and finally to structures in shipping and air transport (section I). The chapter also looks at more traditional treaty approaches to problems such as the force of attraction of the PE and the separate treatment of isolated classes of income, also discussing how to protect the PE operation through the non-discrimination clause (sections II–III).

I. OPERATING THROUGH A PERMANENT ESTABLISHMENT

A. The tax PE threshold

1.03 The taxation of business profits within the treaty is organized in two main provisions: on the one hand, Art. 5 defines the concept of PE but does not itself allocate taxing rights, on the other hand, Art. 7 allocates taxing rights with respect to business profits of an enterprise of a CS attributable to a PE. Art. 7 is based on the separate entity and arm's length principles[1] and has been subject to considerable variations in interpretation. Starting from a lack of a common interpretation, the 1984 report and the 1993 report 'Attribution of Income to PEs' eventually led in 2008 to the report 'Attribution of Profits to PEs' ('2008 Report'), and a new version of Art. 7 appeared in Model 2010, while a revised version of 2008 was adopted in 2010 ('2010 Report'). The current version of Art. 7 reflects the approach developed in the 2010 Report and must be interpreted in light of the guidance contained in it.[2]

1.04 Art. 7 § 1 provides that profits of an enterprise of a CS shall be taxable *only* in the RC unless the enterprise carries on business in the SC through a PE situated therein. If the enterprise carries on business as aforesaid, the profits that are attributable to the PE in accordance with Art. 7 § 2 *may be taxed* in the SC (Art. 7 § 1). An additional problem is the non discrimination in the SC of PEs of foreign enterprises. The first principle established by Art. 7 § 1 is that there is extraterritorial tax jurisdiction of the RC in respect to business profits sourced in the SC only if there is a PE in the SC of a taxpayer resident of the RC producing such profits.

1.05 The Commentary remarks that there is international consensus on this principle: 'until an enterprise of one state has a PE in another state, it should

---

1 Commentary to Art. 7 § 1–3. The 2010 Report is divided into four parts: attribution of profits to PEs in general; PEs of banks; PEs of enterprises carrying on global trading; and PEs of enterprises carrying on insurance activities.

2 On this evolution see: Burgers, Irene, 'Commentary on Art. 7 of the OECD Model treaty' in: Burgers, Irene et al. (eds), *The Taxation of Permanent Establishments* (IBFD 1994); Gutman, Daniel, 'French Swiss Point of View on the Societe Schneider Electric Case: Some Thoughts on the Personal Attribution of Income Requirement in International Tax Law' (2003) 31 *Intertax* 156; IFA, 'The Attribution of Profits to Permanent Establishment' *Cahiers Droit Fisc. Intl.* (2006) 91b; Malherbe, Jacques, 'Permanent Establishments Claim their Share of Profits: Does the Taxman Agree?' (2011) 66 *Bull. Intl. Tax.* 359; Nouel, Luis, 'The New Art. 7 of the OECD Model Tax Convention: the End of the Road?' (2011) 65 *Bull. Intl. Tax.* 1; OECD, *2010 Report on the Attribution of Profits to Permanent Establishments* (OECD 2010); Pijl, Hans, 'Morgan Stanley: Issues Regarding Permanent Establishment and Profit Attribution in Light of the OECD View' (2008) 62 *Bull. Intl. Tax.* 164; Pijl, Hans, 'Interpretation of Art. 7 of the OECD Model, Permanent Establishment Financing and Other Dealings' (2011) 65 *Bull. Intl. Tax.* 294; Russo, Roberto, *The Attribution of Profits to Permanent Establishments: the Taxation of Intra-Company Dealings* (IBFD 2005).

not properly be regarded as participating in the economic life of that other state to such an extent that the other state should have taxing rights on its profits', adding that the right to tax of the state where the PE is situated does not extend to profits that an enterprise may derive from that state but that are not attributable to the PE.[3] National courts affirm this principle.[4]

The second principle implicit to Art. 7 § 1 is that extraterritorial tax juris- **1.06** diction of the RC in respect of business profits sourced in the SC is limited to the profits 'attributable' to the PE in the SC. This is a very broad concept that is now more precisely defined by Art. 7 § 2 introduced in 2010, which on the basis of the separate enterprise fiction, provides a method for attributing profits to a PE but courts had already established and applied this principle.[5]

Moreover, when a PE is deemed to exist, the clause of Art. 7 § 1, according to **1.07** which taxation in the SC is limited to profits attributable to the PE in the SC, must be read in combination with Art. 7 § 4 which establishes that if profits include items of income which are dealt with separately in other articles of the Convention, then the provisions of those articles shall not be affected by the provisions of Art. 7. The Commentary notes that even when there is a PE in the SC, Art. 7 § 1 prevents the RC from taxing an enterprise of the other CS (the SC) on profits that are not attributable to the PE: 'the right to tax of the state where the PE is situated does not extend to profits that the enterprise may derive from that state but that are not attributable to the PE'.[6] So the determination of the profits attributable to the PE is then developed through the principle of separate taxation of isolated classes of income established by Art. 7 § 4 by using the concept of 'effectively connected income' within an approach defined as a 'restricted force of attraction' of the PE. Courts have developed that approach, first by defining the concept of foreign 'business profits' that become taxable in the SC, and second by addressing the issues posed by domestic CFC rules to such a principle.

Art. 7 § 1 refers to the '*profits* of an enterprise of a CS which may be taxable in **1.08** the SC if the enterprise carries on business in the SC through a PE situated therein', and specifies that only the '*profits* that are attributable to the PE' in accordance with Art. 7 § 2 may be taxed in the SC. The Commentary notes that the term '*profits*' has a broad meaning which includes all income derived in

---

3 Commentary to Art. 7 § 11.
4 Spain, Tribunal Economico Administrativo Central, 03852/2004, 23 November 2006.
5 Norway, Høyesterett, HR-2011-02245-A, (sak nr. 2011/755), 2 December 2011.
6 Commentary to Art. 7 § 12.

carrying on an enterprise and corresponds to the use of the term made in domestic laws of most OECD Member Countries.[7]

1.09 Domestic laws often include so-called CFC rules under which the profits of a foreign enterprise (the controlled company) are attributed to the parent company (if certain requirements are met) even if they are not actually distributed as dividends. The result is that if the controlled company is resident of a CS and the parent company is in the other CS, the profits of the controlled company are taxed in the CS of the parent company even if the controlled company does not have a PE there, thereby conflicting with Art. 7 § 1, which provides that profits of an enterprise of a CS shall be taxable only in the RC unless the enterprise carries on business in the SC through a PE situated therein.[8] An opposite approach is found in a case decided in Japan in which the court held that CFC rules did not violate the business profits article of the treaty.[9] Brazil is a country that has very broad CFC legislation and this resulted in many important cases.[10] The Commentary affirms now that CFC rules do not conflict with treaties.[11]

B. The tests to determine the existence of a PE

1.10 The main use of the concept of a PE as defined by treaties is to determine the right of a CS (the SC) to tax the profits of an enterprise of the other CS. In fact, once there is a PE in the SC, under Art. 7 such SC has the power to tax the profits of an enterprise of the other CS arising from activities carried out through a PE situated therein. By contrast, the SC does not have the power to tax the profits of an enterprise of the other CS unless it carries on its business through a PE situated therein.

1.11 Before 2000, the income from professional services and other activities of an independent character was regulated by Art. 14 which was eliminated from the Model in 2000. The underlying idea was that there are differences between the concept of PE used in Art. 5 and 7, and the concept of fixed base

---

7   Commentary to Art. 7 § 71; Australia, High Court of Australia, *Thiel v. Federal Commissioner of Taxation*, 22 August 1990; Brazil, Tribunal Regional Federal da 2ª Região Rio de Janeiro, 2004.50.01.001354–5/ES, 16 March 2010, Brazil, Tribunal Regional Federal da 4ª Região (2002.71.00.006530-5/RS), 4 June 2009.
8   France, Conseil d'État, Assemblee 232276, 28 June 2002.
9   Japan, Supreme Court, 2008 (Gyo-hi) 91, 29 October 2009.
10 Brazil, Conselho de Contribuintes 108-08.765, 23 March 2006, 6; Brazil, Primeira Câmara, 16327.000530/ 2005-28, 17/12/2008, *Eagle Distribuidora de Bebidas S.A. v. National Treasury*, 101-97.070, First Taxpayers Council (1st Chamber), 2008 ; Brazil, Supremo Tribunal Federal, DAU 2,588, 10 April 2013.
11 Commentary to Art. 7 § 14; Commentary to Art. 10 § 37.

used in Art. 14 (independent personal services), with the result that the definition of PE is applicable to what previously constituted a *fixed base*.[12]

In 2017 important changes were made to Art. 5 of the Model (new § 4.1 **1.12** modification of §§ 4, 5 and 6 as a result of the adoption of the Report on Action 7 of the BEPS Project. Therefore the Commentary was also modified significantly. The position of the Commentary is that some of these changes are for the application of conventions concluded before their adoption because they reflect the consensus of the OECD member countries, while parts of the Commentary related to the change of the Model are prospective only and do not affect the interpretation of treaties in which these provisions are not included.

A 'PE' is a fixed place of business, through which the business of an enterprise **1.13** is wholly or partly carried on. So there are three requirements for a PE to exist which are determined through a set of tests:

1. the existence of a 'place of business' (*place of business test* and *right of use test*), i.e., a facility such as premises or, in certain instances, machinery or equipment;
2. the place of business must be 'fixed', i.e. it must be established at a distinct place with a certain degree of permanence (*location test* and *duration test*); and
3. the carrying on of the business of the enterprise through this fixed place of business (*business connection test*), i.e., personnel of the enterprise conduct the business of the enterprise in the state in which the fixed place is situated.[13]

---

12 Austria, Verwaltungsgerichtshof, 2000/15/0118, 18 March 2004; Canada, Federal Court of Appeal, *Dudney v. Her Majesty the Queen*, 24 February 2000.
13 On the concept of PE before the BEPS Project see in general: Arnold, Brian J., 'The Taxation of Income from Services and Tax Treaties: Cleaning Up the Mess' (2011) 65 *Bull. Intl. Tax.* 59; Brugger, Florian, and Plansky, Patrick (eds), *Permanent Establishments in International and EU Tax Law* (Linde 2011); De Vries, David, 'The Concept of Permanent Establishment: A Comparative Analysis of Tax Treaty and Domestic Tax Law' (2010) 38 *Intertax* 577; IFA, 'Is There a Permanent Establishment?' *Cahiers Droit Fisc. Intl.* (2009) 94a; IFA, 'The Development in Different Countries of the Concept of a Permanent Establishment' *Cahiers Droit Fisc. Intl.* (1967) 52; IFA, 'The Position of Permanent Establishments in National and International Fiscal Law' *Cahiers Droit Fisc. Intl.* (1957) 34a; Kobetsky, Michael, *International Taxation of Permanent Establishments. Principles and Policy* (Cambridge University Press 2011); Konnov, Oleg, *Permanent Establishment in Tax Law* (M3 Press 2002); Rawal, Radhakishan, *The Taxation of Permanent Establishments – an International Perspective* (Spiramus 2006); Reamer, Ekkehart, *Permanent Establishments: A Domestic Taxation, Bilateral Tax Treaty and Prospective* (Kluwer Law International 2014); Rust, Alexander, 'Situs Principle V. Permanent Establishment Principle in International Tax Law' (2002) 56 *Bull. Intl. Fisc. Doc.* 15; Sasseville, Jacques, 'Is There a Permanent Establishment? General Report' (2009) 94a *Cahiers Droit Fisc. Intl*; Skaar, Arvid, *Permanent Establishment, Erosion of Tax Treaty Principle* (Kluwer 1991).

1.   The place of business and right of use tests

1.14   The existence of a place of business is ascertained through the *place of business test*, which looks at whether the place is at the taxpayer's disposal (*right of use test*) often disregarding the legal right to use in favour of the analysis of the actual presence, and of course the place of business must be a place 'through which' actual activities are carried out.

1.15   A place of business is any premises, facilities or installations used for carrying on the business of the enterprise whether or not they are used exclusively for that purpose (*place of business test*),[14] such as a pitch in a market place or a permanently used area in a customs depot, and in particular a PE that exists within the premises of another enterprise when a foreign enterprise has at its constant disposal certain premises or a part thereof owned by the other enterprise. This situation is ascertained through the *right of use test.*[15] Quite often there is a place of business because activities are carried out within the premises of the recipients.[16] A place of business can occur through 'virtual technological facilities'.[17]

1.16   The right of use test when applied in isolation (i.e., not bundled together with the permanence test) dictates that for a place of business to exist a certain amount of space must be at the disposal of the taxpayers, it being irrelevant whether premises, facilities or installations are owned, rented, or otherwise.[18] When there is no actual right of use of the premises or facilities there is no place of business.[19]

1.17   The Commentary 2017 has clarified this concept: whether a location is at the disposal of an enterprise depends on that enterprise having the effective power

---

14   Commentary to Art. 5 § 10.

15   Austria, Verwaltungsgerichtshof, 96/14/ 0084, 21 May 1997; Germany, Bundesfinanzhof, IR 80–81/91, 3 February 1993.

16   Germany, FinanzgerichtMünster 9K 6931/98, 6 November 2000.

17   India, Income Tax Appellate Tribunal Delhi, *Amadeus Global Travel v. ADIT*, 30 November 2007. In a wider sense this is the problem of taxing certain models of business of the digital economy, see for example: Hellerstein, Walter, 'Jurisdiction to Tax in the Digital Economy: Permanent and Other Establishments', (2014) 68 *Bull. Intl. Tax.* 6; IFA, 'Taxation of Income Derived from Electronic Commerce' *Cahiers Droit Fisc. Intl.* (2001) 86a; Schaffner, Jean, *How Fixed Is a Permanent Establishment?* (Kluwer Law International 2013).

18   India, Income Tax Appellate Tribunal (ITAT), *Ericsson Radio Systems AB (EAB), Motorola Inc. (MI) and Nokia Networks OY (NOY) v. Deputy Commissioner of Income Tax*, 22 June 2005, (2005) 96 TTJ Delhi; Austria, Verwaltungsgerichtshof, 2000/15/0118, 18 March 2004.

19   Commentary to Art. 5 § 12. See: Belgium, Rechtbank van EersteAanleg Luik, 9 December 2004; Germany, Bundesfinanzhof, IR 30/07, 4 June 2008; India, Income Tax Appellate Tribunal (ITAT), *Ericsson Radio Systems AB (EAB), Motorola Inc. (MI) and Nokia Networks OY (NOY) v. Deputy Commissioner of Income Tax*, 22 June 2005.

to use that location as well as the extent of the presence of the enterprise at that location and the activities that it performs there. This occurs if there is legal possession of the location, but also occurs when an enterprise is allowed to use a specific location that belongs to another enterprise or that is used by a number of enterprises and performs its business activities at that location on a continuous basis during an extended period of time. By contrast, the place is not at the disposal of an enterprise if the enterprise's presence at that location is intermittent or incidental (for example the carrying on of business activities at the home of an individual), or if an enterprise does not have a right to be present at a location. This occurs for example when a plant is owned and used exclusively by a contract-manufacturer.[20]

The right of use test often implies a multi-level analysis of the organization of **1.18** the firm[21] as the mere presence of an enterprise at a particular location does not necessarily mean that location is at the disposal of that enterprise.[22] The place of business must be a place 'through which' actual activities are carried out, and this includes any situation where business activities are carried on at a particular location at the disposal of the enterprise.[23]

2. The location and duration tests

Not only must a place of business exist and be effectively available (place of **1.19** business test and right of use test), but must it must be 'fixed'. This concept of the *'fixed'* place of business implies a *location test* that also looks at a commercial and geographic coherence for mobile activities, as well as a *duration test* in terms of a certain degree of permanency of the place of business. The *location test* focuses on the link between the place of business and a specific geographical point, in the sense that the equipment 'remains on a particular site' (*'spatial delimitation approach,'* but see § 20 of the Commentary), it being irrelevant that the place of business is actually fixed to the soil.[24]

Business activities carried on by an enterprise often move between neighbour- **1.20** ing locations in the SC, so that a concept of commercial and geographic coherence should be used for those mobile activities.[25] Examples of activities

---

20 Commentary to Art. 5 § 12 and 18.
21 Canada, Tax Court of Canada, *Knights of Columbus v. Her Majesty the Queen*, 16 May 2008.
22 Commentary to Art. 5 § 11, Commentary to Art. 5 § 16, Commentary to Art. 5 § 12.
23 Germany, Finanzgericht Baden-Württemberg 3K 309/91, 11 May 1992; The Netherlands, Gerechtshof's-Gravenhage, 101/82 MII, 28 March 1983.
24 Commentary to Art. 5 § 21; and § 122–126. See: The Netherlands, Rechtbank Breda, AWB09/563, 25 May 2009, 8; Norway, Norwegian Supreme Court, 15B/1984, 25 January 1984. See also: Schaffner, Jean, *How Fixed Is a Permanent Establishment?* (Kluwer Law International 2013).
25 Commentary to Art. 5 § 23.

that amount to a 'fixed' place of business because they are coherent commercially and geographically are a very large mine, an 'office hotel', a consulting firm which regularly rents different offices, an outdoor market in parts of which a trader regularly sets up his stand.[26] The Commentary also refers to activities based on revolving locations, such as a painter who, under a single contract, undertakes work throughout a building for a single client, or a consultant who moves from one office to another training the employees within the same branch location.[27] There is a 'fixed' place of business when, for example, a painter works under a series of unrelated contracts for a number of unrelated clients in a large office building, or when a satellite is in geostationary orbit.[28]

1.21 The place of business to be 'fixed', must have a certain degree of permanency, and not be of a purely temporary nature. The rule of thumb here is that the place of business must last for at least six months.[29] Commentary 2017 however introduces exceptions to this practice. The first exception is when activities are of a recurrent nature even if they extend over a number of years (for example drilling operations at a remote arctic location). The second exception is when activities constitute a business that was carried on exclusively in that country, possibly of short duration (for example the operation of a cafeteria during a four-month period in support to activities conducted in a remote place).[30]

1.22 It is also possible that a place of business exists for a very short period of time for activities of a recurrent nature, so that the duration of each period of time should be multiplied by the number of times.[31] It is however possible that the business carried on in a specific SC is short in terms of time but intense in terms of effective presence, so that the duration test is met.[32]

---

26 Norway, Tingrett Stavanger, 99-00421, 9 December 1999.
27 Commentary to Art. 5 § 25. See: Belgium, Rechtbank van EersteAanleg Luik, 9 December 2004; Norway, Høyesterett, 56/994, 10 June 1994.
28 Commentary to Art. 5 § 27.
29 Commentary to Art. 5 § 28. See: The Netherlands, Rechtbank Breda, AWB09/563, 25 May 2009; Norway, Høyesterett, 2004-01003-A, 8 June 2004.
30 Commentary to Art. 5 §§ 29–30.
31 Art. 4 § 4 of the Belgium-France treaty. See: Belgium, Rechtbank van EersteAanleg Gent, G1 2008/0446, 15 May 2008.
32 Commentary to Art. 5 § 32. See: Norway, Lagmannsrett Bergen, *Scanwell AB and Mats Johanson v. Municipality of Stavanger*, Gulating, 330-1989, 15 March 1991.

3. The business connection test

A place of business to become a PE must exist and be effectively available **1.23** (*place of business test* and *right of use test*), must be '*fixed*' (*location test*), but also it must be a place of business 'through which' an enterprise carries on its business, a feature that is assessed by using the *business connection test*. The business connection test dictates that a place of business becomes a PE if the enterprise using it carries on (wholly or partly) its business activity through that place of business but on a *regular basis*, so that the fact that the place of business is actually productive or permanent is not a feature required to meet the business connection test.[33]

Leasing activities pose a business connection problem in so far as the lessor of **1.24** leasing equipment to the lessee continues to operate it within the premises of the lessee on a regular basis with its own personnel. The Commentary indicates that leasing activities may lead to the fixed place of business qualifying as a PE depending: (i) on whether the lessor supplies personnel after installation to operate the equipment under its responsibility; and (ii) on whether the fixed place of business (constituted by the leased facilities, industrial, commercial or scientific equipment, buildings, or intellectual property) is under the control of lessor.[34]

So a fixed place of business is not a PE if facilities, industrial, commercial or **1.25** scientific equipment, buildings, or intellectual property leased to third parties through a fixed place of business are not maintained by an enterprise in the SC, and the contract is limited to the mere leasing even if the lessor supplies personnel after installation to operate the equipment, provided that their responsibility is limited solely to the operation/maintenance of the equipment.[35], if a telecommunications operator in the RC enters into a 'roaming' agreement with an operator in the SC to allow its users in the RC to connect to the SC operator's telecommunications network, any place of the network in the SC is not at the disposal of operator in the RC.[36] The ongoing delivery of spare parts by the seller or producer poses a problem similar to that posed by the leasing of equipment. According to the Commentary there is a PE in these cases if the enterprise maintains a fixed place of business for delivery of spare parts or maintains or repairs machinery, while there is no PE if the fixed place

---

33 Germany, Finanzgericht Baden-Württemberg 3K 309/91, 11 May 1992, 4; Canada, Tax Court of Canada, *Knights of Columbus v. Her Majesty the Queen*, 16 May 2008.

34 Commentary to Art. 5 §§ 36–37. See: Norway, Høyesterett RT 1997 s 653, 29 April 1997.

35 With regard to the leasing of containers report 'The Taxation of Income Derived from the Leasing of Containers' (OECD 1983).

36 Commentary to Art. 5 § 38.

of business furnishes plans, etc. especially developed for the purposes of the individual customer.[37]

1.26 Gaming/vending machines and technological infrastructures such as cables and pipelines also pose a business connection problem in so far as the owner of that equipment operates it automatically and 'on remote'. Gaming and vending machines do not constitute a PE if the enterprise merely sets up the machines and then leases them to other enterprises, while they will constitute a PE if the enterprise which sets up the machines then operates and maintains them for its own account or through a dependent agent.[38] A similar problem is posed by cables/pipelines, which, like vending machines, can be operated remotely and automatically. There is a PE (so the exclusion does not apply) if facilities, such as cables or pipelines, are used to transport property belonging to other enterprises. By contrast there is no PE if the enterprise transports its own property and the transport is merely incidental to the business of enterprise.[39]

1.27 The Commentary 2017 has not changed the traditional approach to the place of business test and right of use test but has made clarifications for subcontractors, remote operation, and joint ventures. The business connection test is met when an enterprise carries on its business through subcontractors at a fixed place of business that is at the disposal of the enterprise. In the absence of employees of the enterprise, other factors show that the enterprise clearly has the effective power to use that site, because the enterprise owns or has legal possession of that site and controls access to and use of the site, for example an enterprise that owns a small hotel and rents out the hotel's rooms through the Internet and has subcontracted the on-site operation of the hotel to a company remunerated on a cost-plus basis. Finally in a 'joint venture' in which different enterprises agree to each carry on a separate part of the same project generally a separate enterprise for the purposes of Artt. 3, 5 and 7 is not established and therefore the business connection test is not met.[40]

---

37 Commentary to Art. 5 § 71.
38 Commentary to Art. 5 § 9.
39 Commentary to Art. 5 § 64. See: Germany, Bundesfinanzhof, IIR 12/92, 30 October 1996.
40 Commentary to Art. 5 §§ 40–44.

C. Building sites

Art. 5 § 2 provides a non-exhaustive list of examples of PEs[41] which must be   **1.28**
interpreted in the light of the general definition of PE. Thus, there is a strict
connection between Art. 5 § 1 and Art. 5 § 2 because a PE can exist in the
form of one of the listed examples only if all the requirements of the basic-rule
PE definition are satisfied.[42] A 'place of management' is another positive
example of Art. 5 § 2.[43] A 'place of management' is not necessarily an 'office'
in the traditional sense, as it is sufficient that facilities are available in a
coordinated way for conducting business.[44] Even within such a concept of
'place of management' a minimal threshold is required for a PE to exist.[45]
Certain treaties contain a clause according to which 'substantial equipment' in
the SC may amount to a PE.[46] Moreover according to Art. 5 § 3 of the Model
a building site or construction or installation project constitutes a PE only if it
lasts more than 12 months.

This simple definition is analysed in the Commentary through five main   **1.29**
issues: the concept of 'building site' or 'construction or installation project'; the
12-month test; how to treat preparatory works; interruptions and time spent
by subsidiary-contractors; and finally projects undertaken by fiscally transparent partnerships.

A 'building site' or a 'construction or installation project' involves the construc-   **1.30**
tion or renovation of buildings, roads, as well as the laying of pipe-lines and
excavations.[47] The rationale of the 12-month test is to establish a workable *de
minimis rule*.[48] The Commentary clarifies that the 12-month test applies to
each individual site or project.[49] A 'coherent whole commercially and geographically' occurs even if the work is based on several contracts and the orders

---

41   Commentary to Art. 5 § 45. The Commentary to Art. 5 at §§ 47–48 acknowledges that there is no common
     view about mines, oil or gas wells, quarries or any other place of extraction of natural resources, all places of
     extraction of hydrocarbons whether on or off-shore, and exploration of natural resources.
42   Switzerland, Verwaltungsgericht Zürich (Administrative Court, Zürich), A 00 131, 28 August 2000,
     Luzerner Gerichts- und Verwaltungsentscheide, 2000, II, 25.
43   Commentary to Art. 5 § 24, 2–3. See: Canada, Supreme Court of Canada, *Crown Forest Industries Ltd. v.
     Her Majesty the Queen*, 22 June 1995, [1995] 2 C.T.C. 64; The Netherlands, Hoge Raad der Nederlanden
     21.286, 24 November 1982. See: Ward, David, 'A Resident of a CS for Tax Treaty Purposes: A Case
     Comment on Crown Forest Industries' (1996) 44 *Canadian Tax J.* 408.
44   Commentary to Art. 5 § 46. See: Germany, Bundesfinanzhof (), I B 101/98, 17 December 1998; Norway,
     Lagmannsrett Hamar (), 91–01618 A, 16 June 1992.
45   Canada, Tax Court of Canada, *Fiebert v. Her Majesty the Queen*, 25 November 1985, [1986] 1 C.T.C. 2034.
46   Art. 4 § 3 b) of the treaty. See: Australia, Federal Court of Australia, *Mcdermott Industries v. Commis-
     sioner of Taxation of the Commonwealth of Australia*, 29 April 2005.
47   Commentary to Art. 5 § 50. See: Denmark, Landsskatteretten LSR 641–1220–1, 24 June 1996.
48   The Netherlands, Hoge Raad der Nederlanden, 32709, 9 December 1998.
49   Commentary to Art. 5 § 51.

are placed by several persons. This approach is meant to counteract abuses in which enterprises divide their contracts up into several parts, each covering a period less than 12 months and attributed to a different company which is, however, owned by the same group.[50] The 'aggregate approach' is supported by tax authorities but Courts often reject it. The typical situation is one in which several building projects, each lasting less than the treaty threshold (usually nine or 12 months), are carried out in the SC for the same customer, but under different contracts.[51]

1.31 The 12-month test becomes quite relevant with the presence of sub-contractors, that is when an enterprise (general contractor) in a comprehensive project subcontracts parts of that project to other enterprises (subcontractors), the period spent by a subcontractor working on the building site must be considered as time spent by the general contractor and the subcontractor has a PE at the site if it lasts more than 12 months. Commentary 2017 also clarifies with an example how the 12-month test is applied when fiscally transparent partnerships undertake projects at the level of the partnership, with the result that each partner has a PE regardless of the time each has spent on the site.

1.32 The splitting-up of contracts is a potential strategy for the artificial avoidance of PE status. There is no significant modification in the Model 2017 about this issue, but the Commentary 2017 states that Art. 29 addresses this situation, or alternatively CSs should introduce a special provision. This proposed rule provides that where an enterprise of a CS carries on activities in the other CS at a place that constitutes a building site, construction project, installation project or other specific project, or carries on supervisory or consultancy activities in connection with such a place, and these activities are carried on during one or more periods of time that, in the aggregate, exceed 30 days; and where connected activities are carried on in that other CS at the same building site, construction or installation project, each exceeding 30 days, by one or more enterprises closely related to the first-mentioned enterprise, then these different periods of time are added to the aggregate period of time during which the first-mentioned enterprise has carried on activities at that building site, construction or installation project. This provision is also found in Art. 14 of the MLI.

1.33 The Commentary 2017 clarifies that the determination of whether activities are connected depends on the facts and circumstances of each case, relying on

---

50   France, Conseil d'État, 16095, 29 June 1981; Germany, Bundesfinanzhof I R 99/97, 21 April 1999.
51   Belgium, Hof van Beroep Antwerpen 1982-07-29, 29 June 1982; Belgium, Hof van Beroep Antwerpen, 1984-04-12, 12 April 1984; Norway, Tingrett Stavanger, 00-260A, 18 September 1980.

key questions, such as whether: the contracts covering the different activities were concluded with the same person or related persons; the conclusion of additional contracts with a person is a logical consequence of a previous contract concluded with that person or related persons; the activities would have been covered by a single contract absent tax planning considerations; the nature of the work involved under the different contracts is the same or similar; the same employees are performing the activities under the different contracts.[52]

A site begins to exist on the date when the contractor begins preparatory work **1.34** in the SC, and continues to exist until work is completed or abandoned or temporarily discontinued and that interruptions do not count (seasonal or other temporary interruptions should be included in determining the life of a site).[53] This practical rule is in a different form than that generally adopted to determine when a PE begins to exist. That rule dictates that this happens when the enterprise commences carrying on its business through a fixed place of business, so the period of time during which the fixed place of business itself is being set up is not counted. By contrast a PE ceases to exist when it is disposed of, when activities are discontinued. If a fixed place of business is leased to another enterprise, the lessor's PE ceases to exist, except where the lessor continues carrying on a business activity of its own through the fixed place of business.[54]

D. Preparatory/auxiliary activities and the anti-fragmentation rule

Activities of multinational groups are often a seamless range of functions in **1.35** which integrated services are performed. So it is difficult to distinguish the 'core' between other functions that are somehow related to core function. The problem here is to identify the threshold between those functions which constitute a PE and those which do not. Art. 5 § 4 lists a number of activities which are not PEs, even if the activity is carried on through a fixed place of business. The common feature of those activities is that the enterprise of the RC cannot, in principle, be taxed in the SC, if it carries on preparatory or auxiliary activities, i.e., activities that are not directly productive and do not belong to the core business of that enterprise. This list must be read in connection with Art. 5 § 4 f) together with the final statement which operates as a residual clause and has been introduced by Model 2017 (see

---

52 Commentary to Art. 5 § 53.
53 Commentary to Art. 5 § 54.
54 Commentary to Art. 5 § 44. See: France, Conseil d'État, 16095, 29 June 1981; Austria, Verwaltungs-gerichtshof), 2004/15/0001, 22 April 2009.

below).[55] Under the exception provided by Art. 5 § 4, activities carried out through a fixed place of business are not PEs if these activities are *'remote'* from the actual realization of profits, so this approach has also been extended to more complex activities.[56] The Commentary to Art. 5 § 130 discusses in detail the core functions of enterprise in e-commerce.

1.36 Under the language adopted by Art. 5 § 4 f) before the changes made by Model 2017 the combination of preparatory or auxiliary activities did not mean of itself that a PE existed. So an enterprise could fragment a cohesive operating business into several small operations to argue that each was merely engaged in preparatory or auxiliary activities. More specifically Art. 5 § 4 letters a)–e) provided that the term 'PE' did not include: a) the use of facilities solely for the purpose of storage, display or delivery of goods or merchandise belonging to the enterprise; b) the maintenance of a stock of goods or merchandise belonging to the enterprise solely for the purpose of storage, display or delivery; c) the maintenance of a stock of goods or merchandise belonging to the enterprise solely for the purpose of processing by another enterprise; d) the maintenance of a fixed place of business solely for the purpose of purchasing goods or merchandise or of collecting information, for the enterprise; and e) maintenance of a fixed place of business solely for the purpose of carrying on, for the enterprise, any other activity of a preparatory or auxiliary character.

1.37 So Art. 5 § 4 listed several exceptions to the basic PE rule of Art. 5 § 1, each of them serving a specific purpose, for example usually storage space fell under the exception of Art. 5 § 3 a).[57] To address that issue the Commentary affirmed that several fixed places of business in the SC carrying out preparatory or auxiliary activities did not amount to a PE if they were *'separated organizationally'*, i.e., if each place of business operated in isolation. By contrast, those fixed places of business were deemed not to be 'separated organizationally' (and amounted to a PE) *if* each place of business performed complementary functions, such as receiving and storing goods in one place, distributing those goods through another, etc.[58] Moreover a fixed place of

---

55 Belgium, Hof van Beroep Gent) 2004–11–30, 30 November 2004; India, Delhi High Court, *UAE Exchange Centre Ltd v. Union of India*, 13 February 2009.

56 India, Indian Supreme Court, *Morgan Stanley & Co., United States v. Commissioner of Income Tax*, 9 July 2007; Switzerland, Bundesgericht/Tribunal fédéral), 102 ATF 264, 17 September 1977.

57 Belgium, Hof van Beroep Gent 2005/AR/477, 16 January 2007; Belgium, Hof van Beroep Gent, 2002–06–18, 18 June 2002, *Jurisprudence Fiscale*, 2003; Denmark, Landsskatteretten, 1988-4-564, 15 December 1988.

58 Commentary to Art. 5 § 74, which has been eliminated in Commentary 2017.

business used for preparatory or auxiliary activities and other activities was a single PE and taxable as regards both types of activities.[59]

Art. 5 § 4 of the Model 2017 has now modified this approach with a more **1.38** restrictive rule because the work on Action 7 led to changes to the wording of Art. 5 § 4 of the Model to address situations in which the specific activity exemptions give rise to BEPS concerns.[60] Art. 13 of the MLI is very similar, but includes two options A and B and the latter differs from Art. 5 § 4 of the Model 2017. Letters a)–f) are substantially the same as before (the reference of preparatory and auxiliary activities has been taken out in individual letters) so that those exclusions continue to operate, but a final statement has been added which clarifies that the term 'PE' shall be deemed not to include each of the individual activities listed in letters a)–e) provided that each of those activities is of a preparatory or auxiliary character.

This final statement also clarifies that the maintenance of a fixed place of **1.39** business solely for any combination of activities mentioned in subparagraphs a)–e), is not a PE if the *overall activity* of the fixed place of business is of a preparatory or auxiliary character. This implies that one not only has to conduct an analysis of each individual activity to check whether it is indeed of a preparatory or auxiliary nature, but also to develop an holistic approach of all the different places of business to determine whether, in their synergy, they effectively are just of a preparatory or auxiliary character.

The Model 2017 reflects a restrictive judicial trend which had previously **1.40** denied, even under the pre-2017 language of Art. 5 § 4, for example, that storage space as such constituted an exception.[61] Another example of a PE was a company resident of the US which established a representative office in India to purchase materials from India, Egypt and Bangladesh,[62] while another case took a different view.[63] The collecting of information has also been considered to be a preparatory activity because information flows create a

---

59 The Netherlands, Hoge Raad der Nederlanden, 17.812, 24 March 1976.
60 On Action 7 BEPS Project: Dos Santos, António Carlos and Cidália Mota Lopes, 'Tax Sovereignty, Tax Competition and the Base Erosion and Profit Shifting Concept of Permanent Establishment' (2016) 25 *EC Tax Review*, 296; Storck, Alfred and Mechtler, Lukas, 'Permanent Establishment: Proposals Related to Art. 5(3) and (4) of the OECD Model Convention' in: Lang, Michael, et al., (eds) *Base Erosion and Profit Shifting* (BEPS), (Linde 2016) p. 57.
61 Spain, Tribunal Económico Administrativo Central, 0657/2003, 2 March 2003; Belgium, Hof van Beroep Gent, 2005/AR/477, 16 January 2007; Germany, Finanzgericht, II 1224/97, 6 September 2001.
62 India, Authority for Advance Rulings (AAR), *Columbia Sportswear Company v. DIT*, 8 August.
63 India, Income Tax Appellate Tribunal (ITAT) Mumbai, *M. Fabrikant and Sons Inc. v. DIT*, 31 March 2011.

PE.[64] This approach was confirmed by other judicial decisions dealing with the management of information in a broad sense.[65]

1.41 The restrictive judicial trend by national courts was also to consider that the preparatory or auxiliary natures of activities carried on through a fixed place of business are, in any event, within the core of a complex structure of trans-national business. There were different judicial patterns in that respect. One approach was simply to consider preparatory activities as belonging to the core business.[66] Moreover, according to the '*attraction approach*', a place of business that in a broad sense supported a core business activity was deemed to be a PE.[67] The criterion to decide whether preparatory or auxiliary activities of a fixed place of business are a PE traditionally was the fact that they formed an essential or significant part of the activity of enterprise 'as a whole',[68] and that it could be relevant how 'remote' an activity is from the actual realization of profits.[69] Even before 2017 the Commentary focused on the residual clause of Art. 5 § 4 e) and pointed out that a fixed place of business through which the enterprise exercises solely an activity which has for the enterprise a preparatory or auxiliary character is deemed *not* to be a PE.[70]

1.42 The Commentary modified in 2017 with respect to these different situations clarifies with more precision the requirement for exemption from the status of PE. For example a stock of goods or merchandise belonging to an enterprise maintained by another person in facilities operated by that other person is not a PE when that enterprise does not have the facilities at its disposal.[71] A bonded warehouse with special gas facilities that an exporter of fruit from one state maintains in another state for the sole purpose of storing fruit in a controlled environment during the customs clearance process in that other state also is not a PE. Likewise a fixed place of business that an enterprise

---

64 Germany, Bundesfinanzhof IR 292/81, 23 January 1985, *Bundessteuerblatt*, 1985, II, 13, 417 *contra:* Belgium, Hof van Beroep Gent 2004–11–30, 30 November 2004.

65 India, Income Tax Appellate Tribunal (ITAT) Delhi, *Pioneer Overseas Corporation v. ADIT*, Nos. 1868, 1869, 1870 and 1871/Del/2005, 24 December 2009; Italy, Corte Suprema di Cassazione, 7682, 25 May 2002; Germany, Bundesfinanzhof, IR 292/81, 23 January 1985; India, Income Tax Appellate Tribunal Delhi, *Amadeus Global Travel v. ADIT*, 30 November 2007; Germany, Finanzgericht II 1224/97, 6 September 2001; *contra:* Belgium, Hof van Beroep Gent 2004–11–30, 30 November 2004.

66 Austria, Verwaltungsgerichtshof, 98/14/0026, 19 March 2002.

67 Germany, Bundesfinanzhof, IR 130/83, 18 December 1986.

68 Commentary to Art. 5 § 59.

69 Commentary to Art. 5 § 23, which has been eliminated in Commentary 2017 and transposed in other paragraphs.

70 Ibid.

71 Commentary to Art. 5 § 65.

maintains solely for the delivery of spare parts to customers for machinery sold to those customers is not a PE.[72]

Subparagraph c) covers the situation in which a stock of goods or merchandise **1.43** belonging to one enterprise is processed by a second enterprise, on behalf of, or on the account of, the first-mentioned enterprise. So situations of toll-manufacturers when a stock of goods belonging to an enterprise of the RC is maintained by a toll-manufacturer located in the SC for the purposes of processing are not PEs, unless the foreign enterprise is allowed unlimited access to the facilities of the toll-manufacturer for inspecting. The mere maintenance of a stock of goods for the purposes of processing by another enterprise is not a PE. By contrast, a fixed place of business used for the purchase of goods or merchandise where the overall activity of the enterprise consists in selling these goods and where purchasing is a core function of the business of the enterprise is a PE.[73]

The second part of subparagraph d) refers to the maintenance of a fixed place **1.44** of business solely for the purpose of collecting information, so it is necessary to determine whether the collection of this information goes beyond the preparatory or auxiliary threshold: for example an office established by an investment fund solely to collect information of investment opportunities is not a PE. By contrast, a fixed place of business used to furnish plans etc. specially developed for the purposes of the individual customer is a PE.[74]

Subparagraph e) provides that a fixed place of business maintained solely for **1.45** the purpose of carrying on, for the enterprise, any activity that is not expressly listed in subparagraphs a)–d) is not a PE if that activity is of a preparatory or auxiliary character. Examples of places of business covered by subparagraph e) are fixed places of business used solely for the purpose of advertising or for the supply of information or for scientific research or for the servicing of a patent or a know-how contract, if such activities have a preparatory or auxiliary character. By contrast, there is a PE if the fixed place of business used for the supply of information also furnishes plans, etc. specially developed for the purposes of the individual customer, or if a research establishment carries out actual manufacturing. There is also a PE if an enterprise that sells goods worldwide establishes an office in a state and the employees working at that office take an active part in the negotiation of important parts of contracts for

---

72 Commentary to Art. 5 § 63.
73 Commentary to Art. 5 §§ 68–69.
74 Commentary to Art. 5 § 69.

the sale of goods to buyers in that state without habitually concluding contracts or playing the principal role leading to the conclusion of contracts (e.g., by participating in decisions related to the type, quality or quantity of products covered by these contracts).[75]

1.46 Art. 5 § 4.1. of the Model 2017 also introduced a so called '*anti-fragmentation rule*'. Art. 13 MLI contains a similar rule. The purpose of Art. 5 § 4.1 is to prevent an enterprise or a group of closely related enterprises from fragmenting a cohesive business operation into several small operations in order to argue that each is merely engaged in a preparatory or auxiliary activity. Under Art. 5 § 4.1, the exceptions provided for by Art. 5 § 4 do not apply to a place of business that would otherwise constitute a PE where the activities carried on at that place and other activities of the same enterprise or of closely related enterprises exercised at that place or at another place in the same state constitute 'complementary functions that are part of a cohesive business operation'.

1.47 So there are two situations covered by Art. 5 § 4.1. in which the exemptions listed by Art. 5 § 4 do not apply. The first situation is the following: a fixed place of business is used or maintained by an enterprise when the same enterprise or a closely related enterprise carries on business activities at the same place or at another place in the same CS, if that place or other place constitutes a PE for the enterprise or the closely related enterprise under the provisions of Art. 5. The second situation is the following: a fixed place of business is used or maintained by an enterprise if the same enterprise or a closely related enterprise carries on business activities at the same place or at another place in the same CS, if the overall activity resulting from the combination of the activities carried on by the two enterprises at the same place, or by the same enterprise or closely related enterprises at the two places, is not of a preparatory or auxiliary character. In both situations, in order to have a PE the business activities carried on by the two enterprises at the same place, or by the same enterprise or closely related enterprises at the two places, must constitute 'complementary functions that are part of a cohesive business operation'. Art. 5 § 8 explains the meaning of the concept of a person or enterprise 'closely related to an enterprise' for the purposes of Art. 5 § 4.1.

E. The Agency-PE: functional analysis

1.48 The purpose of Art. 5 § 5 is to address those situations in which an enterprise does not have a fixed place of business in the SC within the meaning of Art. 5

---

75   Commentary to Art. 5 §§ 70–72.

§§ 1 and 2, and yet that enterprise should be treated as having a PE in that country if a person is acting for it in that country and, at the same time, certain requirements are met ('agency-PE').[76] The re-characterization of a certain situation as an agency-PE covers all actions of a 'dependent agent' for the principal,[77] and if there is a material PE there is no need to conduct the agency-PE test.[78] The Commentary to Art. 5 § 131 addresses the general issue of whether the Internet service provider is a dependent agent.

The Model 2017 introduced significant changes to Art. 5 § 5 which imply a **1.49** different approach from the past. Before these changes, the traditional approach under the previous Art. 5 § 5 was that the definition of 'dependent agent' was a negative one: dependent agents were persons who were *not* independent agents falling under Art. 5 § 6, who involved the enterprise to a particular extent in business activities in the SC in view of the scope of their authority or the nature of their activity,[79] bearing in mind that only persons having the *authority to conclude contracts* repeatedly and not merely in isolated cases could lead to a PE authority.[80]

Under that analysis – which is maintained but expanded now by Model 2017 – **1.50** an agent having the 'authority to conclude contracts in the name of the enterprise' is a person who enters into *contracts which are binding on the enterprise*, even if those contracts are not actually in the name of the enterprise. Previous Commentary to Art. 5 § 32 indicated that the phrase 'authority to conclude contracts in the name of the enterprise' was not limited to contracts literally in the name of the enterprise but extended to contracts 'binding' on the enterprise even if those contracts were not actually in the name of the enterprise, clarifying that an agent could possess actual authority to conclude contracts if he solicited and received (but did not formally finalize) orders which were sent directly to a warehouse from which goods are delivered and where the foreign enterprise routinely approved the transactions.[81]

This substantial approach was quite minimal, but judicial cases have expanded **1.51** it, for example stating that the lack of active involvement by an enterprise in transactions may be indicative of a grant of authority to an agent when, for example, the agent solicits and receives (but does not formally finalize) orders

---

76 Commentary to Art. 5 § 82.
77 Commentary to Art. 5 § 99.
78 Commentary to Art. 5 § 100.
79 Commentary to Art. 5 § 83.
80 Denmark, Landsskatteretten, 1988-4-564, 15 December 1988.
81 Commentary 2014 to Art. 5 § 32.1-1, which has been deleted in Commentary 2017. See: Belgium, Cour d'Appel Bruxelles, 1992–02–18, 18 February 1992.

and the enterprise routinely approves the transactions,[82] or clarifying that the activity of an agent who exercises authority to conclude contracts 'habitually' is more than 'merely transitory' and depends on the nature of contracts or business.[83] The authority to conclude contracts must cover contracts relating to operations that constitute the business proper of the enterprise. Therefore, the authority of a person to engage employees for the enterprise, or to conclude contracts relating to internal operations only, is irrelevant.

1.52 As mentioned, the authority to conclude contracts has to be habitually exercised in the SC, and it is deemed that a person is authorized to negotiate a contract in a way binding on the enterprise, in spite of the fact that the contract is formally signed by another person, or in spite of the fact that such negotiating person has no power of representation. So in commercial practice the issue arose of what was exactly the impact of participation by the foreign enterprise in the negotiation of contracts. The Commentary observes that the mere fact that a person has attended or participated in negotiations is not, by itself, authority to conclude contracts because the relevant factor is determining the exact functions performed by that person on behalf of the enterprise. This concept was applied in an Indian case.[84] National tax authorities have, however, adopted a restrictive approach and claimed that persons who have attended or participated in negotiations may constitute an agency-PE.[85]

1.53 Art. 5 § 5 as amended in Model 2017 expands significantly the pre-existing approach of the 'authority to conclude contracts' and adopts now a view that looks beyond that traditional analysis in so far as it adopts a functional approach based on a three-pronged test. Art. 13 MLI contains a similar rule. The work on Action 7 led to these changes to the wording of Art. 5 § 5 mainly to address the artificial avoidance of PE status through commissionnaire arrangements and similar strategies.[86] Pursuant to Art. 5 § 5, where a person is acting in a CS on behalf of an enterprise and has, and habitually exercises, in a CS, an authority to conclude contracts, in doing so, habitually concludes

---

82 Russia, Federal Arbitration Court, N A40-58575/11-129-248, 2 August 2012.

83 Commentary to Art. 5 § 98. See: Germany, Bundesfinanzhof, I R 87/04, 3 August 2005.

84 Commentary to Art. 5 § 97. India, Income Tax Appellate Tribunal (ITAT) Delhi, *Rolls Royce plc. v. ADIT*, 19 April 2005.

85 See: Italy, Corte Suprema di Cassazione, 7682, 25 May 2002, Italy, Corte Suprema di Cassazione, 8488, 9 April 2010.

86 On the agency-PE Action 7 BEPS Project: Eisenbeiss, Justus, 'BEPS Action 7: Evaluation of the Agency Permanent Establishment', (2016) 44 *Intertax* 481; Pleijsier, Arthur, 'The Agency Permanent Establishment in BEPS Action 7: Treaty Abuse or Business Abuse?', (2015) 43 *Intertax* 147–54, etc.; Uslu, Yasin, 'An Analysis of 'Google Taxes' in the Context of Action 7 of the OECD/G20 Base Erosion and Profit Shifting Initiative', (2018) 72 *Bull. Intl. Taxn.*

contracts, or habitually plays the principal role leading to the conclusion of contracts that are routinely concluded without material modification by the enterprise, and these contracts are a) in the name of the enterprise, or b) for the transfer of the ownership of, or for the granting of the right to use, property owned by that enterprise or that the enterprise has the right to use, or c) for the provision of services by that enterprise, that enterprise shall be deemed to have a PE in that state in respect of any activities which that person undertakes for the enterprise.

Even if the three-pronged test is not met the foreign enterprise is not deemed **1.54** to have a PE if the activities of such a person are limited to the activities covered by Art. 5 § 4 which are not PE. In practice even if the conditions of the three-pronged test are met, Art. 5 § 5 does not apply if the activities performed by the person on behalf of the enterprise are limited to activities mentioned in Art. 5 § 4. Likewise, as before Model 2017, even if the conditions of the three-pronged test are met, Art. 5 § 5 does not apply if the activities are covered by the independent agent exception of Art. 5 § 6.

Art. 5 § 5 does not apply to situations where a person concludes contracts on **1.55** its own behalf and obtains goods or services from other enterprises or arranges for other enterprises to deliver such goods or services to comply with the obligations deriving from these contracts. For example a distributor of products who sells to customers in the SC products that it buys from an enterprise, it is neither acting on behalf of that enterprise nor selling property that is owned by that enterprise since the property that is sold to the customers in the SC is owned by such distributor. In these cases, the person is not acting 'on behalf' of other enterprises and the contracts concluded by the person are neither in the name of these enterprises nor for the transfer to third parties of the ownership or use of property that these enterprises own.

The Commentary now clarifies that there is a 'conclusion of contracts' in all **1.56** situations where, under the relevant law governing contracts, a contract is considered to have been concluded by a person. A contract may be concluded without any active negotiation of the terms of that contract when, for example, the relevant law provides that a contract is concluded by reason of a person accepting, on behalf of an enterprise, the offer made by a third party to enter into a standard contract with that enterprise. Also, a contract may, under the relevant law, be concluded in a state even if that contract is signed outside that state; this occurs for example when the conclusion of a contract results from the acceptance, by a person acting on behalf of an enterprise, of an offer to enter into a contract made by a third party.[87]

1.57 Art. 5 § 5 of Model 2017 not only looks at the authority to conclude contracts or to the habitual conclusion of contracts as before, but also extends to a situation in which a person 'habitually plays the principal role leading to the conclusion of contracts that are routinely concluded without material modification by the enterprise'. The Commentary clarifies that these situations occur when the conclusion of a contract directly results from the actions that the person performs in a CS on behalf of the enterprise even though, under the relevant law, the contract is not concluded by that person in that state. In practice there is an agency-PE when activities that a person exercises in a state result in the regular conclusion of contracts to be performed by a foreign enterprise, i.e., where that person acts as the sales force of the enterprise.[88]

1.58 The Commentary further clarifies that the reference to 'contracts that are routinely concluded without material modification by the enterprise' implies that the person who 'habitually plays the principal role leading to the conclusion of contracts' in the SC is an agency-PE even if the contracts are not formally concluded in that state, for example, where the contracts are routinely subject, outside that state, to review and approval without such review resulting in a modification of the key aspects of these contracts. So there is an agency-PE when, for example, a person solicits and receives (but does not formally finalize) orders which are sent directly to a warehouse from which goods belonging to the enterprise are delivered and where the enterprise routinely approves these transactions. By contrast, there is no agency-PE when a person merely promotes and markets goods or services of an enterprise in a way that does not directly result in the conclusion of contracts, for example when representatives of a pharmaceutical enterprise promote drugs produced by that enterprise by contacting doctors who subsequently prescribe these drugs.[89]

1.59 Contractual arrangements setting up commissionaire structures have in the past traditionally posed the issue of whether the commission agent was an agency-PE. In a commissionaire arrangement, a commission agent in the SC acts on behalf of a foreign enterprise but, in doing so, concludes in its own name contracts with third parties that do not create rights and obligations that are legally enforceable between the foreign enterprise and the third parties

---

87 Commentary to Art. 5 § 87.
88 Commentary to Art. 5 § 88.
89 Commentary to Art. 5 § 89.

even though the foreign enterprise directly transfers to these third parties the ownership or use of property that it owns or has the right to use that property.

Before the changes to Model 2017 it was excluded that a commission agent **1.60** was an agency-PE if his activities were limited to those mentioned at the end of Art. 5 § 5, even if the agent sold the goods or merchandise of the enterprise in his own name, and this was confirmed by leading cases.[90] Even if the Model 2017 does not refer explicitly to commissionaire structures, the Commentary now explicitly affirms that these structures are covered by Art. 5 § 5, when contracts are concluded with clients by an agent, a partner or an employee of an enterprise so as to create legally enforceable rights and obligations between the enterprise and these clients.[91]

Under Art. 5 § 5 there is an agency-PE where a person is acting in a CS on **1.61** behalf of an enterprise and has, and habitually exercises, in a CS, an authority to conclude contracts, and these contracts – even if they are not in the name of the foreign enterprise – are for (i) the transfer of the ownership of property owned by that enterprise or (ii) the provision of services by that enterprise. These situations occur when the contracts that relate to the transfer of the ownership of property, or the provision of services, are performed by the foreign enterprise, and not by the person who acts on the enterprise's behalf. It is worth noting that under Art. 5 § 5 there is an agency-PE in the above situations also when there is (i) the granting of the right to use property owned by that enterprise or (ii) the granting of the right to use property that the enterprise has the right to use or (iii) the transfer of the ownership of property that the enterprise has the right to use.[92]

The work on Action 7 led to changes to the wording of Art. 5 § 6 to address **1.62** the artificial avoidance of PE status. Art. 5 § 6 defines the concept of 'independent agent' which is not an agency-PE. Art. 5 § 6 was replaced in Model 2017 and Art. 13 MLI contains a similar rule.

Before the change Art. 5 § 6 provided that an enterprise was not to be deemed **1.63** to have a PE in a CS merely because it carried on business in that state through a broker, general commission agent or any other agent of an independent status, provided that such persons were acting in the ordinary course of their business.

---

90 France, Conseil d'État 304715, 308525; Norway, Høyesterett HR-2011-02245-A (sak nr. 2011/755), 2 December 2011.
91 Commentary to Art. 5 § 92.
92 Commentary to Art. 5 § 94.

Under that provision the independence of the agent was determined essentially by a two-prong test: (i) the agent had to be *independent* of the enterprise *both legally and economically* (this analysis also relied on the lack of detailed instructions by the principal, and the fact that entrepreneurial risk is borne by the agent); and (ii) the agent had to act in the *ordinary course of his business* when acting on behalf of the enterprise.[93] Furthemore the analysis of whether an agent acted in the ordinary course of his business was developed using two basic indicators: (i) whether the activities belonged to agent's own economic sphere or to the sphere of the principal; and (ii) whether the agent had one or more principals. The Commentary suggested that the business activities carried out within agent's trade should be compared to the other business activities carried out by that agent.[94]

1.64 Art. 5 § 6 in the current version now provides that Art. 5 § 5 shall not apply where the person acting in a CS on behalf of an enterprise of the other CS carries on business in the first-mentioned state as an independent agent and acts for the enterprise in the ordinary course of that business. The previous reference to 'a broker, general commission agent or any other agent of an independent status' has been deleted because it created confusion when applied to different civil law or common law systems and now one has to refer to the requirement of the 'ordinary course of business'.

1.65 The Commentary explains that now the central criterion to exclude that a person is an agency-PE under Art. 5 § 6 is that it acts in the 'ordinary course of business'. An agent is independent – and not an agency-PE – when it acts in the ordinary course of its business as agent, i.e., when it performs activities that are related to that agency business. So an agent does not act in the ordinary course of its business as agent when it performs activities that are unrelated to that agency business. Let us take for example company X that (i) acts on its own account as a distributor for companies a, b, c, and (ii) also acts as an agent for company d. In this situation the activities that company X undertakes as a distributor for companies a, b, c, are not part of the activities that company X carries on in the ordinary course of its business as an agent for company d.[95]

---

93 Commentary 2014 to Art. 5 § 37, which has been deleted in Commentary 2017. See: Belgium, Cour d'Appel Bruxelles, 1992–02–18, 18 February 1992.

94 Commentary 2014 to Art. 5 § 38.8, which has been deleted in Commentary 2017. See: India, High Court of Delhi, *Rolls Royce Singapore Pvt. Ltd. v. ADIT*, 30 August 2011; Germany, Bundesfinanzhof (Federal Fiscal Court), I R 116/93, 14 September 1994; Denmark, Højesteret, 7/1991, 25 June 1996.

95 Commentary to Art. 5 § 110.

The Commentary clarifies that Art. 5 § 6 only applies to persons who act on **1.66** behalf of an enterprise in the course of carrying on a business as an independent agent, but does not apply to persons who act on behalf of an enterprise in a different capacity, such as where an employee acts on behalf of her employer or a partner acts on behalf of a partnership.[96]

The Commentary provides a series of *indicators* that can be used, either in **1.67** isolation or in combination, to determine whether an agent is independent. These indicators are: subsidiary's independence, control/detailed instructions, number of principals, limitations on scale of business, and provision of information. With regard to limitations on scale of business, the Commentary observes that the extent to which the agent exercises freedom in the conduct of business on behalf of the principal within the scope of the authority conferred by the agreement is not relevant. With regard to the provision of information, the Commentary notes that the fact that the agent provides substantial information to the principal is not in itself a sufficient criterion, while the fact that the agent provides substantial information to the principal to seek approval is an indication of dependence.[97]

Additional requirements of independence are that: (i) *the agent's commercial* **1.68** *activities for the enterprise are not subject to detailed instructions or to comprehensive control;* and (ii) *the entrepreneurial risk is borne by the agent.*[98] An independent agent is responsible to his principal for the results, but is not subject to significant control on how work is carried out, or to detailed instructions.[99]

Art. 5 § 6 in the current version however provides that a person who acts **1.69** exclusively or almost exclusively on behalf of one or more enterprises to which it is closely related shall not be considered to be an independent agent with respect to any such enterprise. So the number of principals is an important indicator of the independence of the agent: while only one principal is an indicator of the fact that the agent is essentially captive of that principal, the existence of several principals is an indicator of the fact that the agent is

---

96 Commentary to Art. 5 § 103.
97 Commentary to Art. 5 § 108. See: Canada, Tax Court of Canada, *American Life Insurance Co. v. Her Majesty the Queen*, 16 May 2008, United States, US Tax Court, *Taisei Fire and Marine Insurance Co. Ltd. et al. v. Commissioner of Internal Revenue*, 2 May 1995; The Netherlands, Gerechtshof Den Haag, BK 07/00604, 15 July 2008; Denmark, Højesteret (Supreme Court), 1. afdeling, 142/2001, 5 February 2004; India, Income Tax Appellate Tribunal (ITAT), *Delmas France Mumbai v. ADIT*, 11 January 2012.
98 Commentary to Art. 5 § 104.
99 Commentary to Art. 5 § 106. See: United States, US Tax Court, *Taisei Fire and Marine Insurance Co. Ltd. et al. v. Commissioner of Internal Revenue*, 2 May 1995; India, High Court of Delhi, *Rolls Royce Singapore Pvt. Ltd. v. ADIT*, 30 August 2011; Canada, Tax Court of Canada, *American Life Insurance Co. v. Her Majesty the Queen*, 16 May 2008.

operating as an autonomous entity (i.e., in the ordinary course of business). An agent acts for a number of principals in the ordinary course of its business when none of the principals is predominant in terms of the business carried on by the agent.[100]

1.70 Independent status is less likely if the activities of the person are performed wholly or almost wholly on behalf of only one enterprise, or a group of enterprises that are 'closely related' to each other, over the lifetime of that person's business or over a long period of time. Where, however, a person is acting exclusively for one enterprise to which it is not 'closely related', even if that occurs only for a short period of time (e.g. at the beginning of that person's business operations), it is possible that Art. 5 § 6 applies.[101]

1.71 Art. 5 § 8 explains the meaning of the concept of a person or enterprise 'closely related' to an enterprise for the purposes of Art. § 6. A person or enterprise is closely related to an enterprise if, based on all the relevant facts and circumstances, one has control of the other or both are under the control of the same persons or enterprises. In any case, a person or enterprise shall be considered to be closely related to an enterprise if one possesses directly or indirectly more than 50 per cent of the beneficial interest in the other (or, in the case of a company, more than 50 per cent of the aggregate vote and value of the company's shares or of the beneficial equity interest in the company) or if another person or enterprise possesses directly or indirectly more than 50 per cent of the beneficial interest (or, in the case of a company, more than 50 per cent of the aggregate vote and value of the company's shares or of the beneficial equity interest in the company) in the person and the enterprise or in the two enterprises.

F. Structures in shipping and air transport

1.72 The operation of ships/aircraft/boats in international traffic is traditionally kept out of the Art. 5 approach to the PE because of the peculiar structure of firms operating in this field. Before the changes of Model 2017 Art. 8 § in fact provided that profits from the operation of ships/aircraft/boats in international traffic were taxable only in the CS in which the effective place of management of the enterprise was situated, thereby excluding the need to assess whether

---

100 However, the fact that different principals act in concert to control the acts of the agent is an indication of dependence: Commentary to Art. 5 § 110.

101 Commentary to Art. 5 § 111. India, High Court of Delhi, *Rolls Royce Singapore Pvt. Ltd. v. ADIT*, 30 August 2011.

the operation in the SC was indeed a PE.[102] As the country of the effective place of management of the enterprise usually coincides with the RC, Art. 8 § 1 appeared to adopt a principle of exclusive taxation in the RC.

The Commentary, however, already mentioned different models of taxation of **1.73** this kind of income, such as exclusive taxation in the RC, and a combination of exclusive taxation in the CS where effective place of management and in the RC. Art. 8 has now been entirely remodelled by Model 2017. It previously contained four paragraphs and generally adopted the criterion of the effective place of management of the enterprise. Paragraphs 2–4 have been eliminated and Art. 8 § 1 now provides that the profits of an enterprise of a CS from the operation of ships or aircrafts in international traffic shall be taxable only in that state. A review of the treaty practices of OECD and non-OECD countries revealed that the majority of these states preferred to assign the taxing right to the state of the enterprise, rather than to the CS in which the place of effective management of the enterprise was situated. In this respect it should be noted that pursuant to Art. 3 § 1 d) of the Model the term 'enterprise of a CS' means an enterprise carried on by a resident of the CS.

Moreover Model 2017 eliminated within Art. 8 the reference to 'inland **1.74** waterways transport' so that now the reference is exclusively to profits from international shipping and air transport, and all kinds of these activities are regulated by Art. 8 § 1.

It should also be noted that Model 2017 modified the concept of 'international **1.75** traffic'. Before 2017 subparagraph e) of Art. 3 defined the term 'international traffic' as any transport by a ship or aircraft, except when the ship or aircraft was operated solely between places in the other. Now the subparagraph provides that the term 'international traffic' means any transport by a ship or aircraft, except when the ship or aircraft is operated solely between places in a CS and the enterprise that operates the ship or aircraft is not an enterprise of that state. As noted by the Commentary the definition was amended in 2017 to ensure that it also applied to a transport by a ship or aircraft operated by an

---

102 See in general: Beckermann, Florian, 'Conflicts of Qualification and Income Derived from International Shipping, Inland Waterways Transport and Aircraft Business (Art. 8 OECD MC)' in: Lang, Michael, et al., (eds), *Tax Treaties: Building Bridges between Law and Economics* (IBFD 2010); Cutrera, Margherita, 'Art. 8 – Shipping, Inland and Waterways Transport and Air Transport' in: Ecker, Thomas and Ressler, Gernot (eds), *History of Tax Treaties: The Relevance of the OECD Documents for the Interpretaion of tax Treaties* (Linde 2011); Glicklich, Peter A. and Miller, Michael, *U.S. Taxation of International Shipping and Air Transport Activities* (Bloomberg Bna 2005); Maisto, Guglielmo, 'Shipping, Inland Waterways Transport and Air Transport (Art. 8 OECD Model Convention)' in: Lang, Michael (ed.), *Source Versus Residence: Problems Arising from the Allocation of Taxing Rights in Tax Treaty Law and Possible Alternatives* (Kluwer Law International 2008).

enterprise of a third state. The reason for that is the different language which now explicitly allows the application of § 3 of Art. 15 to a resident of a CS who derives remuneration from employment exercised aboard a ship or aircraft operated by an enterprise of a third state. In spite of the change of definition Art. 8 as a whole continues to apply only to the profits of an enterprise of a CS.[103]

1.76 Art. 8 continues to be the same: to ensure that profits from the operation of ships/aircrafts in international traffic are taxed in one state alone and not in the SC.[104] It should be noted that even if Art. 8 § 1 directly attributes taxing power only to one CS, national courts tend to erode this principle (when included in actual treaties) using different strategies. One of them is to circumscribe the application of Art. 8 § 1 only to international operations, or distinguishing activities not included in the exclusive RC taxation principle.[105]

1.77 Exclusive taxation in the country of the enterprise (Art. 8 § 1) applies to core activities and extended activities (which include directly connected activities, and ancillary activities). The profits covered by Art. 8 § 1 are generally the profits directly obtained by the enterprise from *core activities*, i.e. the transportation of passengers or cargo by ships or aircraft (whether owned, leased or otherwise at the disposal of the enterprise) that it operates in international traffic.[106] *Extended activities* are those that permit, facilitate or support their international traffic operations and the profits derived therefrom are covered by Art. 8 § 1, namely they cannot be taxed in the SC.[107]

1.78 Art. 8 § 1 also covers activities which are directly connected with the core and extended activities. Any activity carried on primarily in connection with the transportation, by the enterprise, of passengers or cargo by ships or aircrafts that it operates in international traffic should be considered to be directly connected with that transportation. Art. 8 § 1 also covers activities which are not directly connected with the operation of the enterprise's ships or aircrafts in international traffic as long as they are ancillary to such operations.[108]

---

103   Commentary to Art. 3 § 6.1.

104   Commentary to Art. 8 § 1. See: Zimbabwe, Federation of Rhodesia and Nyasaland – Special Court, *Undisclosed v. The Commissioner*, 24 May 1964, 26 SATC 226(F).

105   Germany, Finanzgericht Berlin-Brandenburg, 8 K 8084/97, 17 January 2000; Canada, Supreme Court of Canada, *Furness, Withy & Co. v. Her Majesty the Queen*, 29 January 1968; Germany, Bundesfinanzhof, I B 40/94, 14 September 1994; France, Conseil d'État, 249801, 15 July 2004; Italy, Corte Suprema di Cassazione 7609, 1 September 1994.

106   Commentary to Art. 8 § 4.

107   Commentary to Art. 8 § 4.

108   Commentary to Art. 8 § 4.1. See: South Africa, Transvaal Tax Court, *Company name not disclosed v. Commissioner for Inland Revenue*, 25 May 1990.

The Commentary focuses on various types of activities which, depending on **1.79** the circumstances, fall or do not fall under the scope of core or extended activities covered by Art. 8 § 1. These activities include leasing of fully equipped ships/aircraft, slot-chartering, international and domestic combinations, sale of tickets, advertising, use of containers, ground operations, pooling arrangements, shipbuilding, and investment income related to shipping activities.[109] Fishing, dredging or hauling activities on the high seas should fall under Art. 8,[110] but this obviously depends on specific circumstances.[111] Leasing of fully equipped ships/aircraft falls under Art. 8 § 1, but national courts often adopt a restrictive view in this matter.[112]

Investment income related to shipping activities (e.g., income from stocks, **1.80** bonds, shares or loans) falls under Art. 8 § 1 if the investment is an integral part of the carrying on of the business of operating the ships or aircraft in international traffic[113] (for example of interest generated by the cash required in a CS for the carrying on of that business or by bonds posted as security where this is required by law in order to carry on the business). By contrast, Art. 8 § 1 does not apply, for example, to interest from cash-flow or other treasury activities for PEs of the enterprise, or to interest from short-term investment of the profits generated by the local operation of the business if the funds invested are not required for that operation.[114] Other examples of profits not covered by Art. 8 § 1 include profits arising from currency gains and damages awarded after the cancellation of a contract to build a ship in so far as they do not constitute profits from the operation of a ship in international traffic (the ship was not currently operating),[115] or income from a paragliding school in so far as it did not constitute an air transport business within the meaning of the relevant international transport article.[116]

The reference in Art. 8 to operation of boats engaged in inland waterways **1.81** transport has been eliminated, but previously Model 2017 Art. 8 § 2 provided that profits from the operation of those boats were taxable only in the CS in which the effective place of management of the enterprise was situated. Art. 8 § 2 applied not only to inland waterways transport between two or more

---

109 Commentary to Art. 8 §§ 6–12, 14 and 17.
110 Commentary to Art. 8 § 18.
111 The Netherlands, Hoge Raad der Nederlanden, 35.769, 20 December 2000.
112 Canada, Federal Court of Appeal, *Gulf Offshore N.S. Ltd. v. Her Majesty the Queen*, 21 September 2007; France, Cour Administrative d'Appel Nancy, 89NC00529–89NC00531, 10 October 1991.
113 Commentary to Art. 8 § 14.1.
114 Commentary to Art. 8 § 14.2. See: United States, US Court of Federal Claims, *Qantas Airways Ltd. v. United States (Internal Revenue Service)*, 4 April 1997.
115 Germany, Bundesfinanzhof I R 31/02, 1 April 2003.
116 Austria, Verwaltungsgerichtshof, 2005/15/0072, 19 March 2008.

countries, but also to inland waterways transport carried on by an enterprise of one country between two points in another country.[117] Art. 8 § 2 has now been eliminated by Model 2017. The goal of Art. 8 § 2 was to apply to inland waterways transport the same treatment as to shipping and air transport in international traffic, so that the rules with respect to the taxing right of the effective place of management country as set forth in Art. 8 § 1 applied also to activities covered by Art. 8 § 2;[118] paragraphs 4–14 of the Commentary to Art. 8 (dealing specifically with Art. 8 § 1) thus continue to apply, with the necessary adaptations, for purposes of determining which profits may be considered to be derived from the operation of boats with respect to inland waterways transport.[119]

1.82 Enterprises exclusively engaged in shipping, inland waterways transport or air transport before Model 2017 came under Art. 8 § 2, as regards profits arising to them from the operation of ships or aircraft belonging to them.[120] The Commentary makes a distinction between foreign PEs exclusively engaged and foreign PEs not exclusively engaged in shipping or air transport. The former situation occurs when an enterprise has in a foreign country PEs exclusively concerned with the operation of its ships or aircrafts, and so the SC does not have a power to tax the profits of the PE.[121] By contrast, a foreign PE exclusively engaged in inland waterways transport was deemed to be a PE that received goods carried by third parties on its own ships: also in this case the SC does not have the power to tax the profits of the PE.[122]

1.83 Before Model 2017, Art. 8 § 3 provided that if the effective place of management of a shipping enterprise or of an inland waterways transport enterprise was aboard a ship/boat, *then* it was deemed to be situated in the CS in which the home harbour of the ship/boat is situated, *or*, if there was no such home harbour, in the CS of which the operator of the ship/boat is a resident.[123] Art. 8 § 3 has now been eliminated by Model 2017.

1.84 Art. 8 § 4 has been maintained in Model 2017 and renamed Art. 8 § 2. It provides that Art. 8 § 1 shall also apply to profits from the participation in a pool, a joint business or an international operating agency. This includes

---

117   Commentary to Art. 8 § 16; Germany, Finanzgericht Nordrhein-Westfalen, 2 K 92/99, 22 June 2001.
118   Commentary to Art. 8 §§ 15–16.
119   Commentary to Art. 8 § 16.1.
120   Commentary to Art. 8 §§ 18–19.
121   Commentary to Art. 8 § 20.
122   Commentary to Art. 8 §§ 21–22.
123   The Netherlands, Hoge Raad der Nederlanden, No. AWB 10/00157, 25 March 2011.

various forms of international company operation that exist in shipping or air transport, such as pooling agreements or other treaties.[124]

II. FORCE OF ATTRACTION OF THE PE

Art. 7 § 4 provides that *if* profits include items of income that are dealt with **1.85** separately in other articles of the Convention, *then* the provisions of those articles shall not be affected by the provisions of Art. 7. This means that the provisions of those articles operate instead of Art. 7 in so far as the situations of *'isolated income'* covered by those articles are not attracted to taxation as business profits of the PE under the concept of the 'limited force of attraction of the PE'. In other words: in these cases the existence of the PE does not, per se, determine that the foreign person is taxable in the SC. This section on separate taxation of business profits under Art. 7 § 4 is preceded by general remarks on the 'effectively connected' concept and then focuses on the relationship between Art. 7 with other articles from the perspective of the treaty in the SC.

If the profits of an enterprise include categories of income which are dealt with **1.86** separately in other articles of the Convention, i.e., dividends, the question that arises is which article should apply to these categories of income, for example in the case of dividends, should Art. 7 or Art. 10 apply (and so on for other treaty articles)?[125] The Commentary summarizes longstanding differences of view. According to the so-called *'full force of attraction'*, income such as other business profits, dividends, interest and royalties arising from sources in the SC are fully taxable by the SC if the beneficiary has a PE therein, even though such income is not attributable to that PE. According to the so-called *'limited (or restricted) force of attraction'* in taxing the profits that a foreign enterprise derives from the SC, tax authorities of the SC should look at separate sources of profit, subject to the possible application of other articles of the Convention.[126]

The Commentary is based on the restricted force of attraction and notes that **1.87** this solution allows simpler and more efficient tax administration and compliance, and is more closely adapted to the way in which business is commonly carried on. The organization of modern business is highly complex.[127] So the

---

124 Commentary to Art. 8 §§ 24–25.
125 Commentary to Art. 7 § 72.
126 Commentary to Art. 7 § 12-1.
127 Commentary to Art. 7 § 12-1 last statement.

restricted force of attraction is a rule of interpretation that ensures that articles applicable to specific categories of income have priority over Art. 7,[128] clarifying that Art. 7 § 4 does not govern the manner in which income will be classified for the purposes of domestic laws.[129]

1.88 The restricted force of attraction, to operate, needs a criterion to distinguish which kinds of income are 'attracted' by the PE, and which other kinds of income are not 'attracted' and are therefore 'isolated'. This criterion is the 'effectively connected' concept. The Commentary affirms that Art. 7 applies *only* to business profits which do not belong to categories of income covered by these other articles, but does not apply to other specific categories of income.[130]

A. Which activities are 'attracted' by the PE?

1.89 There are specific treaty articles that operatively establish when income (otherwise 'isolated') becomes effectively connected (Artt. 10 § 4, 11 § 3, 12 § 2, and 21 § 2, hereinafter the '*EFC rules*'). The Commentary addresses these different situations of effectively connected income, but has a common structure in respect of dividends (Art. 10 § 4), interest (Art. 11 § 4), royalties (Art. 12 § 3), and other income (Art. 21 § 2).

1.90 In the first place the Commentary provides that dividends, interest, royalties, and other income arising in the SC and payable to taxpayers resident in the RC fall outside the scope of arrangements made to prevent those types of income from being taxed both in the SC and in the RC (i.e., the CS of the beneficiary's residence) *if* the beneficiary of those types of income has a PE in the SC.

1.91 The Commentary generally observes that EFC rules are *not* based on the 'full force of attraction of PE', and suggests that those articles do *not* stipulate that dividends, interest, royalties and other income flowing to a resident of the RC from a source situated in the SC must be related to a PE which that resident may have in the SC. By contrast, the Commentary explains that those articles provide that in the SC those dividends, interest, royalties and other income are taxable as part of the profits of a PE there owned by the beneficiary resident in the RC, *only if they meet a specific connection requirement.* In the cases indicated

---

128   Commentary to Art. 7 § 73.
129   Commentary to Art. 7 § 74-2.
130   Commentary to Art. 7 § 74-1.

above each of the EFC rules relieves the SC from any limitations under Arts. 10, 11, 12 and 21.

The Commentary observes that the EFC rules rely on an *'economic ownership'* **1.92** concept. The Commentary also suggests that the 'economic' ownership of participations (dividends), debt claims (interest), right or property (royalties), or assets (other income) is determined under the principles developed in the CFA's report Attribution of Profits to PEs (§§ 72–97). Moreover, according to the Commentary, the requirement that participations (dividends), debt claims (interest), right or property (royalties) or assets (other income) be 'effectively connected' to the PE requires more than merely recording items in the books of the PE for accounting purposes.

The transfer of participations (dividends), debt claims (interest), right or **1.93** property (royalties) or assets (other income) to PEs set up solely for that purpose in countries that offer a preferential tax regime to those classes of income triggers the application of domestic anti-abuse rules.

This part of the chapter focuses more specifically on the relationship of Art. 7 **1.94** with EFC rules.

1. Effectively connected dividends

Art. 10 § 4 provides that Art. 10 §§ 1 and 2 shall not apply if the beneficial **1.95** owner of the dividends, being a resident of the RC, carries on business in the SC (the CS of which the company paying the dividends is a resident) through a PE situated in the SC and the participation in respect of which the dividends are paid is effectively connected with such a PE. In such a case, Art. 7 shall apply.[131]

2. Effectively connected interest

Art. 11 § 5 provides that if the person paying the interest (whether he is a **1.96** resident of the SC, the RC or a third country), has in a CS a PE in connection with which the indebtedness on which the paid interest was incurred, and such interest is borne by such PE, then such interest shall be deemed to arise in the SC (the state in which the PE is situated). The application of this rule has led to distinguish, from the perspective of the SC, situations in which interest is not attracted ('isolated interest'), by the PE and situations in which interest is attracted by the PE.[132] The general principle established by Art. 11 § 1 is that

---

131   Commentary to Art. 10 §§ 31–32.2.
132   Commentary to Art. 11 §§ 24–25.2.

the SC of the interest is the state of which the payer of interest is a resident. An exception is made by Art. 11 § 5 in the case of interest-bearing loans that have an obvious economic link with a PE owned in the SC by the payer of the interest. Art. 11 § 5 provides that: *if* (i) the loan was contracted for the requirements of that PE in the SC; and (ii) the interest is borne by that PE, *then* the source of the interest is in the CS in which the PE is situated (the SC), leaving aside the place of residence of the owner of the PE (a third country or the RC).[133]

1.97 National courts have applied the 'restricted force of attraction of PE' to determine, on the basis of the OECD guidelines described above, in which cases interest is not attracted and therefore subject to isolated treaty treatment and developed various criteria.[134] The link, for example occurs if the management of the PE has contracted a loan, which it uses for the specific requirements of the PE, and shows it among its liabilities and pays the interest thereon directly to the creditor. A second situation is one in which the head office of the enterprise has contracted a loan the proceeds of which are used solely for the purposes of a PE situated in another country (the interest is serviced by the head office but is ultimately borne by the PE). By contrast, if the loan is contracted by the head office of the enterprise and its proceeds are used for several PEs situated in different countries the requirements of the second sentence of Art. 11 § 5 are not met, and the state where the PE is situated is not the SC for the purposes of the treaty (i.e., the state where the interest is deemed to arise). This situation falls outside Art. 11 § 5.[135]

1.98 Art. 11 § 5 regulates the tax treatment of interest borne by a PE situated either in the SC or in a third country and received by a taxpayer resident in the RC, but also indirectly provides a ban on extraterritorial taxation in the SC on interest paid to a recipient in the RC but effectively attributable to a PE in the SC.[136] In the situation just described the state where the PE is situated is not entitled to tax such interest if there is no economic link between the loan on which the interest arises and the PE. In other words, the exception to the general rule made by Art. 11 § 5 operates only where the economic link between the loan and the PE is sufficiently clear-cut. This link occurs in

---

133 Commentary to Art. 11 § 26.
134 Germany, Finanzgericht Bayern 9 K 3576/01, 10 December 2003, 4; Belgium, Hof van Beroep Gent, 1995/FR/59, 1 April 2003; Germany, Bundesfinanzhof, I R 5/06, 17 October 2007.
135 Belgium, Hof van Beroep Gent, 2000/83, 27 April 2000, 7; Spain, Tribunal Económico Administrativo Central, 2007–03–15, 15 March 2007.
136 Germany, Bundesfinanzhof, I R 128/80, 9 October 1985; Germany, Bundesfinanzhof, I R 54/92, 20 January 1993.

several situations in which the requirements of the second sentence of Art. 11 § 5 are met.

3. Effectively connected royalties

Art. 12 § 3 provides that Art. 12 § 1 shall not apply if the beneficial owner of **1.99** the royalties, being a resident of the RC, carries on business in the SC in which the royalties arise through a PE situated therein and the right or property in respect of which the royalties are paid is effectively connected with such PE; in such a case Art. 7 shall apply.[137] In respect of outbound royalties courts of the SCs have generally checked whether a PE of the foreign recipient actually existed in the SC to establish a tax charge leading to the application to the business profit treaty article.[138]

4. Effectively connected capital gains

The allocation rule of Art. 13 § 2 is that gains from the alienation of movable **1.100** property forming part of the business property of a PE which an enterprise of the RC has in the SC, including such gains from the alienation of such a PE (alone or with the whole enterprise), *may be taxed* in that SC. 'Movable property' is defined as all property other than immovable property, which is dealt with in Art 13 § 1, including intangible property, such as goodwill, licences, etc. Art. 13 § 2 applies in two instances: (i) when movable property of a PE is alienated; or (ii) when a PE as such (alone or with the whole enterprise) is alienated. If the whole enterprise is alienated, then Art. 13 § 2 applies to gains deemed to result from the alienation of movable property forming part of the business property of the PE, with the result that Art. 7 applies.[139]

5. Effectively connected other income

The rule adopted by Art. 21 § 2 is the force of attraction on other income **1.101** effectively connected to a PE, i.e., the so-called 'restricted force of attraction of the PE'. Under this rule the other income arising in the SC and payable to taxpayers resident in the RC falls *outside* the scope of Art. 21 § 1 (no tax in the SC) *if* the recipient of that other income has a PE in the SC, and the other income is effectively connected to that PE, so in practice Art. 21 § 2 relieves the SC from any limitations to its treaty taxing power imposed by Art. 21 § 1.

---

137   Commentary to Art. 12 § 20–21.2.
138   Germany, Bundesfinanzhof, I R 84/99–I R 112/94, 29 November 2000.
139   Commentary to Art. 13 § 24–25. See: United States, US Tax Court, *Jan Casimir Lewenhaupt v. Commissioner of Internal Revenue*, 23 April 1953; Germany, Bundesfinanzhof, I B 191/09, 19 May 2010.

1.102 If other income is 'associated' with the activity of a PE (of a taxpayer resident of the RC) situated in the treaty SC, then Art. 7 applies, triggering taxation in the treaty SC of PE's income, including other income.[140] This is an exception authorized by Art. 21 § 2, to Art. 21 § 1, so the treaty SC may tax.[141] National Courts have generally construed this situation as an authorized derogation by the business profits article to the other income article (based under Art. 21 § 1 of the Model), typically in cases involving participations of active partners in small companies.[142]

1.103 Art. 21 § 2 (instead of Artt. 10, 11, or 12) specifically regulates the treatment of dividends, interest or royalties arising in the SC which are 'attributable' to a PE which a taxpayer resident of the RC has in the SC. This concept of dividends, interest or royalties arising in the SC which are 'attributable' to a PE in practice overlaps with the effectively connected concept used by Artt. 10 § 5, 11 § 4, and 12 § 3.

1.104 The situations concerning dividends, interest and royalties are often the result of abuses in which the foreign PE is set up solely to benefit from low taxes in countries that offer preferential treatment to income. These abuses are carried out: (i) for dividends through the transfer of shares to PEs set up solely for that purpose in countries that offer preferential treatment to dividend income; (ii) for interest through the transfer of loans to PEs; and (iii) for royalties through the transfer of intangibles to PEs. The Commentary 2017 fills a gap and directly addresses these abusive structures, stating that they can be addressed by Art. 29 § 8 and that to secure treaty benefits the requirement that a shareholding be 'effectively connected' to such a location requires more than merely recording the shareholding in the books of the PE for accounting purposes.[143]

B. Separate treatment of isolated classes of income

1.105 In many situations courts have not relied on the effectively connected income concept, but have focused directly on whether separate treatment applied, that is whether specific treaty articles on isolated classes of income applied instead of the business profits treaty article. More specifically case law addressed the application of the business profits article vis-à-vis income from immovable

---

140 The term 'other income associated to a PE', in practice has the same meaning as the terms 'income effectively connected to a PE', or 'income attributable to a PE' used by the Commentary to Art. 21.
141 Commentary to Art. 21 § 4-1.
142 Belgium, Hof van Cassatie/Cour de Cassation, F1851N, 21 December 1990; The Netherlands, Hoge Raad der Nederlanden, 42.292, 12 October 2007.
143 Commentary to Art. 10 § 32; 11 § 12, and 12 § 5.

property of an enterprise (Art. 6 § 4), income from personal services (Artt. 15, 16, 17 and 18), and royalties (Art. 12).

Art. 6 § 4 provides that Art. 6 §§ 1 and 3 shall also apply to the income **1.106** from immovable property of an enterprise. The Commentary clarifies that the right to tax the SC has priority over the right to tax of the RC and applies also where the income of an enterprise is only 'indirectly derived' from immovable property.[144] One therefore can distinguish between: (i) income from immovable property which is part of a PE in the SC; and (ii) income from immovable property which is *not* part of a PE in the SC. When income from immovable property is *not* actually part of the income of a PE in the SC the immovable property article of the relevant treaty is applied instead of the business profit article.[145] Courts had to decide whether income from immovable property was actually part of the income of a PE in the SC and whether the immovable property article or the business profits article of the relevant treaty applied.[146]

Case law also addressed the application of Art. 7 vis-à-vis income from **1.107** personal services (Artt. 15, 16, 17 and 18). When a non-resident is employed in individual work in the SC usually the employment article applies, providing tests under which the employment income of such an individual is taxable exclusively in her/his RC. Art. 7, however, can apply when activities are carried out pursuant to a contract *for* services (as opposed to a contract *of* services). In the *contract for services*, the services are rendered under a contract for the provision of services between two separate enterprises so that the foreign enterprise may be taxable in the SC if it has a PE there to which the profits are attributable. By contrast, under the *contract of services* the services: (i) are rendered by an individual to an enterprise; and (ii) are in an employment relationship between the individual and the enterprise so that the employment article applies.[147]

A similar issue is found with regard to the business profits article vis-à-vis the **1.108** directors' fees article and courts held that such latter provision applied to income earned as a working partner in a Belgian limited liability company.[148] With regard to Art. 17 § 1 (taxation in the SC of income of foreign

---

144 Commentary to Art. 6 § 4-1.
145 France, Conseil d'État, 12790, 30 May 1980, France, Conseil d'État, 37377–37378, 27 February 1984; France, Conseil d'État, 93187, 26 November 1975.
146 France, Conseil d'État, 349741, 5 April 2013.
147 Commentary to Art. 15 § 8.4.
148 Belgium, Hof van Beroep Gent, 2000–12–05, 5 December 2000; The Netherlands, Hoge Raad der Nederlanden, 35.242, 20 December 2000; Germany, Bundesfinanzhof, I R 106/09, 11 August 2010.

entertainers and sportspersons in the absence of a PE), the Commentary affirms that such provision is an exception to the rules in Art. 7[149] so the question addressed by courts is how to determine the exact scope of this exception.[150]

1.109 Art. 7 (and not Art. 17) applies to payments for advertising or sponsorship income not attributed to performances or appearances[151] and to other payments, such as payments received in the event of the cancellation of a performance, sponsorship/advertising fees not connected with performances, payments for merchandizing derived from sales in a country not connected with performances in that country, payments for image rights not connected with the entertainer's or sportsperson's performance, and payments for the broadcasting of a performance to the owner of the broadcasting rights.[152] These payments for the broadcasting of a performance to the owner of the broadcasting rights occur for example when the organizer of a soccer tournament is also the owner of the broadcasting rights in the event and, as such, receives payments for broadcasting rights related to the event. The share of these payments, distributed by the owner of the broadcasting rights to participating teams, constitutes business profits for those recipients, provided that the payments are not re-distributed to the players. The payments for the broadcasting rights fall under Art. 7 because they are not related to personal activities of the performer and therefore do not constitute income derived by a person such as an entertainer or sportsperson from that person's personal activities as such.[153]

III. PROTECTING THE PE OPERATION THROUGH THE NON-DISCRIMINATION CLAUSE

1.110 When a PE is effectively existent in the SC, the operation of such PE is protected by Art. 24 § 3 (the PE non-discrimination clause), which provides that the taxation on a PE which an enterprise of the RC has in the SC shall not be less-favourably levied in that SC than the taxation levied on enterprises of that SC carrying on the same activities. This treaty clause essentially establishes a full inbound equal treatment in the SC of PEs of

---

149   Commentary to Art. 17 § 2.
150   Czech Republic, Nejvyšší Správní Soud, 9 Afs 55/2007-76, 22 November 2007.
151   Commentary to Art. 17 § 9-4.
152   Commentary to Art. 17 § 9.4-1.
153   Commentary to Art. 17 § 9.4-1.

foreign enterprises, but the Commentary enumerates derogations to such a clause and describes the actual implications of the same treatment clause for PEs.

The Commentary establishes full inbound equal treatment in the SC of PEs **1.111** of foreign enterprises stating that Art. 24 § 3 is designed to end discrimination based on the actual situs of an enterprise in the SC that affects non-residents in the SC (i.e., residents of the RC) who have a PE in the SC irrespective of their nationality.[154] The Commentary however enumerates derogations to the full inbound equal treatment in the SC of PEs of foreign enterprises. First, specific or limited elements are relevant in establishing the comparable for inbound equal protection, for example, the head offices of the PEs and an enterprise in the SC to be comparable must have similar 'legal structure' or carry out the 'same activities'. Second, it is possible to have a different mode of taxation because the CS where the PE is situated (the SC) can limit/exclude personal allowances and reliefs. Third, the same treatment is not applicable to certain intra-group transactions, such as transfer prices.

The compared entities (i.e., the foreign head office of the PE and an **1.112** enterprise in the SC) first must belong to the *same-sector business activities* because the purpose of Art. 24 § 3 is to end all discrimination in the treatment of PEs as compared with resident enterprises belonging to the same sector of activities, as regards taxes based on business activities, and especially taxes on business profits.[155] Second, the compared entities must have a *similar 'legal structure'*, i.e., tax treatment in the SC of an enterprise of the RC should be compared to that of an enterprise of the SC that has a legal structure that is similar to that of the enterprise to which the PE belongs.

For example, Art. 24 § 3 does not require the SC to apply to the profits of the **1.113** PE of an enterprise the same rate of tax as is applicable to a domestic enterprise in the SC. Third, the compared entities must carry out *'same activities'*. The Commentary notes that regulated and unregulated activities generally do not constitute the 'same activities' for the purposes of Art. 24 § 3, and that for purposes of Art. 24 § 3, a PE whose activities include the borrowing and lending of money is not entitled to the same treatment as domestic banks since the PE does not carry on the same activities.[156]

---

154   Commentary to Art. 24 § 33 and 35. See: Germany, Bundesfinanzhof, I R 54/96, 22 April 1998.
155   Commentary to Art. 24 § 37.
156   Commentary to Art. 24 § 38. See: Germany, Bundesfinanzhof, II R 51/03, 10 March 2005.

1.114 The CS where PE is situated (the SC) can limit/exclude personal allowances and reliefs. Under Art. 24 § 3 it does not constitute discrimination ('more burdensome taxation') to tax non-resident persons differently, for practical reasons, from resident persons, as long as this does not result in more burdensome taxation for residents than for non-residents.[157] Specific mechanisms or administrative practices that apply only for the purposes of determining profits attributable to a PE (Art. 7 § 2) do not per se violate Art. 24 § 3.[158]

1.115 Art. 24 § 3 prevents dual use of allowances, but leaves it open to the SC to give personal allowances and reliefs to the persons concerned in the proportion which the amount of the PE's profits in the SC bears to the worldwide income taxable in the RC.[159] It is also possible to limit incentives to PEs of non-resident taxpayers in the SC because they promote objectives directly related to the proper economic activity of the state concerned. Non-resident enterprises must meet the same requirements as resident enterprises and are not entitled to tax advantages attaching to activities the exercise of which is strictly reserved, on grounds of national interest, defence, protection of the national economy, etc. to domestic enterprises.[160]

1.116 The Commentary notes that the same treatment is not applicable to certain group transactions, such as rules that take account of the relationship between an enterprise and other enterprises (e.g., rules that allow consolidation, transfer of losses or tax-free transfers of property between companies under common ownership), or to the distribution of the profits of a resident enterprise, because those rules do not focus on the taxation of an enterprise's own business activities similar to those of the PE but, instead, focus on the taxation of a resident enterprise as part of a group of associated enterprises.[161]

1.117 The Commentary identifies the following areas of potential non-discrimination of PEs versus domestic companies: deduction of the trading expenses, depreciation and reserves, loss carrying forward or backward, taxation of capital gains realized on the alienation of assets during or on the

---

157 Commentary to Art. 24 § 34.1.
158 Commentary to Art. 24 § 43.2 and last statement. See: United States, US Court of Appeals for the Second Circuit, *Reuters Ltd. v. New York Tax Appeals Tribunal*, 12 October 1993, 603 N.Y.S.2d 795; Austria, Verfassungsgerichtshof (Constitutional Court), B758/88 – B759/88, 15 March 1990.
159 Commentary to Art. 24 § 36.
160 Commentary to Art. 24 § 43.
161 Commentary to Art. 24 § 41. See: Canada, Tax Court of Canada, *Saipem UK Ltd. v. Her Majesty the Queen*, 14 January 2011; Spain, Tribunal Supremo, 8720/1998, 12 April 2003. Commentary to Art. 24 § 42. See: Spain, Tribunal Supremo, 4517/1997, 15 July 2002.

cessation of business. By contrast, equal treatment does not cover other sensitive areas.[162]

An issue addressed by national courts is whether the dividends received by a **1.118** PE in the SC in respect of participations owned by that PE in foreign companies, should be subject, in the same SC, to the same treatment afforded to dividends received by domestic companies in the SC in respect of participations owned by those companies in foreign companies.[163] The Commentary weighs the arguments for and against the extension of dividends exemption to PEs.[164] An argument for the extension of dividends exemption to PEs is that the PE receiving dividends from the subsidiary should likewise be granted the exemption in view of the fact that a profits tax has already been levied in the hands of the subsidiary. This approach, mandated by the EU law, has also been adopted by national courts in respect of treaty issues.[165] There are however arguments against the extension of the dividends exemption to PEs. The Commentary observes that assimilating PEs to local enterprises does not entail any obligation for the country where the PE is located to accord such special treatment to exempt received dividends. This argument has also been applied by national courts.[166]

Another issue concerning PEs of foreign companies is the withholding of tax **1.119** on out-going dividends. The Commentary suggests adapting Art. 10 §§ 2 and 4, so as to enable withholding tax to be levied in the SC on dividends paid by companies which are residents of the SC to PEs of companies which are residents of the RC the same way as if they were received directly, i.e., by the head offices of the RC companies.[167]

The PE is a part of a legal entity which is not under the jurisdiction of the **1.120** SC, so if in applying the progressive scale, the SC takes into account the profits of the whole company to which such a PE belongs there can be a conflict with the PE non-discrimination article. So the Commentary suggests that a minimum tax rate for PEs can be accepted.[168] Moreover, if a *branch tax* (a surcharge) is levied, then the profits of a PE of an enterprise of

---

162 Finland, Korkein Hallinto-oikeus, KHO:2013:169, 25 October 2013; Austria, Verwaltungsgerichtshof, 2005/14/0036, 16 February 2006; Switzerland, Bundesgericht/Tribunal fédéral, 2P.140/2005, 28 November 2005.

163 Gammie, Malcolm, 'Non Discrimination and the Taxation of Cross-Border Dividends', (2010) 2 *World Tax. J.* 162.

164 Commentary to Art. 24 §§ 48–54.

165 France, Conseil d'État, 50643, 18 November 1985.

166 Belgium, Hof van Cassatie/Cour de Cassation, F902F, 30 June 1988.

167 Commentary to Art. 24 §§ 64–66.

168 Commentary to Art. 24 § 56.

the RC are taxed at a higher rate than the profits of enterprises of the SC. This is in theory contrary to Art. 24 § 3, but the justification of a branch tax is that if a subsidiary of the foreign enterprise earned the same profits as the PE and subsequently distributed these profits as dividends an additional withholding tax would be levied on these dividends in accordance with Art. 10 § 2.[169] Similarly, a *'branch level interest tax'* is a tax imposed on amounts deducted, as interest, in computing the profits of a PE, but such a tax is levied on the enterprise to which the interest is paid and therefore is not contrary to Art. 24 § 3.[170]

1.121   *If* foreign income (sourced in a third country) is included in profits attributable to a PE in the SC owned by a parent company in the RC, *then* Art. 24 § 3 requires that the SC grants to the PE the FTC on such income sourced in the third country if such FTC is granted to resident enterprises under domestic laws.[171] The problem that arises in this situation is whether the FTC granted by the treaty between the SC and the third country can be extended to PEs in the SC of a taxpayer resident of the RC.[172] The Commentary establishes that the same treatment should be extended to PEs in the SC that are recipients of dividends, interest, or royalties from a third country, attributing to them the FTC granted by the treaties concluded by the SC with such a third country.

1.122   The Commentary also focuses on the following situation: a PE in the SC of an enterprise resident of the RC receives dividends, interest or royalties from a third country and poses the following question: if and to what extent should the SC (where PE is situated) credit the tax that cannot be recovered from the third country? The Commentary takes the position that the FTC should be extended in those situations to the PE observing that the majority of countries grant credit in these cases on the basis of their domestic laws or under Art. 24 § 3.[173]

1.123   National courts have addressed this problem but excluded the credit in the SC.[174] The Commentary 2017 highlights that in these situations there can be triangular cases of abuses. For example, if a CS applies the exemption method of Art. 23A to the profits attributable to a PE situated in a third state which

---

169   Commentary to Art. 24 § 60.
170   Commentary to Art. 24 § 61. By contrast §§ 62–66 observe that in respect of the withholding tax on dividends, interest and royalties received by a PE the CSs can include in the treaties specific provisions.
171   Commentary to Art. 24 § 67. See: Belgium, Tribunal de Première Instance Bruxelles, 2007/63, *Tijdschrift voor Fiscaal Recht*, 2007; Germany, Finanzgericht Hamburg, II 69/80, 9 August 1985.
172   Commentary to Art. 24 § 68.
173   Commentary to Art. 24, § 70.1–4.
174   Belgium, Hof van Cassatie/Court de Cassation, RF 01718_1, 23 March 1995; Belgium, Hof van Cassatie/Court de Cassation, F930115F, 26 January 1995.

does not tax passive income that arises in the other CS but that is attributable to such PE, there is risk that such income might not be taxed in any of the three states. Art. 29 § 8 addresses this issue. Moreover if the CS of which the enterprise is a resident exempts from tax the profits of the PE located in the other CS, there is a danger that the enterprise will transfer assets such as shares, bonds or patents to PEs in states that offer very favourable tax treatment, and in certain circumstances the resulting income may not be taxed in any of the three states. The Commentary suggests that to prevent such practices, a provision can be included in the convention between the state of which the enterprise is a resident and the third state (the state of source) stating that an enterprise can claim the benefits of the convention only if the income obtained by the PE situated in the other state is taxed normally in the state of the PE.[175]

Art. 24 § 4 provides that, except where Art. 9 § 1, Art. 11 § 6, or Art. 12 § 4, **1.124** apply, interest, royalties and other disbursements paid by an enterprise of the SC to a resident of the RC shall, for the purpose of determining the taxable profits of such an enterprise, be deductible under the same conditions as if they had been paid to a resident of the SC. Similarly, any debts of an enterprise of the SC to a resident of the RC shall, for the purpose of determining the taxable capital of such an enterprise, be deductible under the same conditions as if they had been contracted to a resident of the SC.

This treaty clause essentially establishes a full inbound equal treatment in the **1.125** SC of foreign and domestic enterprises, but the Commentary enumerates derogations in respect to thin cap issues: the country of the borrower can apply its domestic rules on thin cap in so far as these are compatible with arm's length (Art. 9 § 1 Art. 11 § 6 or Art 12 § 4), while limitations of deductions which only apply to non-resident creditors (to the exclusion of resident creditors) are prohibited.[176] The Commentary takes the position that payments of interest to resident/non-resident taxpayers under thin cap rules are outside the scope of Art. 24 § 5.[177] National courts have taken differing views:

---

175   Commentary to Art. 24, §§ 7–72.
176   Commentary to Art. 24 § 73–74. See: Nakhai, Katja, et al., 'Thin Capitalization Rules and Non-discrimination Principles' (2004) 32 *Intertax* 126; Gouthiere, Bruno, 'Thin Capitalization Rules and the Non-discrimination Principle' (2002) 42 *Eur. Tax*, 159; IFA, 'International Aspects of Thin Capitalization', (1996) 81b *Cahiers Droit Fisc. Intl.*
177   Commentary to Art. 24 § 79.2.

a judicial approach bars thin cap rules that adversely ring fence foreign lenders, while an opposing approach protects domestic thin cap rules as anti-abuse rules.[178]

---

178   Spain, Tribunal Supremo, 5871/2006, 17 March 2011; Germany, Bundesfinanzhof, I R 6/09, 8 September 2010; France, Conseil d'État, 233894, 14 November 2001; France, Court Administrative d'Appel Nancy, 98-1741, 10 October 2002; Spain, Tribunal Económico Administrativo Central, 2335/2002; Spain, Tribunal Económico Administrativo Central, 2007-12-20, 20 December 2007; Canada, Tax Court of Canada, *Ramada Ontario Ltd. v. Her Majesty the Queen*, 3 December 1993.

2

ENTITLEMENT TO TAX TREATIES

The perspective of the country of destination of the investment reveals **2.01** important aspects of the BEPS impact on tax treaties, and notably that there are now new limitations to the access to the benefits of a bilateral treaty by entities that are not effectively located in either of the two CSs, in addition to a general ban on double treaty exemption obtained through different techniques.

This chapter focuses on the new set of requirements that need to be met to **2.02** have full entitlement to the tax treaty, by individually looking at each of them: scope of the treaties (section I), residence test for treaty purposes (section II), the limitation of benefits clause (section III), and treaty abuse (section IV), treaty entitlement and non-discrimination (section V).

The analysis of the scope of the treaties includes the basic rules about the **2.03** personal scope, transparency and hybrid mismatches, the saving clause, and the taxes covered by the treaties. The discussion on the residence test for treaty purposes first looks at the notion of 'resident', and then discusses resolution of conflicts for dual residents.

2.04 The limitation of benefits clause is the new BEPS-related subjective require-ment for entitlement to tax treaties. This clause is based on different tests that will be discussed herebelow (qualified person, active conduct test, derivative benefits and discretionary test, anti-abuse rule for permanent establishments situated in third countries).

2.05 The topic of treaty abuse has been newly introduced by the BEPS Project into tax treaties through Art. 29. This provision, together with the Commentary, adopts an integral approach that includes the principal purpose test of Art. 29 § 9, a broad discussion of the method to address the improper use of the Convention, a new concept of double treaty exemption, together with the traditional approach using the 'beneficial owner' concept.

I. SCOPE OF THE TREATIES

A. Personal scope: the basic rule

2.06 The personal scope of the Convention is defined by the combined application of Art. 1, 3 § 1 a) and b), and 4. Art. 1 provides that the Convention shall apply to 'persons' who are 'resident' of one or both of the CSs. The terms 'person' and 'resident' are defined respectively by Art. 3 § 1 a) and b) and by Art. 4 § 1.[1]

2.07 According to Art. 3 § 1 a) for the purposes of the Convention, unless the context otherwise requires, the term 'person' includes an individual, a company and any other body of persons, while according to Art. 3 § 1 b) the term 'company' means any body corporate or any entity that is treated as a body corporate for tax purposes. According to Art. 3 § 1 b) for the purposes of the Convention, the term 'resident of a CS' means any person (as defined by Art. 3 § 1 a)) who, under the laws of the RC, is liable to tax therein by reason of his domicile, residence, place of management or any other criterion of a similar nature, and also includes that state and any political subdivisions or local authorities.

---

1 Hattingh, Johann P., 'Art. 1 of the OECD Model: Historical Background and the Issues Surrounding It' (2003) 57 *Bull. Intl. Fisc. Doc.* 215; Hattingh, Johann P., 'The Role and Function of Art. 1 of the OECD Model' (2003) 57 *Bull. Intl. Fisc. Doc.* 546.

As a result an entity, to be entitled to the Convention, must meet three **2.08** essential requirements: it must be: (i) a *'person'* for the purposes of the Convention; (ii) a person *'resident'* of one of the CSs;[2] and (iii) a person resident of one of the CSs which is *'liable to tax'* therein.[3] The Commentary observes that treaties are applicable to 'residents' of one or both of the CSs irrespective of nationality. As a result of the changes to the Commentary in 2017 however the fact that a person is a resident of a CS does not mean that the person is automatically entitled to the benefits of the Convention since some or all of these benefits may be denied under various provisions of the Convention, including those of Art. 29 (see §§ 3–4 of Chapter 2).[4]

The first requirement for an entity, to be entitled to the Convention is that **2.09** such an entity is a *'person'* for the purposes of the Convention. National courts have addressed this basic issue.[5] The requirement that an entity is a 'person' for the purposes of the Convention has been specifically addressed in a line of US cases concerning trusts.[6]

B. Transparency and hybrid mismatches

1. Transparent entities or arrangements

Tax treaties ideally operate with persons who are non-transparent, that is **2.10** individuals and most types of companies. The problem is that legal entities and other arrangements can be legally organized to be 'transparent', so that legal and tax effects are attributed to the participants rather than to the legal entity. To address this situation Art. 1 § 2 provides that for the purposes of a Convention, income derived by or through an entity or arrangement that is treated as wholly or partly 'fiscally transparent' under the tax law of either CS shall be considered to be income of a resident of a CS but only to the extent that the income is treated, for purposes of taxation by that state, as the income of a resident of that state.

---

2   Dual residence is regulated by Art. 4 § 2.
3   Vogel, Klaus, *Tax Treaty News: Liable to Tax Under Art. 4 of the OECD Model Convention* (IBFD 2001).
4   Commentary to Art. 1 § 1.
5   France, Conseil d'État, 144211, 4 April 1997; Germany, Finanzgericht Nordrhein-Westfalen, 2 K 4034/05, 20 April 2007.
6   United States, US Supreme Court, *Andre Maximov v. United States*, 29 April 1963. See also: United States, US District Court for the Southern District of New York, *Raymond E. Burdick v. Commissioner*, 29 May 1963, 63-2 USTC (CCH) 9527; United States, US Tax Court, *Lambert Tree Trust Estate v. Commissioner*, 25 June 1962, 38 T.C. 392 (1962); United States, US District Court for the Northern District of California, *American Trust Company v. James G. Smyth, Collector of Internal Revenue and United States of America*, 6 April 1956, 56-2 USTC (CCH) 9683, reversed 57-2 USTC (CCH) 9824; Australia, Federal Court of Australia, *Resource Capital Fund III LP v. Commissioner of Taxation*, 26 April 2013.

2.11   Art. 1 § 2 was introduced by Action 2 'Neutralising the Effects of Hybrid Mismatch Arrangements' and addresses income earned through transparent entities or arrangements. An entity or arrangement is 'fiscally transparent' when, the income (or part thereof) of the entity or arrangement is not taxed at the level of the entity or the arrangement but at the level of the persons who have an interest in that entity or arrangement. This fiscal transparency is determined by the domestic laws of a CS. Art. 3 § 1 (Transparent Entities) of the MLI replicates the text of Art. 1 § 2, with changes made solely to conform the terminology used in the model provision to the terminology used in the Convention.

2.12   The Commentary to Art. 1 clarifies that Art. 1 § 2 addresses the situation of the income of entities or arrangements that one or both CSs treat as wholly or partly fiscally transparent for tax purposes and ensures that income of such entities or arrangements is treated in accordance with the 1999 report of the Committee on Fiscal Affairs entitled: 'The Application of the OECD Model Tax Convention to Partnerships'. That report dealt exclusively with partnerships and other non-corporate entities, but now the Model covers also transparent trusts because it refers to entities that are 'wholly or partly' treated as fiscally transparent.

2.13   Art. 1 § 2 ensures that the benefits of the Convention are not granted where neither CS treats, under its domestic laws, the income of an entity or arrangement as the income of one of its residents. Art. 1 § 2 also ensures that if the benefits of the Convention are actually granted because this test is met, then the relevant income is attributed to that resident for the purposes of the application of the various allocative rules of the Convention. So its goal is attributing the taxing power to the proper CS but it does not require a CS to change the way in which it attributes income or characterizes entities for the purposes of its domestic law. Neither does Art. 1 § 2 restrict the CSs' obligation to provide relief of double taxation under Artt. 23A and 23B where the income of a resident of that state may be taxed by the other state in accordance with the Convention.

2.14   So CSs should not grant the benefits of a Convention where they cannot verify whether a person is truly entitled to these benefits. This situation may occur, for example, when an entity is established in a jurisdiction from which a CS cannot obtain tax information. The situation covered by Art. 1 § 2 is illustrated by the following example: state A and state B have concluded a treaty. State A considers that an entity established in state B is a company and taxes that entity on interest that it receives from a debtor resident in state A. Under the domestic law of state B, however, the entity is treated as a partnership and the two members in that entity, who share equally all its income, are each taxed on half of the interest. One of the members is a resident of state B and the other one is a resident of a country with which states A and B do not have a treaty. Art. 1 § 2 provides that in such case half of the interest shall be considered, for the purposes of Art. 11, to be income of a resident of state B.

The Commentary specifies that it is irrelevant to the view taken by each CS **2.15** about who is the entity that derives that income for domestic tax purposes because the reference by Art 1 § 2 to 'income derived by or through an entity or arrangement' covers any income that is earned by or through an entity or arrangement. Likewise it is irrelevant where the entity or arrangement is established, so Art 1 § 2 applies to an entity established in a third state to the extent that, under the domestic laws of one of the CSs, the entity is treated as wholly or partly fiscally transparent and income of that entity is attributed to a resident of that state.[7]

When an entity or arrangement is treated as partly fiscally transparent under **2.16** the domestic law of one of the CSs, only part of the income of the entity or arrangement might be taxed at the level of the persons who have an interest in that entity or arrangement while the rest would remain taxable at the level of the entity or arrangement

2. Partnerships

The 1999 report of the Committee on Fiscal Affairs entitled: 'The Appli- **2.17** cation of the OECD Model Tax Convention to Partnerships' had already addressed the situation of the income of entities or arrangements that one or both CSs treat as wholly or partly fiscally transparent partnerships and other non-corporate entities. This report was transposed in the Commentary, but Commentary 2017 has eliminated this section. Because now the Model covers all fiscally transparent entities or arrangements the deleted part of the Commentary was no longer necessary.[8]

Domestic laws differ in the treatment of partnerships: in most countries **2.18** partnerships are treated as tax-transparent entities (i.e., profits are directly

---

7 Commentary to Art. 1 § 7.
8 Gouthiere, Bruno, *L'application des Conventions Fiscales Aux Societes de Personnes* (Francis Lefebvre 2000); Wheeler, Joanna, The Attribution of Income to a Person for Tax Treaty Purposes (IBFD 2005); Lang, Michael, *The Application of the OECD Model Tax Convention to Partnerships-A Critical Analysis of the Report Prepared by the OECD Committee on Fiscal Affairs* (Kluwer Law International 2000); Murray, Paul, 'OECD Partnership Report: Reshaping Treaty Interpretation?' (2000) 45 *Brit. Tax Rev.* 71; Avery Jones, John F., et al., 'Characterization of other States' Partnerships for Income Tax' (2002) 56 *Bull. Intl. Fisc. Doc.* 288.

attributed *pro quota* to the partners), while in some countries partnerships are treated as taxable units (i.e., tax-opaque entities or non-tax-transparent entities). The Commentary,[9] before the changes in 2017 complemented by the report by the CFA, 'The Application of the OECD Model Treaty to Partnerships', devoted considerable attention to the mismatches created by domestic laws which treat partnerships as taxable units or as fiscal transparent entities.

2.19 The preliminary issue was which CS has the treaty entitlement to tax partnerships when the domestic laws of the RC (the country of residence of the partners) and of the SC (the country of the partnership) are not aligned in considering the partnership tax transparent.

2.20 When the partnership is entitled to treaty benefits as a person, the Convention does not restrict the right of a CS to tax the partners on their share of the income.[10] If the partnership is treated as a company resident of a CS and 'liable to tax' therein (Art. 4 § 1), then the partnership is entitled to treaty benefits as a person, for example, the profits are subject to the dividends article when distributed.[11] By contrast, if the partnership is fiscally transparent in a CS2 and is not 'liable to tax' therein, then the partnership is *not* entitled to treaty benefits and the other CS1 can tax the partners with respect to their share of income.[12]

2.21 Moreover when fiscally transparent partnerships or separate taxable entities are not a resident of the CS1 on the basis of its domestic laws, the partners liable to tax are the appropriate persons to claim treaty benefits because they are the recipient of the profits of the partnership.[13] Fiscally transparent partnerships do not qualify as residents of a CS under Art. 4 because the concepts of 'employer' and 'resident' for the purposes of Art. 15 § 2 b) are applied at the level of the partners rather than at the level of a transparent entity.[14]

2.22 With regard to the taxation of partnerships there can be conflicts in the allocation of taxing rights of the two CSs. For example, *if* the SC treats a domestic partnership as fiscally transparent and the non-resident partner of

---

9 Commentary to Art. 1 § 2–6.7.
10 France, Conseil d'État, 317024, 11 July 2011.
11 See: The Netherlands, Hoge Raad der Nederlanden, 29 084, 23 March 1994.
12 This point was specified by Commentary to Art. 1 § 5 which however has been deleted in 2017.
13 South Africa, Free State High Court – Bloemfontein, *J.J. Grundlingh v. Commissioner for the South African Revenue Service*, 17 September 2009.
14 This point was specified by Commentary to Art. 1 § 6.1 which however has been deleted in 2017.

such a partnership is resident of a state that taxes partnerships as companies, *then* the partner is not able to claim in the RC treaty benefits because that income is not allocated in the RC of the partner. The same situation occurs if a partnership is not resident in the SC and is regarded by the SC as a separate taxable entity to which the income would be attributed.

The pre-2017 Commentary noted that in these situations the income alloca- **2.23** tion in the RC was decisive: according to the Commentary conflicts of allocation were solved because income 'allocated' to partners was deemed to be 'paid' in so far as partners satisfied the condition that income concerned was 'paid to a resident of the other CS' or 'derived by a resident of the other CS'. These conditions were satisfied even if the partnership was not resident in the SC and was regarded by the SC as a separate taxable entity to which the income would be attributed. This position is confirmed by the Commentary to Art. 23 which affirms that when double taxation results from conflicts of qualifications, the RC is obliged to provide relief (credit or exemption).[15]

The Commentary also addressed triangular cases involving partnerships and **2.24** acknowledged that difficulties could arise and referred to § 19.1 (now § 56) of Commentary to Art. 5 and §§ 6.1 and 6.2 of Commentary to Art. 15. Moreover, in case of conflicts of qualification §§ 32.1 and 56.1 of the Commentary to Art. 23 apply.

3. Collective investment vehicles

Another problem is the treaty eligibility of CIVs. The main question **2.25** addressed by the Commentary is whether a CIV should qualify for treaty benefits in its own right.[16] To do so a CIV must qualify as a 'person' and 'resident' of a CS for the purposes of the dividends or interest article being the 'beneficial owner' of the income. In light of the fact that there are differences in the tax treatment of CIVs from country to country the problem that often arises is whether a CIV is a 'person' or whether a CIV is a 'resident'. Whether a CIV is a 'person' depends on the legal form of the CIV, i.e., whether it is regulated by domestic law as a taxable unit. Whether a CIV is a 'resident'

---

15 For details see Commentary to Art. 23A and 23B § 32.2–3. See: Belgium, Hof van Cassatie/Cour de Cassation F030006F, 2 December 2004. OECD: *The Granting of Treaty Benefits with Respect to the Income of CIV* (OECD-TAG 2010); Chew, Victor, 'The Application of Tax Treaties to Collective Investment Vehicles: Beneficial Owner Requirement Explained?' (2015) 17 *Derivatives & Financial Instruments* 6; Da Silva, Bruno, 'Granting Tax Treaty Benefits to Collective Investment Vehicles: a Review of the OECD Report and the 2010 Amendments to the Model Tax Convention' (2011) 39 *Intertax* 195.
16 A special report was issued by the OECD: *The Granting of Treaty Benefits with Respect to the Income of CIV*, complementing §§ 6.8–6.30 of the Commentary to Art. 1.

depends on its tax treatment in the state in which it is established, on the basis of the criteria established by domestic laws.

2.26 The Commentary addresses these policy issues and advances five approaches proposing possible treaty clauses respectively based on the following rules:

1. CIVs are expressly entitled to treaty benefits by the treaty in so far as they are attributed the quality of being a person for treaty purposes;
2. CIVs are entitled to treaty benefits under the 'equivalent beneficiaries' requirement;
3. CIVs are entitled to treaty benefits on the condition that CIV investors are residents of the same country as the CIV;
4. CIVs are entitled to treaty benefits by adopting a look-through approach which ensures that the benefits of investors are maintained; and
5. CIVs are entitled to treaty benefits if they are publicly traded.

CIV rules are essentially inspired to the beneficial owner approach for dividends and to the improper use of treaty policies, with adaptations.[17]

C. The saving clause

2.27 Art. 1 § 3 of the Model 2017 introduces a new provision denominated 'saving clause'. This is a novelty which is transposed from the US Model and addresses a specific problem of tax treaties: most of the provisions of the Convention restrict the right of the SC to tax the residents of the other RC. In some limited cases, the provisions of the Convention limit a CS's right to tax its own residents and the saving clause clarifies which are the cases in which the RC is limited by the convention in taxing its own resident taxpayers.[18]

2.28 According to Art. 1 § 3 the Convention shall not affect the taxation, by a CS, of its residents, except with respect to the benefits granted under Art. 7 § 3, Art. 9 § 2, Artt. 19, 20, 23 [a] [b], 24, 25 and 28. Art. 1 § 3 has two parts. First it affirms (in the first statement) the principle that the right of a CS to tax its own residents must be preserved, and, as a general rule, cannot be affected by the Convention ('the Convention shall not affect the taxation, by a CS, of its residents'). Second, it introduces several relevant derogations to this principle, in so far as it provides (in the second statement) that the Convention

---

17 Commentary to Art. 1 § 6.17.
18 Schuch, Joseph and Neubauer, Nikolaus, 'The Saving Clause – Art 1 Para 3 OECD MC' in: Lang, Michael, et al., (eds) *Base Erosion and Profit Shifting (BEPS)*, (Linde 2016).

shall affect the taxation, by a CS, of its residents, with respect to the benefits granted under Art. 7 § 3, Art. 9 § 2, Artt. 19, 20, 23 [a] [b], 24, 25 and 28.

In practice the RC cannot deny to its residents certain benefits granted by **2.29** Art. 1 § 3 second statement. Art. 11 of the MLI includes very similar provisions. In other words: the Convention does not restrict a CS's right to tax its own residents except where this is explicitly provided.

Art. 1 § 3 covers the situations in which a Convention imposes restrictions on **2.30** a CS's right to tax its own residents. A very good example of the saving clause is when it is explicitly provided that a CS does not have the right to grant to an enterprise of that state a correlative adjustment following an initial adjustment made by the other CS (Art. 7 §§ 2 and 3), to the amount of tax charged on the profits of a PE of the enterprise. Similarly Artt. 19 and 20 are included in the saving clause, so that a CS is not allowed to tax an individual who is resident of that state if that individual derives income in respect of government services rendered to the other CS or if that individual is a student who meets the conditions of Art. 20. Art. 28 also falls in the list of the saving clause with the result that a CS is prevented from taxing an individual who is resident of that state when that individual is a member of the diplomatic mission or consular post of the other CS.

Finally Artt. 23A and 23B, which require a CS to provide relief of double **2.31** taxation to its residents with respect to the income sourced in the other state, are affected by the Convention because they are included in the saving clause. The saving clause finally covers administrative safeguards: Art. 24 – which protects residents of a CS against discriminatory taxation practices – and Art. 25 – which allows residents of a CS to request a MAP.

D. Taxes covered by the Treaties

Art. 2 ensures the identification of the CSs' taxes covered by treaty to avoid **2.32** the necessity of concluding a new treaty whenever the CSs' domestic laws are modified, and also ensures that the CS reciprocally notify significant changes in their domestic laws.[19] The structure of Art. 2 is the following: provisions that define the objective scope of the Convention as covering taxes on income

---

19   Commentary to Art. 2 § 1–2. In general: Brandstetter, Patricia, *Taxes Covered. A Study of Art. 2 of the OECD Model Conventions* (IBFD 2011); Kasaizi, Abeid, 'Interpretation of the Material Scope of Taxes Covered by the OECD-MC (Art. 2 OECD-MC)' in: Schilcher, Michael and Weninger, Patrick (eds), *Fundamental Issues and Practical Problems in Tax Treaty Interpretation* (Linde 2008); Lang, Michael, 'Taxes Covered – What is a 'Tax' According to Art. 2 of the OECD Model?', (2005) 59 *Bull. Intl. Fisc. Doc.* 216; Tenore, Mario, 'Taxes Covered: The OECD Model (2010) versus EU Directives' (2012) 66 *Bull. Intl. Tax.* 27.

and on capital (§ 1); the definition of taxes on income and on capital (§ 2); a list of those taxes (§ 3), and a clause about new taxes (§ 4).

2.33 The scope of the Convention is defined by Art. 2 § 1 which provides that it shall apply to taxes on income and on capital imposed on behalf of a CS or of its political subdivisions or local authorities, irrespective of the manner in which they are levied. What matters in identifying the covered taxes is how they are levied, while it is immaterial on behalf of which authorities such taxes are imposed. A distinction should be made, however, when one of the CS is a federal system, as state and local taxes are often excluded.[20]

2.34 Art. 2 § 2 provides that there shall be regarded as taxes on income and on capital all taxes imposed on total income, on total capital, or on elements of income or capital, including taxes on gains from the alienation of movable property/immovable property, taxes on the total amounts of wages/salaries paid by enterprises, as well as taxes on capital appreciation. So Art. 2 § 1 includes duties or charges accessory to taxes (increases, costs, interest, etc.), but does not include social security charges, or any other charges if there is a direct connection between the levy and individual benefits; the Commentary now recognizes interest and penalties accessory to taxes as taxes covered under the operation of MAPs.[21]

2.35 The core of judicial decisions concerning Art. 2 consists of the analysis of whether domestic taxes fall either in the category of income tax or in that of capital taxes which are covered by the treaties. Extraordinary taxes and local taxes in federal systems are not considered, but domestic taxes (such as municipal business taxes on payroll, net wealth taxes, forfeit taxes, taxes on lottery prizes) are deemed by courts to fall under the treaties.[22] Lottery prizes are also covered by the treaties if included in income tax.[23] In certain cases extraordinary taxes are deemed to be covered by treaties in so far as they have, in substance, the structure of an income tax, for example, the so-called 'windfall tax' in the UK is characterized as an excess profit tax.[24] Local business taxes tend to be excluded when they do not constitute a local layer of

---

20   Finland, Korkein Hallinto-oikeus, 2004:12, 6 February 2004.
21   Commentary to Art. 2 § 3–4. See: New Zealand, Court/Chamber Taxation, *Not disclosed at Taxation Review Authority v. Commissioner of Inland Revenue*, 18 January 1990.
22   Austria, Verwaltungsgerichtshof, 2000/13/0134, 28 March 2001; Austria, Verwaltungsgerichtshof, 99/15/0265, 3 August 2000; France, Tribunal de Grande Instance Paris, 1985–01–17, 17 January 1985; The Netherlands, Hoge Raad der Nederlanden, 42.211, 1 December 2006; The Netherlands, Hoge Raad der Nederlanden, 42.211, 1 December 2006.
23   Switzerland, Verwaltungsgericht Bern 1996–08–30, 30 August 1996.
24   United States, US Supreme Court, *PPL Corporation and Subsidiaries v. the Commissioner of Internal Revenue*, 20 May 2013.

the national income taxes.[25] Extraordinary taxes also tend to be excluded from the coverage of the treaties in so far as they pursue regulatory or policy goals, like for example the Greek extraordinary social responsibility contribution.[26]

Taxes on the gains derived from the alienation of movable or immovable **2.36** property are generally covered by the capital gains article, but it is left to domestic laws to decide whether to levy a special tax on capital gains or treat them as ordinary income.[27] As a result the issue arose in case law whether treaties apply to capital gains when domestic laws do not specify whether capital gains are treated separately or as ordinary income.[28]

Countries are free to clarify in their treaties whether 'extraordinary taxes' are **2.37** covered. What happens generally is that only ordinary taxes are covered by the treaty, while extraordinary taxes are excluded as a result of judicial qualifications in so far as they pursue regulatory or policy goals.[29] Taxes on capital are generally included in the covered taxes article or in the capital taxes article. In certain cases, it is relatively easy to exclude the capital nature of a tax, but in other situations the capital tax characterization is not linear.

Art. 2 § 3 simply lists the taxes in force at the time of signature of the treaty.[30] **2.38** The general approach, however, is that such a list not exhaustive.[31] Art. 2 § 4 provides that the Convention shall also apply to any identical or substantially similar taxes that are imposed after the date of signature of the Convention in addition to, or in place of, the existing taxes and that the Competent Authorities of the CSs shall notify each other of any significant changes that have been made in their taxation laws.[32] This criterion of 'substantially similar taxes' has been used flexibly by national courts, so that the objective purpose of treaties is open-ended and geared to domestic changes, preventing the need to negotiate new treaties when new taxes are introduced.[33]

---

25 France, Conseil d'État, 249801, 15 July 2004, *Revue de jurisprudence fiscale*, 11/2004, 1089. On a similar fact situation, a Russian decision: Russia, Commercial Court for Moscow Circuit A40-1164/11-99-7, 20 February 2012.

26 Greece, Administrative Court of Appeals of Athens, 481/2012, 7 February 2012.

27 Commentary to Art. 13 § 4.

28 Australia, Federal Court of Australia – Full Court, *Virgin Holdings SA v. Federal Commissioner of Taxation*, 10 October 2008, [2008] FCA 1503; Australia, Federal Court of Australia, *Undershaft Ltd. v. Commissioner of Taxation*, 3 February 2009.

29 Greece, Administrative Court of Appeals of Athens, 481/2012, 7 February 2012.

30 Commentary to Art. 2 § 5.

31 Belgium, Tribunal de Première Instance Bruxelles, 2008/16347/A, 23 November 2011; Belgium, Tribunal de Première Instance Bruxelles, 2006/2662/A, 2 August 2011.

32 Commentary to Art. 2 §§ 7–8.

33 Austria, Verwaltungsgerichtshof 99/15/0265, 3 August 2000; Austria, Verwaltungsgerichtshof, 98/13/0021, 15 December 1999; Luxembourg, Tribunal Administratif 18793/19298, 11 July 2005; The Netherlands, Hoge Raad der Nederlanden, 42.211, 1 December 2006.

II. RESIDENCE TEST FOR TREATY PURPOSES

A. The notion of 'resident'

2.39 The treaty's personal scope of application is to relieve double taxation from double residence, not only double taxation from taxation in the RC and in the SC. Therefore Art. 4 defines the meaning of the term 'resident of a CS' and solves cases of double residence which may be created by the domestic laws of states which impose 'full tax liability' based on the taxpayers' personal attachment to the RC.[34]

2.40 In respect to individuals the definition of a resident covers various forms of personal attachment to a state. According to Art. 4 § 1 the term 'resident of a CS' includes any person who, under the laws of that state, is liable to tax therein by reason of his domicile, residence, place of management or any other criterion of a similar nature, government of each state or political subdivision or local authority thereof,[35] as well as recognized pension funds. These funds have been added to the list of resident persons by the Model 2017 which also, at Art. 3 § 1 i), expressly provides a definition.[36] Art. 4 § 2 however, provides that the term 'resident of a CS', does not include any person who is liable to tax in RC in respect only of income from sources in the RC or capital situated therein. Pension funds, charities and other organizations may be exempted from tax only if they meet all of the requirements for exemption specified in domestic laws.[37]

2.41 National courts have addressed situations in which the issue was whether a taxpayer was *effectively liable to tax* and therefore entitled to the benefits of the treaty.[38] The concept of a person 'liable to tax' also applies to individuals.[39] In many states the concept of 'liable to tax' is meant to include situations in which the RC does *not* in fact impose tax but the taxpayer is simply 'subject to tax' under the domestic laws of a CS.[40] In other cases courts have applied the concept of 'liable to tax' as including persons who are not residents for Convention purposes (unless expressly covered by a specific clause). Fiscally

---

34 Commentary to Art. 4 §§ 1–7. Model Art. 4 §§ 1–3.

35 Commentary to Art. 4 § 8.

36 Commentary to Art. 1 § 10.3–10.18.

37 Commentary to Art. 4 § 8.11.

38 Canada, Tax Court of Canada, *TD Securities LLC v. Her Majesty the Queen*, 8 April 2010; Canada, Supreme Court of Canada, *Crown Forest Industries Ltd. v. Her Majesty the Queen*, 22 June 1995; The Netherlands, Hoge Raad der Nederlanden (Supreme Court), 28 February 2001.

39 Canada, Tax Court of Canada, *McFadyen v. Her Majesty the Queen*, 11 September 2000.

40 Sweden, Regeringsrätten, RÅ 1996 ref 84 (6301-1994), 2 October 1996, *Skattenytt*, 1997 s. 219. See also: France, Conseil d'État 370054, 9 November 2015.

transparent partnerships are not a resident of the relevant country because the partners liable to tax are the appropriate persons to claim Convention benefits.[41]

For the purposes of the Convention, the term 'resident of a CS' also includes **2.42** that state and any political subdivision or local authority thereof. The Commentary deals with the issue of application of Art. 4 § 1 to sovereign wealth funds and notes that these are special purpose investment funds or arrangements created by a state or a political subdivision for macroeconomic purposes, which hold, manage or administer assets to achieve financial objectives and invest in foreign financial assets.[42]

The term 'resident of a CS' does not include any person who is liable to tax in **2.43** that state on the basis of its domestic laws in respect only of income from sources in that state, or capital situated therein. A resident of state A according to state A's domestic laws (i.e., the domestic laws of the RC), but subject in the RC only to taxation limited to the income from sources in that country on the basis of the domestic laws of that country, is *not* resident for treaty purposes because it is not taxable on income sourced outside the RC. The Commentary provides examples of this situation: foreign diplomatic and consular staff serving in the RC, 'offshore' companies held by foreign shareholders and exempted by domestic laws of the RC on their foreign income, companies and other persons not subject to comprehensive liability in the RC because residents of state A according to state A's domestic laws, but residents of state B pursuant to a treaty between A and B.[43] The Commentary notes that the second sentence, if interpreted literally, would exclude from the scope of Convention all residents of countries adopting a territorial principle, but clarifies that this is not the case.[44]

B. Dual residents

Treaties do not lay down standards on 'residence' for domestic laws which **2.44** therefore can significantly differ in the choice of the tests to determine residence of taxpayers. There are different cases. In the first place there are situations in which there is no conflict at all between the domestic laws of the

---

41 The Netherlands, Hoge Raad der Nederlanden, 29 084, 23 March 1994.
42 Commentary to Art. 4 § 8.5. OECD-TAG, *Discussion Draft on the Application of the Tax Treaties to State-owned Entities, Including Sovereign Wealth Funds* (OECD-TAG 2009).
43 Commentary to Art. 4 § 8.1.
44 Commentary to Art. 4 § 8.3.

CSs on the residence of taxpayers, so that for the purposes of the treaty a taxpayer is deemed to be resident *only* in one CS.

2.45 By contrast, in other situations there is a conflict between the domestic laws of the CSs on the residence of taxpayers, so that, on the basis of the domestic laws of the CSs, a taxpayer is deemed to be resident of both CSs. There is no solution to such a conflict by recourse to the domestic laws concept of residence of each CS and so there is a conflict between two residences: a choice must be made between the two claims and Art. 4 is aimed at resolving the conflict. When there is a different timing of the charging of taxes the juridical double taxation is not from dual residence and this is not prevented by Art. 4 tie-break rules.

2.46 Art. 4 § 1 provides that for the purposes of the Convention, the term 'resident of a CS' means any individual who, *under the laws of that state*, is liable to tax therein by reason of his domicile, residence or any other criterion of a similar nature, and therefore when an individual is resident in just one CS on the basis of domestic laws of that CS, there is no issue of dual residency and no need to apply the tie-break rules. National courts have often limited themselves to the analysis of domestic laws to plainly determine that, on the basis of such domestic laws, a taxpayer is resident just in one of the CSs. This approach is evident in a series of Canadian cases.[45]

2.47 Art. 4 § 2 relates to the cases where, under § 1, an individual is a resident of *both CSs* and is aimed at solving this conflict through so called 'tie-break rules' in which the attachment of the taxpayer to one state prevails over attachment to the other state, leading to the determination of just one the RC for the purposes of the treaty.[46]

1. Tie-break rules for individuals

2.48 Art. 4 § 2 a) first sentence provides that *if* by reason of § 1 an individual is a resident of both CSs, then he shall be deemed to be a resident only of the state in which he has a permanent home available to him. So if the taxpayer is a dual

---

45   Canada, Tax Court of Canada, *Fisher v. Her Majesty the Queen*, 29 September 1994, [1995] 1 C.T.C. 2011; Canada, Tax Court of Canada, *McFadyen v. Her Majesty the Queen*, 11 September 2000; Canada, Tax Court of Canada, *Valentina Sobolev v. Her Majesty the Queen*, 29 November 2001; Portugal, Supremo Tribunal Administrativo, 0876/10, 24 February 2011. See in general: Maisto, Guglielmo, *Residence of Individuals Under Tax Treaties and EC Law* (IBFD 2010).

46   Sasseville, Jacques, 'History and Interpretation of the Tie-breaker Rule in Art. 4(2) of the OECD Model Tax Convention' in: Maisto, Guglielmo (ed.), *Residence of Individuals under Tax Treaties and EC Law* (IBFD 2010); Van Raad, Cornelius, '2008 OECD Model: Operation and Effect of Art. 4(1) in Dual Residence Issues Under the Updated Commentary' (2009) 63 *Bull. Intl. Tax.* 187.

resident preference is given to the CS where the individual has a permanent home available to him, provided that the individual has a permanent home in *only* one CS.[47] In practice this tie-break rule is based on a double condition: (i) the existence of a permanent home; (ii) which is 'available' only in one CS. National courts have applied this tie-break rule consistently through a substantial analysis.[48]

The definition of permanent home for the purposes of Art. 4 § 2 a) first **2.49** sentence includes two features: the dwelling must effectively be a 'home' and must be 'permanent'. The Commentary defines a 'home' tautologically as 'any form of home (house or apartment) belonging to or rented by the individual, rented furnished room',[49] and specifies that for a home to be 'permanent' 'the individual must have arranged and retained it for his permanent use as opposed to staying at a particular place under such conditions that it is evident that the stay is intended to be of short duration'.[50] Courts often conduct a practical analysis of a dwelling use.[51] In addition to the fact the individual has 'arranged' to stay in that specific home, effective continuous permanence there is decisive. Courts often conduct a negative analysis to exclude that a dwelling has an 'effective and continuous' permanent nature.[52] Other courts elucidate which are the factors to positively assess the permanence of the home as continuous and not occasional.[53]

Art. 4 § 2 a) second sentence provides that: (i) if by reason of Art. 4 § 1 an **2.50** individual is a resident of both CSs; and (ii) if he has a permanent home available to him in both states, then he shall be deemed to be a resident only of the state with which his personal/economic relations are closer. This is the centre of vital interests test. In practice this tie-break rule is based on a *double condition*: permanent home available to the taxpayer in both CSs and prevailing (i.e., 'closer') centre of vital interests in one CS. If the individual has a permanent home in both CSs, then Art. 4 § 2 a) second sentence gives preference to the state where the centre of vital interests is located, i.e., the state with which the personal and economic relations of the individual are closer.[54]

---

47 Commentary to Art. 4 § 19.
48 Canada, Tax Court of Canada, *Garcia v. Her Majesty the Queen*, 28 September 2007, [2008] 1 C.T.C. 2215; Canada, Tax Court of Canada, *McFadyen v. Her Majesty the Queen*, 11 September 2000.
49 Commentary to Art. 4 § 13.
50 Commentary to Art. 4 § 13. See: Canada, Tax Court of Canada, *Garcia v. Her Majesty the Queen*, 28 September 2007.
51 Canada, Tax Court of Canada, *Salt v. Her Majesty the Queen*, 2 March 2007, 2007 TCC 118; Poland, Naczelny Sąd Administracyjny, II FSK 972/08, 13 November 2009.
52 Denmark, Østre Landsret, SKM2013.394.ØLR / B-2077-12, 19 March 2013.
53 Germany, Bundesfinanzhof, I R 22/06, 5 June 2007; Germany, Finanzgericht Baden-Württemberg, 13 K 166/01, 22 February 2006,
54 Commentary to Art. 4 § 14.

2.51 The centre of vital interests is identified on the basis of several indicators, such as family and social relations, occupations, political, cultural or other activities, place of business, place from which he administers his property, etc. and clarifies that circumstances must be examined as a whole, but considerations based on the personal acts of the individual must receive special attention.[55] National courts have applied this tie-break rule consistently through detailed substantial analysis of the actual conduct of life.[56] Often economic and personal ties are so closely intertwined that the court conducts an analysis which balances the economic and the personal ties in a kind of global view.[57] The place of business is one of the factors to be used to apply the centre of vital interests test, and in certain circumstances it can amount to the existence of a PE, thereby defining the tax prerogatives of the SC rather than the RC.[58]

2.52 The fact that the taxpayer has both a permanent home and habitual abode in one CS is an indication that he or she is resident there for treaty purposes. In practice this tie-break rule – which can be defined as the 'modified centre of vital interests test' – is based on *two conditions*: (i) a doubt in the application of the general centre of vital interests test, and (ii) permanent home and habitual abode in the same CS.[59]

2.53 Art. 4 § 2 b) establishes the 'habitual abode test' and provides that if by reason of Art. 4 § 1 an individual is a resident of both CSs, and if the state in which he has his centre of vital interests cannot be determined, *or* if he has no permanent home available to him in either state, he shall be deemed to be a resident only of the state in which he has a habitual abode.

2.54 This rule is actually made up of two tests. The first test is Art. 4 § 2 b), first sentence which establishes a pre-requisite for the application of the habitual abode test, i.e., that the centre of vital interests state cannot be determined (*negative centre of vital interests test*). The second test is Art. 4 § 2 b), first sentence, i.e., no permanent home is available in either state (*negative permanent home test*). If both the negative centre of vital interests test and the

---

55 Commentary to Art. 4 § 15. See: Baker, Philip, 'The Expression Centre of Vital Interests in Art. 4(2) of OECD Model Convention' in: Maisto, Guglielmo (ed.), *Residence of Individuals under Tax Treaties and EC Law* (IBFD 2010); Pittman, Shauna, 'The Centre of Vital Interests Rule: Do Personal Interests Prevail over Economic Interests?' in: Hofstätter, Matthias and Plansky, Patrick, *Dual Residence in Tax Treaty Law and EC Law* (Linde 2009).

56 Canada, Tax Court of Canada, *Gaudreau v. Her Majesty the Queen*, 22 December 2004; France, Conseil d'État 28831, 13 May 1983; France, Conseil d'État, 8046, 14 March 1979.

57 France, Conseil d'État 76534, 19 May 1972.

58 Italy, Corte Suprema di Cassazione, 24246/2011, 18 November 2011.

59 Canada, Tax Court of Canada, *Gaudreau v. Her Majesty the Queen*, 22 December 2004; Canada, Tax Court of Canada, *Yoon v. Her Majesty the Queen*, 22 July 2005.

negative permanent home test are met, then the *habitual abode* test in the proper sense can be applied.

The *first mode* of application of the habitual abode test is one in which the **2.55** centre of vital interests state cannot be determined (negative centre of vital interests test) and no permanent home is available to the taxpayer in either state (negative permanent home test), so that the taxpayer is resident in the country where he or she has her/his habitual abode (*if* the centre of vital interests cannot be determined and a permanent home is in neither state, *then* the habitual abode test). In respect of the concept of 'habitual abode' the Commentary observes that: 'If the permanent home is in neither state, for example, a person going from one hotel to another (...) also all stays made in a state must be considered without it being necessary to ascertain the reasons for them'.[60]

The term 'habitual abode' has been clarified in the Commentary 2017 as a **2.56** notion that refers to the frequency, duration and regularity of stays that are part of the settled routine of an individual's life and are therefore more than transient. As recognized in subparagraph c), it is possible for an individual to have a habitual abode in the two states, which would be the case if the individual was customarily or usually present in each state during the relevant period, regardless of the fact that he spent more days in one state than in the other.

The Commentary also implies a *second mode* of application of the habitual **2.57** abode test in which the centre of vital interests state cannot be determined (negative centre of vital interests test) and the taxpayer has a permanent home in both states,[61] so that the taxpayer is resident in the country where he or she has her/his habitual abode.

Art. 4 § 2 c) establishes the nationality test and provides that if by reason of **2.58** Art. 4 § 1 an individual is a resident of both CSs, then if he has a habitual abode in both states or in neither of them, he shall be deemed to be a resident only of the state of which he is a national (of course it is assumed that neither the permanent home test nor the centre of vital interests test has been met). In practice this tie-break rule is based on *a double alternative condition*: (i) habitual abode in both CSs, or (ii) habitual abode in neither of them. This creates a hierarchy of tests that courts tend to follow strictly to apply the

---

60 Commentary to Art. 4 § 18.
61 It is further assumed here that also the modified centre of vital interests test is not met, i.e., that the taxpayer does not have a permanent home and habitual abode in one state.

nationality test.[62] Care should be taken, however, to consider a period of time during which there were no major changes of personal circumstances that would clearly affect the determination (such as separation or divorce).[63]

2.59 Art. 4 § 2 d) provides that if by reason of Art. 4 § 1 an individual is a resident of both CSs, then if he is a national of both states or of neither of them, the Competent Authorities of the CSs shall settle the question by mutual agreement. In practice this tie-break rule is based on a *double alternative condition*: (i) the taxpayer is a national of both CSs, or (ii) the taxpayer is a national of neither of them (of course it is assumed that neither the permanent home test, the centre of vital interests, nor the habitual abode test, nor the nationality test has been met).

2. Allocating residence for companies

2.60 Art. 4 § 1 provides that for the purposes of the Convention, the term 'resident of a CS means any person who, under the laws of that state, is liable to tax therein by reason of his effective place of management or any other criterion of a similar nature', and therefore when a person, such as a company is resident of just one CS on the basis of the domestic laws of both CSs, there is no issue of dual residency and no need to apply the tie-break rules. This rule has a broad scope as it covers companies and other bodies of persons, irrespective of whether they are or are not legal persons. National courts have often limited themselves to the analysis of domestic laws to plainly determine that, on the basis of such domestic laws, a company is resident just in one of the CSs.[64] Often the question of the company residence is a question of proof.[65]

2.61 A situation of dual residence for legal entities, as for individuals, occurs when the criteria adopted by the two CSs are different, for example, the domestic laws of one CS attribute importance to the registration and those of the other CS to the effective place of management. In these cases, the tie-break rules of Art. 4 § 3 apply. A purely formal criterion like registration is not an adequate solution, and it is preferable to adopt a tie-break test based on the place where the company is actually managed (effective place of management).[66] As a matter of fact Art. 4 § 1 adopts the effective place of management test when

---

62 France, Conseil d'État, 69853, 26 January 1990.

63 Commentary to Art. 4 § 19–19.1

64 Italy, Commissione Tributaria Centrale, Case 4992, 10 October 1996, The Netherlands, Hoge Raad der Nederlanden, 23 877, 1 July 1987.

65 The Netherlands, Hoge Raad der Nederlanden 11/05198, 30 November 2012; The Netherlands, Gerechtshof Den Haag, 100/81 M III, 22 January 1982. See in general: Couzin, Robert, *Corporate Residence and International Taxation* (IBFD 2002); Maisto, Guglielmo, *Residence of Companies Under Tax Treaties and EC Law* (IBFD 2009).

66 Commentary to Art. 4 § 22.

applied to companies as it provides that for the purposes of the Convention, the term 'resident of a CS' means any person (as defined by Art. 3 § 1 which includes companies) who, under the laws of the RC, is liable to tax therein by reason of place of management or any other criterion of a similar nature.[67]

The tie-break rules for companies before the Model 2017 were established **2.62** by Art. 4 § 3 which provided that *if* by reason of § 1 a person other than an individual is a resident of both CSs, *then* it shall be deemed to be a resident only of the state in which its effective place of management is situated. The concept of effective place of management was derived from the treaties on income from shipping and air transport as the place where *key management and commercial decisions* that are necessary for the conduct of the entity's business as a whole are in substance made, an assessment that should be made on the basis of all relevant facts and circumstances. An entity may have more than one place of management, but it can have only one effective place of management.[68]

The analysis of effective place of management is factual.[69] This implies that **2.63** the effective place of management used by the Commentary and the Model and the 'management and control' concept applied under UK domestic laws are similar but there are some differences, and several UK cases have addressed this distinction.[70]

---

67 Avery Jones, John F., et al, 'Place of Effective Management As Residence-Tiebreaker' (2005) 59 *Bull. Intl. Fisc. Doc.* 20; Burgers, Irene, 'Some Thoughts on Further Refinement of the Concept of Place of Effective Management for Tax Treaty Purpose' (2007) 35 *Intertax* 378; Burgstaller, Eva and Hasliger, Katharin, 'Place of Effective Management as Tie-Breaker-Rule' (2004) 32 *Intertax* 376; OECD-TAG, *Place of Effective Management Concept: Suggestions for Changes to the OECD Model Tax Convention* (OECD-TAG 2003); OECD-TAG, *The Impact of the Communications Revolution on the Application of 'Place of Effective Management' as a Tie Breaker Rule* (OECD-TAG 2001); Romano, Carlo, *The Evolving Concept of Place of Effective Management As a Tie Breaker Rule Under the Oecd Model Convention and Italian Law* (2001) 41 *Eur. Tax.* 339; Sasseville, Jacques, *The Meaning of Place of Effective Management* (IBFD 2009); Shalhav, Sarig, 'The Evolution of the Art. 4 (3) and Its Impact on the Place of Effective Management Tie Breaker Rule' (2004) 32 *Intertax* 460.

68 Commentary to Art. 4 § 2. France, Conseil d'État 371435, 7 March 2016. See also: Brood, Edgar, 'Dual Residence of Companies' (1990) 18 *Intertax* 1.

69 Belgium, Cour d'Appel, Bruxelles, 1982–06–29, 29 June 1982; United Kingdom, UK First-tier Tribunal (Tax Chamber), *Laerstate BV v. Commissioners for Her Majesty's Revenue and Customs*, 11 August 2009; Germany, Finanzgericht Nordrhein-Westfalen Düsseldorf, II 170/83 A(E), 1 March 1984.

70 United Kingdom, Commissioners for Her Majesty's Revenue and Customs, *Wensleydale's Settlement Trustees v. Inland Revenue Commissioners*, 14 March 1996, [1996] STC 24; United Kingdom, Court of Appeal of England and Wales (Civil Division), *Smallwood (Trevor Smallwood and Mary Caroline Smallwood, Trustees of the Trevor Smallwood Trust, and Trevor Smallwood, Settlor of the Trevor Smallwood Trust) v. Commissioners for HM Revenue and Customs*, 8 July 2010; United Kingdom, Court of Appeal of England and Wales (Civil Division), *Mr and Mrs R J Wood v. Mrs L M Holden*, 26 January 2006. See: Hattingh, Johann P., 'Can Effective Management Be Distinguished from Central Management and Control' (2003) 48 *Brit. Tax Rev.* 296; Cleave, Brian, 'The Smallwood Case: Dual Residence of Trustees' (2011) 65 *Bull. Intl. Tax.* 8.

2.64   Art. 4 § 3 of the Model 2017 introduced a radical change and replaced § 3 of Art. 4, which now reads as follows:

> 3. Where by reason of the provisions of § 1 a person other than an individual is a resident of both CSs, the Competent Authorities of the CSs shall endeavour to determine by mutual agreement the CS of which such person shall be deemed to be a resident for the purposes of the Convention, having regard to its place of effective management, the place where it is incorporated or otherwise constituted and any other relevant factors. In the absence of such agreement, such person shall not be entitled to any relief or exemption from tax provided by this Convention except to the extent and in such manner as may be agreed upon by the Competent Authorities of the CSs.

Art. 4 § 3 of the Model 2017 is equivalent to Art. 4 § 1 of the MLI.

2.65   This a brand new approach under which, essentially, when a company is dual resident under the domestic laws of CSs, the Competent Authorities of the CSs step in and try to determine by MAP the CS of which such person is resident for the purposes of the Convention, looking at different factors which include the place of effective management, but also extending to the place of incorporation in a broad sense or to any other relevant factors. In 2017 the CFA recognized that there had been a number of tax avoidance cases involving dual resident companies and concluded that a better solution to the issue of dual residence of entities other than individuals was to deal with such situations on a case-by-case basis. The important change is that, if the MAP is not concluded, then the dual resident person is not entitled to any relief or exemption from tax provided by the Convention, but the Competent Authorities of the CSs may stipulate specific arrangements. In other words: if there is no agreement by the Competent Authorities, there is no treaty protection for the dual resident company.

2.66   With regard to the identification of the effective place of management the Commentary before 2017 noted that some countries follow a case-by-case approach as the best way to deal with difficulties in determining the effective place of management that may arise from the use of new communication technologies.[71] Competent Authorities should take account of various factors, i.e., where the meetings of the board of directors or equivalent body are usually held, CEO and other senior executives usually carry on their activities, the senior day-to-day management of the person is carried on, the person's headquarters are located, accounting records are kept, and which country's laws govern the legal status of the person.

---

71   Commentary 2014 to Art. 4 § 24.1 has been deleted in 2017 (it originally envisaged the same solution introduced now in Model 2017).

III. THE LIMITATION OF BENEFITS CLAUSE

Art. 29 §§ 1–7 contains broad guidelines for a treaty '*Limitation of Benefit* **2.67**
Rule' ('LOB rule' or 'LOB clause'). The purpose of the LOB rule is to deny
treaty benefits in the case of structures that result in the indirect granting of
treaty benefits to persons that are not directly entitled to these benefits. Art.
29 § 1 provides that a resident of a CS shall not be entitled to the benefits of
the Convention unless it constitutes a 'qualified person' under Art. 29 § 2 or
unless benefits are granted under the provisions of Art. 29 §§ 3, 4, 5 or 6. So
Art. 29 § 1 constitutes the core of the LOB rule, which restricts treaty benefits
to a resident of a CS who is a 'qualified person' as defined in Art. 29 § 2,
subject to certain exemptions provided for by Art. 29 §§ 3–6.

Art. 29 § 2 then determines who constitutes a 'qualified person' by reference to **2.68**
the nature or attributes of various categories of persons; any person to which
that paragraph applies is entitled to all the benefits of the Convention. Under
Art. 29 § 2 a qualified person is: an individual; a CS, its political subdivisions
and their agencies and instrumentalities; certain publicly-traded companies
and entities; certain affiliates of publicly-listed companies and entities; certain
non-profit organizations and recognized pension funds; other entities that
meet certain ownership and base erosion requirements; and certain collective
investment vehicles.

Art. 29 §§ 3–6 provide exclusions from the principle of the treaty entitlement **2.69**
for qualified persons. These provisions recognize that in some cases persons
who are not residents of a CS may establish an entity in that state for
legitimate business reasons. So, under Art. 29 § 3, a person is entitled to the
benefits of the Convention with respect to an item of income even if it does
not constitute a 'qualified person' under Art. 29 § 2 as long as that item of
income emanates from, or is incidental to, the active conduct of a business in
that person's state of residence (subject to certain exceptions). Art. 29 § 3
recommends rules that extend treaty benefits to certain income derived by
such a person that is not a qualified person if the person is engaged in the
active conduct of a business in its state of residence and the income emanates
from, or is incidental to, that business.

Art. 29 § 4 is a 'derivative benefits' provision that allows certain entities owned **2.70**
by residents of third states to obtain treaty benefits provided that these
residents would have been entitled to equivalent benefits if they had invested
directly. Art. 29 § 5 is a 'headquarters company' provision under which a
company that is not eligible for benefits under Art. 29 § 2 may nevertheless
qualify for benefits with respect to particular items of income.

2.71 Finally Art. 29 § 6 contemplates the introduction of provisions that allow the Competent Authority of a CS to grant certain treaty benefits to a person where benefits would otherwise be denied under Art. 29 § 1. Art. 29 § 7 provides definitions applicable for the purposes of Art. 29 §§ 1–7.

2.72 The domestic laws of certain states include anti-abuse rules but also need a LOB rule. In these cases a state can rely on the detailed LOB rule of Art. 29 §§ 1–7, together with rules for conduit arrangements not covered by the detailed LOB rule. These rules for conduit arrangements which are other than the LOB rule essentially deny the benefits of the provisions of the Convention (e.g., those of Artt. 7, 10, 11, 12 and 21), in respect of any income obtained through a conduit arrangement. These rules can take the form of beneficial ownership doctrines, can be domestic anti-abuse rules or other judicial doctrines that would achieve a similar result.

A. Qualified person

2.73 Model 2017 simply provides guidelines for the text of Art. 29 § 1, while the Commentary provides a draft text for Art. 29 § 1, in one single version, both for the simplified and the detailed version, as follows:

> 1. Except as otherwise provided in this article, a resident of a CS shall not be entitled to a benefit that would otherwise be accorded by this Convention (other than a benefit under § 3 of Art. 4, § 2 of Art. 9 or Art. 25) unless such resident is a 'qualified person', as defined in § 2, at the time that the benefit would be accorded.

The Commentary also provides a single text of both the simplified and detailed versions of Art. 29, § 2 which contains the definition of 'qualified person', as follows:

> 2. A resident of a CS shall be a qualified person at a time when a benefit would otherwise be accorded by the Convention if, at that time, the resident is:
> a) an individual;
> b) that CS or political subdivision or local authority thereof, or an agency or instrumentality of that state, political subdivision or local authority;
> c) a company or other entity, if the principal class of its shares is regularly traded on one or more recognised stock exchanges;
> d) a person, other than an individual, that:
>   i. is [an agreed description of the relevant non-profit organisations found in each CS],
>   ii. is a recognised pension fund;
> e) a person other than an individual if, at that time and on at least half of the days of a twelve-month period that includes that time, persons who are residents of that

CS and that are entitled to benefits of this Convention under subparagraphs a) to d) own, directly or indirectly, at least 50 per cent of the shares of the person … .

Art. 29 § 1 provides that a qualified person under Art. 29 § 2 is entitled to the 'benefits otherwise accorded to residents of a CS under the Convention'. These benefits include all limitations to the CSs' taxing rights under Artt. 6–22, the elimination of double taxation provided by Art. 23 and the protection afforded to residents of a CS under Art. 24. The Commentary clarifies however that the LOB clause does not restrict the availability of treaty benefits under Art. 4 § 3, Art. 9 § 2 or Art. 25, or under the few provisions of the Convention that do not require that a person be a resident of a CS in order to enjoy the benefits of those provisions (e.g., the provisions of Art. 24 § 1, to the extent that they apply to nationals who are not residents of either CS). **2.74**

A resident of a CS who constitutes a 'qualified person' under Art. 29 § 2 must still meet the conditions of the other provisions of the Convention to obtain these benefits (e.g., that the resident must be the beneficial owner of dividends in order to benefit from the provisions of § 2 of Art. 10) and these benefits may be denied or restricted under applicable anti-abuse rules such as the rules in Art. 29 §§ 8 and 9. **2.75**

Subparagraph a) of both the simplified and detailed versions provides that any individual who is a resident of a CS will be a qualified person. Under some treaty provisions, a CIV must be treated as an individual for the purposes and constitutes a qualified person by virtue of subparagraph a).[72] **2.76**

Subparagraph b) of both the simplified and detailed versions provides that the CSs and any political subdivision or local authority thereof constitute qualified persons. These words apply to any part of a state, such as a separate fund established by the state that does not constitute, and is not owned by, a separate person. Under the last part of the subparagraph, a separate legal person which is a resident of a CS and is an agency or instrumentality of a CS, or a political subdivision or local authority thereof, will also be a qualified person and, therefore, will be entitled to all the benefits of the Convention while it qualifies as such. The concept of 'agency or instrumentality' is restricted to entities set up by a state (or a political subdivision or local authority thereof) to perform exclusively functions of a governmental nature.[73] **2.77**

---

72 Commentary to Art. 29 §§ 13 and 61.
73 Commentary to Art. 29 § 14.

2.78 Subparagraph c) of the simplified version provides that a company or other entity, if the principal class of its shares is regularly traded on one or more recognised stock exchanges, constitutes a qualified person. The terms 'shares', covers comparable interests in entities, other than companies, to which the subparagraph applies; this includes, for example, publicly-traded units of a trust. The Commentary provides only a detailed version of subparagraph d) about affiliates of publicly-traded companies and entities.

2.79 Subparagraph d) of the simplified version provides that a person, other than an individual, that is a non-profit organization or a recognized pension fund constitutes a qualified person. A non-profit organization is a person that does not pay tax in its state of residence and that is constituted and operated exclusively to fulfil certain social functions (e.g., charitable, scientific, artistic, cultural, or educational). The description of such entities refers to domestic laws of that state that describe these entities or to the domestic law factors that allow the identification of these entities.

2.80 Subparagraph e) of the simplified version provides an additional method to qualify for treaty benefits to any entity that is a resident of a CS which, at the time when the relevant treaty benefit otherwise would be accorded and on at least half the days of a 12-month period that includes that time, at least 50 per cent of the shares of that entity are owned, directly or indirectly, by persons who are residents of that CS and that are themselves entitled to the benefits of this Convention.[74]

B. Active conduct test

2.81 The Commentary contemplates only one version for both the simplified and the detailed versions of Art. 29 § 3 relating to the active conduct of a business, as follows:

> 3. a) A resident of a CS shall be entitled to benefits under this Convention with respect to an item of income derived from the other CS, regardless of whether the resident is a qualified person, if the resident is engaged in the active conduct of a business in the first-mentioned state and the income derived from the other state emanates from, or is incidental to, that business. For purposes of this article, the term 'active conduct of a business' shall not include the following activities or any combination thereof:
> (i)   operating as a holding company;
> (ii) providing overall supervision or administration of a group of companies;
> (iii) providing group financing (including cash pooling); or

---

74   Commentary to Art. 29 § 43.

(iv) making or managing investments,

unless these activities are carried on by a bank or [...], insurance enterprise or registered securities dealer in the ordinary course of its business as such.

b) If a resident of a CS derives an item of income from a business activity conducted by that resident in the other CS, or derives an item of income arising in the other state from a connected person, the conditions described in subparagraph a) shall be considered to be satisfied with respect to such item only if the business activity carried on by the resident in the first-mentioned state to which the item is related is substantial in relation to the same or complementary business activity carried on by the resident or such connected person in the other CS. Whether a business activity is substantial for the purposes of this paragraph shall be determined based on all the facts and circumstances.

c) For purposes of applying this paragraph, activities conducted by connected persons with respect to a resident of a CS shall be deemed to be conducted by such resident.

Subparagraph a) sets forth the general rule that a resident of a CS engaged in **2.82** the active conduct of a business in that state may obtain the benefits of the Convention with respect to an item of income derived from the other CS. The item of income, however, must emanate from, or be incidental to, that business. Active conduct of a business includes the performance of professional services and of other activities of an independent character. An entity generally will be considered to be engaged in the active conduct of a business only if persons through whom the entity is acting (such as officers or employees of a company) conduct substantial activities.

The Commentary 2017 (§§ 68–81) introduces a so-called '*active conduct test*' **2.83** under which treaty benefits are granted even if the requirements to be a qualified person are not met. Under the active-conduct test of Art. 29 § 3, a person (typically a company) will be eligible for treaty benefits if it satisfies two conditions: 1) it is engaged in the active conduct of a business in its state of residence and 2) the payment for which benefits are sought emanates from, or is incidental to, the business. In certain cases, an additional requirement that the business be substantial in size relative to the activity in the state of source generating the income must be met.

So Art. 29 § 3 a) recognizes that where an entity resident of a CS actively **2.84** carries on business activities in that state, including activities conducted by connected persons, and derives income from the other CS that emanates from, or is incidental to, such business activities, granting treaty benefits with respect to such income does not give rise to treaty-shopping concerns regardless of the nature and ownership of the entity.

2.85 Subdivisions (i)–(iv) of subparagraph a) identify specific functions that, either on their own or in combination, will be considered, for purposes of Art. 29 § 3, not to constitute the active conduct of a business in a CS, even when all such functions are conducted in the same state. The Commentary takes the position that, on the basis of such a list, the administrative support functions of multinationals, as well as the activities of operating as a holding company, do not constitute the active conduct of a business and, therefore, income that emanates from, or is incidental to, such activities cannot be entitled to treaty benefits under Art. 29 § 3.

2.86 An item of income 'emanates from' the active conduct of a business in the state of residence if there is a factual connection between the actively conducted business and the item of income for which benefits are sought ('factual connection test'). For example, if a company conducts research and development in its state of residence and develops a patent for a new process, royalties from licensing the patent would be factually connected to the actively conducted business in the state of residence. For determining the factual connection one should compare the lines of business in each state. The line of business in the state of source may be upstream or downstream to the activity conducted in the state of residence. Thus, the line of business in the state of source may provide inputs for a manufacturing process that occurs in the state of residence, or the line of business in the state of source may sell the output of the manufacturing process conducted by a resident.

2.87 The Commentary provides an example to illustrate these principles: ACO is a company resident of state A and is engaged in the active conduct of a business in that state consisting in manufacturing product X. ACO owns 100 per cent of the shares of BCO, a company resident of state B. BCO acquires product X from ACO and distributes it to customers in state B. Since the distribution activity by BCO of product X is factually connected to ACO's manufacturing of that product, dividends paid by BCO to ACO will be treated as emanating from ACO's business.[75]

2.88 An item of income derived from the state of source is 'incidental to' the business carried on in the state of residence if production of the item facilitates the conduct of the business in the state of residence. For example income derived from the temporary investment of working capital of a person in the state of residence in securities issued by persons in the state of source is 'incidental income'.[76]

---

75   Commentary to Art. 29 § 75.
76   Commentary to Art. 29 § 76.

Subparagraph b) of Art. 29 § 3 requires a further condition – the substantiality **2.89** test – to the general rule in subparagraph a) in cases where the business generating the item of income in question is carried on either by the person deriving the income or by a connected person in the SC. Under the substantiality test the business carried on in the RC under those circumstances must be substantial in relation to the activity in the SC. The determination of substantiality is based upon all the facts and circumstances, including the comparative sizes of the businesses in each CS, the relative sizes of the economies and markets in the CSs, the nature of the activities performed in each state, and the relative contributions made to that business in each state.[77] Art. 29 § 3, subparagraph c) also includes attribution rules in the case of activities conducted by connected persons for determining whether a person meets the active conduct of business test and the substantiality test and the Commentary provides several examples.

The Commentary also clarifies that the substantiality test is made separately **2.90** for each item of income derived from the SC, with reference to the business in the RC from which the item of income in question emanates. It is therefore possible that a person is entitled to the benefits of the Convention with respect to one item of income but not with respect to another. By contrast, the substantiality test does not apply if the business generating the item of income in question is not carried on in the SC by the resident seeking benefits or by a connected person in the SC. For example, if a small research firm in one state develops a process that it licenses to a very large pharmaceutical manufacturer in another state that is not a connected person with respect to the small research firm, the size of the business activity of the research firm in the first state would not have to be tested against the size of the business activity of the manufacturer. Another example is that of a small bank of one state that makes a loan to a very large company that is not a connected person and that is operating a business in the other state.[78]

C. Derivative benefits and discretionary test

The simplified version of Art. 29 § 4 introduces a derivative benefits clause, as **2.91** follows:

> 4. A resident of a CS that is not a qualified person shall nevertheless be entitled to a benefit that would otherwise be accorded by this Convention with respect to an item of income if, at the time when the benefit otherwise would be accorded and on at least

---

77 Commentary to Art. 29 § 77.
78 Commentary to Art. 29 §§ 78–79.

half of the days of any twelve month period that includes that time, persons that are equivalent beneficiaries own, directly or indirectly, at least 75 per cent of the shares of the resident.

2.92 Art. 29 § 4 of the simplified version sets forth a derivative benefits test that is potentially applicable to all treaty benefits, although the test must be applied to each individual item of income. This derivative benefits test entitles companies and entities that are residents of a CS but that are not qualifying persons under Art. 29 § 2 to be entitled to treaty benefits with respect to an item of income if, at the time that the benefit would otherwise be granted with respect to that item of income and on at least half of the days of any 12-month period that includes that time, at least 75 per cent of the shares (as defined in Art. 29 § 7) of that company or entity are owned, directly or indirectly, by persons that satisfy the definition of 'equivalent beneficiary' found in Art. 29 § 7.

2.93 An 'equivalent beneficiary', for the purposes of Art. 29 § 4, is a person who would have been entitled to equivalent or more favourable benefits from the state of source if it had received the same income directly. Art. 29 § 6 (e) explicitly provides that the term 'equivalent beneficiary' means any person who would be entitled to benefits with respect to an item of income accorded by a CS under the domestic law of that CS, the applicable Convention or any other international agreement which are equivalent to, or more favourable than, benefits to be accorded to that item of income under the applicable Convention.

2.94 The Commentary introduces a version for both the simplified (Art. 29 § 5) and the detailed version (Art. 29 § 6) of the clause relating to discretionary relief, as follows:

> 5. If a resident of a CS is neither a qualified person pursuant to the provisions of § 2 of this article, nor entitled to benefits under § 3 or 4 (simplified version) […], the Competent Authority of the CS in which benefits are denied under the previous provisions of this article may, nevertheless, grant the benefits of this Convention, or benefits with respect to a specific item of income or capital, taking into account the object and purpose of this Convention, but only if such resident demonstrates to the satisfaction of such Competent Authority that neither its establishment, acquisition or maintenance, nor the conduct of its operations, had as one of its principal purposes the obtaining of benefits under this Convention. The Competent Authority of the CS to which a request has been made, under this paragraph, by a resident of the other state, shall consult with the Competent Authority of that other state before either granting or denying the request.

To obtain discretionary relief, a person must establish, that 1) there are **2.95** non-tax business reasons for its operations and, 2) the benefits would not otherwise be contrary to the object and purpose of the Convention. The Commentary notes that one of the factors that the Competent Authority will typically take into account is whether the resident has a substantial non-tax nexus to its state of residence. For example, in the case of a resident subsidiary with a parent in a third state, the fact that the relevant withholding rate provided in the Convention is at least as low as the corresponding withholding rate in the income tax convention between the SC and the third state is not by itself evidence of a nexus or relationship to the other CS. Another relevant factor is whether there is no or minimal tax imposed on the item of income in both the state of residence of the applicant and the state of source (typically in cases of hybrid structures under domestic laws), unless such level of taxation is properly granted by the treaty, for example outbound dividends are subject to low or no taxation in both states when the recipient company resident of the other state owns a substantial part of the shares of the paying company.[79]

The discretionary relief can be denied if at least one of the principal purposes **2.96** was to obtain treaty benefits, because Art. 29 § 5 provides that neither the establishment acquisition or maintenance of the taxpayer, nor the conduct of its operations, had as one of its principal purposes the obtaining of benefits under this Convention. So to obtain discretionary relief it is necessary to prove that the benefits obtained under a tax treaty are not the sole or dominant purpose.

The request for discretionary relief may be presented before (e.g., through a **2.97** ruling request) or after the establishment, acquisition or maintenance of the person for whom the request is made, but before benefits may be claimed. The discretionary relief granted by the Competent Authority may be limited to only certain benefits and subject to conditions, such as setting time limits on the duration of any relief granted.

D. Anti-abuse rule for PEs in third countries

Art. 29 § 8 addresses potential abuses which may result from the transfer of **2.98** shares, debt-claims, rights or property to PEs set up in countries that impose no or low tax on the income from such assets. For example, an enterprise of CS1 sets up a PE in a third country that imposes no or low tax on the profits of the PE which are also are exempt in CS1 (because of treaty exemption under Art. 23A between CS1 and the third country where the PE is located or

---

79   Commentary to Art. 29 §§ 103–104.

because of the domestic law of CS1). The enterprise derives interest arising from CS2 which is included in the profits attributable to the PE in the third country. CS2 (the state in which the interest arises), in the absence of Art. 29 § 8, would be obliged to grant the benefits of the limitation of tax provided for in Art. 11 § 2 despite the fact that the interest is exempt from tax in CS2 and is subject to little or no tax in the third country where the PE is situated. In that situation, Art. 29 § 8 denies the benefits of the Convention between CS1 and CS2 with respect to that income.

2.99 The situation described in the above example is captured by Art. 29 § 8 a) which provides that if (i) an enterprise of a CS derives income from the other CS and the first-mentioned state treats such income as attributable to a PE of the enterprise situated in a third jurisdiction, and (ii) the profits attributable to that PE are exempt from tax in the first-mentioned state, then the benefits of this Convention shall not apply to any item of income on which the tax in the third jurisdiction is less than the lower of [rate to be determined bilaterally] of the amount of that item of income and 60 per cent of the tax that would be imposed in the first-mentioned state on that item of income if that PE were situated in the first-mentioned state. In such a case any income to which the provisions of this paragraph apply shall remain taxable according to the domestic law of the other state, notwithstanding any other provisions of the Convention.

2.100 Art. 29 § 8 b) however provides that Art. 29 § 8 a) does not apply if the income derived from the other state emanates from, or is incidental to, the active conduct of a business carried on through the PE (other than the business of making, managing or simply holding investments for the enterprise's own account, unless these activities are banking, insurance or securities activities carried on by a bank, insurance enterprise or registered securities dealer, respectively).

2.101 Moreover Art. 29 § 8 c) provides that if benefits under the Convention are denied under Art. 29 § 8 a) with respect to an item of income derived by a resident of a CS, the Competent Authority of the other CS may, nevertheless, grant these benefits with respect to that item of income if, in response to a request by such resident, such Competent Authority determines that granting such benefits is justified in light of the reasons such resident did not satisfy the requirements of this Art. 29 § 8 c) (such as the existence of losses). The Competent Authority of the CS to which a request has been made under the preceding sentence shall consult with the Competent Authority of the other CS before either granting or denying the request.

IV. TREATY ABUSE

A. An integral approach

Model 2017 includes a new Art. 29, *'Entitlement of Benefits'*, which introduces **2.102** for the first time in tax treaties provisions that explicitly restrict the availability of those bilateral agreements, transposing concepts developed in Action 6. Art. 29 of the Model is substantially similar to Art. 7 ('Prevention of Treaty Abuse'), and Art. 10 ('Anti-abuse Rule for Permanent Establishments Situated in Third Jurisdictions') of the MLI. These changes reflect a recent evolution toward more regulation of aggressive tax planning through anti-abuse rules.[80]

Art. 29 § 9 contains a general anti-abuse rule denominated *'Principal Purpose* **2.103** *Test'* ('PPT') which reads as follows: 'Notwithstanding the other provisions of this Convention, a benefit under this Convention shall not be granted in respect of an item of income or capital if it is reasonable to conclude, having regard to all relevant facts and circumstances, that obtaining that benefit was one of the principal purposes of any arrangement or transaction that resulted directly or indirectly in that benefit, unless it is established that granting that benefit in these circumstances would be in accordance with the object and purpose of the relevant provisions of this Convention.'

Model 2017 also provides at Art. 29 §§ 1–7 broad guidelines for a treaty of the **2.104** LOB rule, while the Commentary provides a draft text for such a rule both in a simplified and a detailed version. Art. 29 § 8 is a specific anti-abuse rule for PEs situated in a third country and applies when an enterprise of a CS derives income from the other CS and the first-mentioned state treats such income as attributable to a PE of the enterprise situated in a third jurisdiction, and (ii) the profits attributable to that PE are exempt from tax in the first-mentioned state. In these situations Art. 29 § 8 provides that the benefits of this Convention shall not apply to any item of income on which the tax in the third country is taxed at a significantly lower rate or is exempt (see Section III of this Chapter).

---

80 On anti-abuse rules before the BEPS Project: de Broe, Luc, *International Tax Planning and Prevention of Abuse* (IBFD 2008); Avi-Yonah, Reuven, and Panayi, Christiana H., 'Rethinking Treaty Shopping: Lessons for the European Union' in: Lang, Michael, et al., (eds), *Tax Treaties: Building Bridges between Law and Economics* (IBFD 2010); Ward, David, 'Abuse of Tax Treaties' (1995) 23 *Intertax* 176; CD-TAG, *International Tax Avoidance and Evasion – Four Related Studies* (OECD-TAG 1987); Duff, David G, 'Responses to Treaty Shopping: A Comparative Evaluation' in: Lang, Michael, et al., (eds), *Tax Treaties*, ibid.

2.105   The rationale of Art. 29 as a whole is to prevent treaty shopping through which persons who are not residents of a CS establish an entity that is a resident of that state to reduce or eliminate taxation in the other CS through the benefits of the tax treaty concluded between these two states (such as the reduction or elimination of withholding taxes on dividends, interest or royalties).[81]

2.106   This goal is aligned with the intention of the CSs, incorporated in the preamble of the Convention, to eliminate double taxation without creating opportunities for non-taxation or reduced taxation through tax evasion or avoidance, including through treaty shopping arrangements. The fact that persons who are not directly entitled to treaty benefits obtain these benefits indirectly through treaty shopping clearly frustrates the bilateral and reciprocal nature of tax treaties.[82]

2.107   Art. 29 constitutes a 'minimum standard' agreed to as part of the BEPS Project, to eliminate double taxation without creating opportunities for non-taxation or reduced taxation through tax evasion or avoidance, including through treaty-shopping arrangements. The implementation of this minimum standard however depends on the choice by CSs. Depending on the circumstances the CSs may decide a) to adopt only the PPT rule of Art. 29 § 9, or b) to adopt the detailed LOB rule of Art. 29 §§ 1–7 together with the implementation of certain anti-conduit mechanisms not covered by the LOB rule, or c) to adopt the PPT rule of Art. 29 § 9 in combination with any variation of Art. 29 §§ 1–7.

2.108   The Commentary suggests that states that do not include the PPT rule should adopt the detailed LOB rule and this is the reason why the Commentary includes a detailed version of the LOB rule, in addition to a simplified version.

B.   The principal purpose test

2.109   The provisions of Art. 29 § 9 have the effect of denying a benefit under a tax convention where one of the principal purposes of an arrangement or transaction that has been entered into is to obtain a benefit under the convention ('treaty shopping'). This treaty abuse is also discussed in the section 'Improper

---

81   On anti-abuse rules in the BEPS Project: Pinetz, Erik, 'Final Report on Action 6 of the OECD/G20 Base Erosion and Profit Shifting Initiative: Prevention of Treaty Abuse', (2016) 70 *Bull. Intl. Taxn.*; Pinetz, Erik, 'Use of a Principle Purpose Test to Prevent Treaty Abuse', in: Lang, Michael, et al., (eds) Base Erosion and Profit Shifting (BEPS), (Linde 2016).

82   Commentary to Art. 29 §§ 1–2.

use of treaties' of the Commentary to Art. 1 and therefore the Commentary to Art. 29 § 9 is connected to such section.[83]

According to the Commentary on Art. 1, the benefits of a tax convention **2.110** should not be available where one of the principal purposes of certain transactions or arrangements is to secure a benefit under a tax treaty, because obtaining that benefit in these circumstances would be contrary to the object and purpose of the tax convention.

The PPT rule is a broad rule against treaty shopping and must be read in **2.111** combination with the LOB rule, which focuses on the legal nature, ownership in, and activities of, residents of a CS, and in the context of the Convention, including its preamble. The PPT rule supplements and does not restrict the scope or application of Art. 29 §§ 1–7 (the LOB rule) and of Art. 29 § 8 (the rule applicable to a PE situated in a third country), so the benefits to which a person is entitled under the LOB rule can be denied under the PPT rule.

The Commentary makes the example of a public company whose shares are **2.112** regularly traded on a recognized stock exchange in the CS of which the company is a resident which derives income from the other CS and enjoys certain treaty benefits. The fact that such a company is a qualified person under the LOB rule does not imply that under the PPT rule these (or other) benefits could not be denied. Denial of benefits can occur if, for example, such a company is a bank that enters into a conduit financing arrangement intended to provide indirectly to a resident of a third state the benefit of lower source taxation under a tax treaty. These reasons are unrelated to the ownership of the shares of that company and the LOB rule, so they can trigger the application of the PPT rule.[84] By contrast, a benefit which is denied by the LOB rule is not necessarily denied by the PPT.

The PPT rule applies if one the principal purposes of an arrangement or **2.113** transaction is to obtain benefits under the Convention. In that respect Art. 29 § 9 last part contains an escape clause which allows the person who enjoys the benefits allegedly disallowed by the PPT rule to prove that obtaining those benefits in those circumstances was in accordance with the object and purpose of the relevant provisions of the Convention. Such a person, however, cannot avoid the application of Art. 29 § 9 by merely asserting that the arrangement or transaction was not undertaken or arranged to obtain the benefits of the Convention. The Commentary notes that all of the evidence must be weighed

---

83   See: Kok, Reinout. 'The Principal Purpose Test in Tax Treaties under BEPS 6', (2016) 44 *Intertax* 406–12.
84   Commentary to Art. 29 §§ 171–173.

to determine whether it is reasonable to conclude that an arrangement or transaction was undertaken or arranged for such a purpose.[85]

2.114 In more general terms, to determine whether or not one of the principal purposes of an arrangement or transaction is to obtain benefits under the Convention, one has to undertake an objective analysis of the aims and objects of all persons involved in putting that arrangement or transaction in place or being a party to it. The determination of the purposes of an arrangement or transaction, according to the Commentary, is a 'question of fact' which can only be answered by considering all circumstances surrounding the arrangement or event on a case-by-case basis.

2.115 Although such a 'question of fact' should be amenable to conclusive proof, the Commentary takes the position that it is sufficient to reasonably conclude that one of the principal purposes of the arrangement or transaction was to obtain the benefits of the tax convention. In particular the Commentary remarks that a purpose is not a 'principal purpose' when it is reasonable to conclude that obtaining the benefit was not a principal consideration and would not have justified entering into any arrangement or transaction that has, alone or together with other transactions, resulted in the benefit. In particular, where an arrangement is inextricably linked to a core commercial activity, and its form has not been driven by considerations of obtaining a benefit, it is unlikely that its principal purpose will be considered to be to obtain that benefit.[86] The Commentary provides an exhaustive list of examples which illustrate the application of the PPT rule as well as in the case of conduit arrangements.

C. Improper use of the Convention

1. *The evolution of the comprehensive approach*

2.116 Domestic anti-abuse rules are aimed at protecting the benefit of domestic laws and treaties against treaty shopping. This aim is aligned with one of the purposes of treaties, which is to prevent tax avoidance and evasion. As a consequence, the Commentary takes the position that domestic anti-abuse rules do not conflict with treaties, and benefits of treaties cannot be granted when transactions constitute an abuse of such treaties. This principle applies independently from the PPT rule established by Art. 29 § 9.[87]

---

85 Commentary to Art. 29 § 179.
86 Commentary to Art. 29 §§ 178 and 181.
87 Commentary to Art. 1 § 61.

In practice, therefore, an abuse of a treaty is as an abuse of domestic laws. **2.117** There is however the need for the inclusion of anti-abuse rules in treaties, such as the concept of 'beneficial owner' (in Artt. 10, 11, and 12), the look-through approach adopted by Art. 17 § 2, the requirement that a subsidiary be managed by the parent in such a way that the subsidiary is not a PE of the parent. To address those issues the CFA issued two reports ('Treaties and the Use of Base Companies' and 'Treaties and the Use of Conduit Companies') which are now included in the Commentary to Art. 1, which now also includes consideration about Art. 29 introduced in 2017.

The Commentary, before the changes of 2017, addressed the policy issues **2.118** raised by improper use of the treaties and advanced five approaches proposing possible treaty clauses. The approaches were: the look-through approach; the subject-to-tax approach; the channel approach; the bona fide safeguard clauses; and the limitation-of-benefits approach. This part of the Commentary has been replaced by a completely revised section about the 'Improper use of the Convention' which is inspired by the main principles of the BEPS project in this area. An entirely new section of the Commentary has also been added and focuses on restricting treaty benefits when the income that is subject to certain preferred tax regimes may lead to double exemption.

The pre-2017 *look-through approach* disallowed treaty benefits to a company **2.119** not owned, directly or indirectly, by residents of the RC (state of which the company is a resident). This approach could be adopted in treaties with countries that have no or very low taxation and where little business activity is carried on, but requires to be complemented by derogations to protect bona fide business activities. In practice when income was paid to an intermediary company which in turn paid that income to a recipient, the treatment accorded by the treaty between the SC and the RC of the recipient was applied only to the recipient which was resident of the same CS but not to the recipient which was not resident of the same CS. This latter company in such a case was viewed as a pass-through. National courts often apply the look-through approach.[88]

According to the *subject-to-tax approach* (which has now been deleted from the **2.120** Commentary) treaty benefits are granted in the SC only if the income is subject to tax in the RC. This approach can be used in states with well-developed economic structures and complex laws, but bona fide derogations for flexibility are needed; this approach does not provide adequate protection

---

[88] Australia, High Court of Australia, *Anthony Whitworth Russell v. Commissioner of Taxation of Commonwealth of Australia*, 10 February 2012.

against advanced tax avoidance schemes such as 'stepping-stone strategies'.[89] The subject-to-tax approach has been used in cases about beneficial ownership of interest, dividends and royalties.

2.121 The *channel approach* (which has now been deleted from the Commentary) singles out cases of improper use with reference to the conduit arrangements themselves and is aimed at counteracting 'stepping-stone' schemes.[90] This approach has been used in cases about beneficial ownership of interest and royalties by looking at the criterion of real disposition of funds. *Bona fide safeguard clauses* (which have now been deleted from the Commentary) were aimed at ensuring that treaty benefits were granted only in bona fide cases.[91] A bona fide provision usually included a general clause which was complemented by different additional provisions (activity provisions, amount of tax provisions, stock exchange provisions, alternative relief provisions) which could be combined in different ways. Bona fide safeguard clauses have been used as indicators in cases about beneficial ownership of dividends, interest and royalties by looking at the criterion of real disposition of funds.

2.122 The *limitation-of-benefits* approach (which has now been deleted from the Commentary) addressed 'treaty shopping' adopting a LOB clause which is now codified in the Model 2017. According to such a clause a resident of a CS who derives income from the other CS was entitled to all the benefits of the treaty otherwise accorded to residents of a CS only if such a resident was a 'qualified person' as defined by the various tests of the LOB clause and also met the other conditions of the treaty for the obtaining of such benefits. The Commentary proposed a LOB clause but is now entirely replaced by detailed guidelines included in the Model together with extensive Commentary to Art. 29.[92]

2.123 The sections of the Commentary that are now replaced by the BEPS changes also described other provisions addressing different types of improper use of the treaties and advanced the following approaches: provisions aimed at entities benefiting from preferential tax regimes; provisions aimed at particular types of income; anti-abuse rules dealing with source taxation of specific types of income; provisions aimed at preferential regimes introduced after the signature of the treaty; and remittance-based taxation. The provisions aimed at entities benefiting from preferential tax regimes adopted an *ad hoc* exclusion

---

89 Commentary 2014 to Art. 1 § 15.
90 Commentary 2014 to Art. 1 § 17, now deleted.
91 Austria, Verwaltungsgerichtshof, 2001/13/0018 and 0019, 10 August 2005.
92 Commentary 2014 to Art. 1 § 20, deleted by Commentary 2017.

approach and a preferential tax regime approach. These provisions have been both eliminated from the Commentary.

The *ad hoc exclusion approach* denied treaty benefits to companies enjoying tax **2.124** privileges in their RC and was based on the following clause: 'No provision of the Convention conferring an exemption from, or reduction of, tax shall apply to income received or paid by a company as defined under section ... of the ... Act, or under any similar provision enacted by ... after the signature of the Convention'.[93] The scope of this provision could be further limited by referring only to specific types of income, such as dividends, interest, capital gains, or directors' fees. The *preferential tax regime approach* denied treaty benefits to entities that would otherwise qualify as residents of a CS but which enjoyed in that state a preferential tax regime restricted to foreign-held entities.[94]

Provisions aimed at particular types of income were essentially passive income **2.125** clauses which denied treaty benefits in respect of income that was subject to low or no tax under a preferential tax regime. A passive income clause covered income derived from activities which did not require a substantial presence in that state,[95] and also defined what was a preferential tax regime.[96] *Anti-abuse rules dealing with source taxation* of specific types of income adopted the main purpose approach and denied the benefits of specific articles of the treaties that restricted source taxation where transactions (Artt. 10, 11, 12 and 21) were entered into for the main purpose of obtaining these benefits.[97] Finally the *provisions aimed at preferential regimes* protected a CS from having to give treaty benefits with respect to income benefiting from a special regime for certain offshore income,[98] or adopted the 'substance-over-form', 'economic substance' and general anti-abuse rules as established by domestic laws.[99]

In the new section of the Commentary 'Improper use of the Convention' these **2.126** different approaches have been replaced by a comprehensive approach tailored to aggressive tax planning and BEPS strategies, also in light of the new Art. 29 about entitlement to the benefits of tax treaties.

---

93   Commentary to Art. 1 § 21–21.1, deleted in Commentary 2017.
94   Commentary 2014 to Art. 1 § 21.2, deleted in Commentary 2017.
95   Commentary 2014 to Art. 1 § 21.3, deleted in Commentary 2017.
96   Commentary 2014 to Art. 1 § 21.3, deleted in Commentary 2017.
97   Commentary 2014 to Art. 1 § 21.4, deleted in Commentary 2017.
98   Commentary 2014 to Art. 1 § 21.5, deleted in Commentary 2017.
99   Commentary 2014 to Art. 1 § 22, deleted in Commentary 2017.

2.127 The extension of the network of tax conventions increases the risk of abuse by facilitating the use of arrangements aimed at securing the benefits of both the tax advantages available under certain domestic laws and the reliefs from tax provided for in these double taxation conventions. There is treaty abuse, for example, if a person acts through a legal entity created in a state to obtain treaty benefits that would not be available directly.

2.128 The Commentary introduces now an in-depth discussion of different approaches to addressing tax avoidance, that is through (i) tax conventions, (ii) domestic anti-abuse rules and judicial doctrines, (iii) general legislative anti-abuse rules, or (iv) controlled foreign company provisions. The Commentary also adds an entirely new section which is about restricting treaty benefits with respect to income that is subject to certain features of another state's tax system, advancing possible provisions on (i) special tax regimes, (ii) subsequent changes to domestic law, and (iii) notional deductions for equity.

2. Different approaches to address tax avoidance

2.129 Art. 29 § 9 and the specific treaty anti-abuse rules included in tax conventions are aimed at these and other transactions and arrangements entered into for the purpose of obtaining treaty benefits in inappropriate circumstances. Where, however, a tax convention does not include such rules, the question may arise whether the provisions of tax conventions prevent the application of domestic anti-abuse provisions. The position of the Commentary is that there is no conflict between such rules and the provisions of tax conventions because the benefits of a tax convention are not available when a main purpose for entering into certain transactions or arrangements is to secure a more favourable tax position and obtaining that more favourable treatment. In fact the use of the convention in these circumstances is contrary to the object and purpose of the relevant provisions and the position of the Commentary is that this overarching principle applies independently from Art. 29 § 9, which merely confirms it.[100]

2.130 Domestic anti-abuse rules and judicial doctrines often address transactions and arrangements which have the purpose of obtaining domestic or treaty benefits in inappropriate circumstances. The Commentary clarifies that this domestic dimension does not limit the scope of application of these domestic rules. Moreover, domestic anti-abuse rules apply in cross-border situations which often imply application of tax treaties, because these rules include thin capitalization rules, transfer pricing rules, exit tax rules, dividend stripping

---

100   Commentary to Art. 1 §§ 57 and 61.

rules, and anti-conduit rules.[101] The Commentary takes the position that treaty anti-abuse provisions prevail over domestic anti-abuse provisions only if there is a conflict. The rationale is found in the principle of '*pacta sunt servanda*' (Art. 26 of the VCLT). Thus, if the application of specific anti-abuse rules found in domestic law results in a tax treatment that is not in accordance with the provisions of a tax treaty, this conflicts with the provisions of that treaty and the provisions of the treaty should prevail under public international law.[102]

The case in which treaty anti-abuse provisions prevail over domestic anti-abuse provisions can be avoided by preventing such conflicts. First, a treaty may specifically allow the application of certain types of specific domestic anti-abuse rules. For example, Art. 9 specifically authorizes the application of domestic rules in the circumstances defined by that article. Also, many treaties include specific provisions clarifying that there is no conflict or, even if there is a conflict, allowing the application of the domestic rules, for example, when treaties expressly allow the application of the domestic thin capitalization rule. Second, many provisions of the Convention depend on the application of domestic law, so that it is virtually impossible that there will be a conflict, for example the residence of a person must be determined on the basis of Art. 4 § 1. Third, the application of tax treaty provisions may be denied under Art. 29 § 9, or under judicial doctrines or principles applicable to the interpretation of the treaty, so by definition there is no conflict between treaty provisions (Art. 29 § 9) and the relevant domestic specific anti-abuse rules.[103]   **2.131**

The same conclusions can be reached with regard to domestic general legislative anti-abuse rules. There is no conflict between treaty rules and Art. 29 § 9, so these rules apply in the same circumstances in which the benefits of the Convention are denied under Art. 29 § 9, or, in the case of a treaty that does not include that paragraph, under the guiding principle in § 61 of the Commentary to Art. 1.   **2.132**

The same problems about conflict between treaty and domestic rules arise in respect of judicial doctrines that are part of domestic law, such as substance over form, economic substance, sham, business purpose, step-transaction, abuse of law and *fraus legis*. The position of the Commentary is that Artt. 31–33 of the VCLT do not prevent the application of judicial doctrines in so far as they operate as principles to the interpretation of tax treaties. For   **2.133**

---

101 Commentary to Art. 1 § 66.
102 Commentary to Art. 1 § 70.
103 Commentary to Art. 1 §§ 72–75.

example, the approach according to which domestic tax provisions are applied to the basis of the economic substance of certain transactions can be extended to tax treaty provisions.[104]

2.134 Finally the Commentary resolves the problem of whether domestic controlled foreign company provisions conflict with treaties. These measures result in a CS taxing its residents on income attributable to their participation in certain foreign entities and, according to certain views, they conflict with Art. 7 § 1 and Art. 10 § 5. The Commentary excludes that there is such a conflict for two reasons. First, Art. 1 § 3 (the saving clause) confirms that provisions (such as the CFC rules) which result in a CS taxing its own residents do not conflict with tax conventions. Second, in a specific treaty lacking the saving clause, the interpretation according to which these articles prevent the application of CFC rules conflicts with Art. 7 § 1 and Art. 10 § 5.[105]

3. *Addressing low-taxed treaty income*

2.135 In addition to the restrictions related to the improper use of the tax treaties, the Commentary 2017 introduces further restrictions to treaty benefits with respect to income that is subject to certain features of another state's tax system. What can occur in practice is that the other CS, on the basis of domestic legislation, may subject to low or no taxation certain items that, under the treaty, are subject to tax in that state. The concern of the other CS is that such features of the tax system of the treaty partner could increase the risk of non-taxation, which may include tax advantages that are ring fenced from the domestic economy.

2.136 The Commentary before the changes of 2017 advanced five approaches (look-through approach, the subject-to-tax approach, the channel approach, the bona fide safeguard clauses, and the limitation-of-benefits approach) which are now superseded by an entirely new section added to the Commentary which is about restricting treaty benefits with respect to income that is subject to certain features of another state's tax system. The Commentary now advances possible provisions on (i) special tax regimes, (ii) subsequent changes to domestic law, and (iii) notional deductions for equity. Furthermore the Commentary makes a distinction between the situation in which (i) the relevant features of the tax system of the other state are known at the time the treaty is being negotiated, and (ii) the situation in which such features are introduced in the tax system of the other CS after the conclusion of the tax treaty. The Commentary in the former case suggests different types of provisions on special tax regimes, while

---

104   Commentary to Art. 1 §§ 72–75.
105   Commentary to Art. 7 § 14; Commentary to Art. 10 § 37.

in the latter case it advances possible provisions on subsequent changes to domestic law.

The Commentary suggests that a tax treaty could include specific provisions to **2.137** deny the application of the treaty to income which benefits from regimes that meet the requirements of what are defined as 'special tax regimes'. For instance, the benefits of the provisions of Artt. 11 and 12 could be denied with respect to interest and royalties derived from a connected person if such interest and royalties benefited, in the state of residence of their beneficial owner, from such a special tax regime.

Of course these ad hoc provisions restricting the application of treaties require **2.138** a definition of 'special tax regime'. In summary a 'special tax regime' is a preferential rate of taxation for, or a permanent reduction in the tax base with respect to, interest, royalties or any combination thereof, as compared to income from sales of goods or services.

These advantages are usually achieved through: 1) an exclusion from gross **2.139** receipts; 2) a deduction not related to an effective payment; 3) a deduction for dividends paid or accrued; or 4) taxation that is inconsistent with the principles of Arts. 7 or 9, for example a regime under which no interest income is imputed on an interest-free note that is held by a company resident of a CS and is issued by an associated enterprise that is a resident of the other CS. A special tax regime can be achieved not only by statutes or regulations, but also by administrative practices, for example routine rulings. Generally applicable provisions that are not deemed to be a 'special tax regime' are standard deductions, accelerated depreciations, corporate tax consolidation, dividends received deductions, loss carryovers and foreign tax credits.

An additional type of 'special tax regime' for companies that do not engage in **2.140** the active conduct of a business in a CS is identified when a preferential rate of taxation or a permanent reduction in the tax base is granted by that CS in respect to substantially all of a company's income or substantially all of a company's foreign source income. This occurs for example in regimes granting to offshore companies standard deductions, accelerated depreciation, corporate tax consolidation, dividends received deductions, loss carryovers and foreign tax credits. In general the rate of taxation is determined on the basis the income tax principles of the CS that has implemented the regime in question.

In all the above cases there is a 'special tax regime' if the rate of taxation is **2.141** 60 per cent of the general statutory rate of company tax applicable in the other

CS, or less then a certain rate predetermined bilaterally. Some exclusions are possible for royalties when research and development activities take place in the CS, or when expenditures are effectively incurred by the person enjoying the benefits for the purpose of actual research and development activities.

2.142 Moreover a 'special tax regime' does not apply to: a) recognized pension funds; b) organizations that are established and maintained exclusively for religious, charitable, scientific, artistic, cultural or educational purposes; and c) persons the taxation of which achieves a single level of taxation either in the hands of the person or the person's shareholders (with at most one year of deferral), that hold (i) a diversified portfolio of securities subject to investor-protection regulation and marketed primarily to retail investors; or (ii) predominantly immovable property.

2.143 The Commentary also contemplates a situation in which a preferential regime is introduced in the tax system of one CS after the conclusion of the tax treaty, which might have prevented the conclusion of the treaty if it had existed at that time. The Commentary suggests the following provision that would address these concerns:

> 1. If at any time after the signing of this Convention, a CS a) reduces the general statutory rate of company tax that applies with respect to substantially all of the income of resident companies with the result that such rate falls below the lesser of either (i) [rate to be determined bilaterally] or (ii) 60 per cent of the general statutory rate of company tax applicable in the other CS, or b) the first-mentioned CS provides an exemption from taxation to resident companies for substantially all foreign source income (including interest and royalties), the CSs shall consult with a view to amending this Convention to restore an appropriate allocation of taxing rights between the CSs.

2.144 In the proposed provision there is also a clause according to which a CS may notify the other CS through diplomatic channels that it shall cease to apply the provisions of Artt. 10, 11, 12 and 21 if consultations do not progress; the provisions of such articles cease to have effect in both CSs with respect to payments to resident companies six months after the date that the other CS issues a written public notification stating that it shall cease to apply the provisions of these articles.

2.145 The provision suggested by the Commentary addresses two types of subsequent changes. The first type is when the other state reduces the general statutory rate of company tax that applies with respect to substantially all of the income of its resident companies, with the result that such a rate falls below the lesser of a minimum rate that would need to be determined bilaterally or 60 per cent of the general rate of company tax applicable in the other state. The second type of subsequent change in domestic tax law is when a state provides an exemption from taxation to companies resident of that state with respect to substantially all foreign source income (including interest and royalties) derived by these companies. The reference to an exemption does not include taxation systems under which only foreign source dividends or business profits from foreign PEs are exempt from tax by the residence state (so-called 'dividend exemption' systems).

An example of a tax regime with respect to which treaty benefits might be **2.146** specifically restricted relates to domestic law provisions that provide for a notional deduction with respect to equity. CSs which agree to deny the application of Art. 11 to interest that is paid to connected persons who benefit from such notional deductions may do so by adding the following provision to Art. 11:

> 2. Notwithstanding the provisions of § 1 of this article, interest arising in a CS and beneficially owned by a resident of the other CS that is connected to the payer (as defined in Art. 5 § 8) may be taxed in the first-mentioned CS in accordance with domestic law if such resident benefits, at any time during the taxable year in which the interest is paid, from notional deductions with respect to amounts that the CS of which the beneficial owner is a resident treats as equity.

D. Using the 'beneficial owner' concept

The Commentary provides common concepts in regard to the beneficial **2.147** owner of, respectively, dividends, interest, royalties and capital gains. Essentially the Commentary clarifies that the term 'beneficial owner' is not used in a narrow technical sense (such as the meaning that it has under the trust laws of many common law countries), rather, it should be understood in its context, in particular in relation to the words *'paid … to a resident'*, and in light of the object and purposes of the Convention, including avoiding double taxation and the prevention of fiscal evasion and avoidance.[106] Most situations of beneficial ownership are now addressed by Art. 29 which is aimed at preventing treaty shopping situations.[107]

---

106   See for example Commentary to Art. 10 § 12.
107   Blanluet, Gauthier, 'La Notion de Bénéficiaire Effectif en Droit Fiscal International' in: Martial Chadefaux et al. (eds), *Ecrits de fiscalité des entreprises: Etudes à la mémoire du professeur Maurice Cozian* (Litec 2009); Duff, David G., 'Beneficial Ownership: Recent trends' in: Lang, Michael, et al. (eds), *Beneficial Ownership: Recent Trends* (IBFD 2013); Baumgartner, Bobath, *Das Konzept des Beneficial Owner im Internationalen Steuerrecht der Schweiz* (Schultess 2010).

2.148 National courts have autonomously developed judicial criteria to identify beneficial ownership and conduit structures in the different economic and legal contexts in which respectively, dividends, interest, royalties and capital gains are paid or realized within cross-border group structures. So the analysis developed below looks at the specific judicial applications in these different areas. The beneficial ownership concept in judicial applications is often aligned with the policies discussed in the Commentary about the improper use of treaties.

2.149 When an item of income is paid to a resident of a CS acting in the capacity of *agent or nominee* it is inconsistent with the object and purpose of the Convention for the SC to grant relief or exemption merely on account of the status of the direct recipient of income as a resident of the other CS. So in these cases the treaty is not applied because the agent is not a beneficial owner.[108]

2.150 Similarly if a resident of a CS simply acts as a 'conduit' for another person who in fact receives the benefit of the income, then it is inconsistent with the object and purpose of the Convention for the SC to grant relief or exemption.[109] The term 'conduit' is further defined in the CFA report 'Double Taxation Treaties and Use of Conduit Companies' which clarifies that 'a conduit company cannot normally be regarded as beneficial owner if, though formal owner, it has, as a practical matter, very narrow powers which render it, in relation to income concerned, a mere fiduciary or administrator acting on account of interested parties'. So limitation of the tax in the SC is available only when an intermediary, such as an agent or nominee located in a CS or in a third country, is interposed between beneficiary and payer, and qualifies as a beneficial owner resident of the other CS.[110]

2.151 Moreover the Commentary affirms that 'the meaning of "beneficial owner" (...) must be distinguished from the different meaning that has been given to that term in the context of other instruments that concern the determination of the persons (typically the individuals) that exercise ultimate control over entities or assets'.[111] These indicators highlighted by the Commentary are found in judicial applications that conclude that an intermediary entity factually did not act as a conduit.[112] By contrast, the same indicators are often

---

108   Commentary to Art.10 § 12.2. See: Italy, Corte Suprema di Cassazione, 4600, 1 March 2009.
109   Commentary to Art. 10 § 12.3.
110   Commentary to Art. 10 § 12.2 and 12.4.
111   Commentary to Art. 10 § 12.6.
112   Denmark, Østre Landsret, B-2152-10, 20 December 2011; Denmark, Landsskatteretten; Czech Republic, Nejvyšší Správní Soud, 2 Afs 86/2010-141, 10 June 2011.

used to characterize an intermediary entity as a conduit.[113] National courts have applied the indicators of the Commentary to determine whether intermediary entities are actually beneficial owners. Certain cases positively indicate the requirements for such entities to be considered as such, so that the treaty between the SC of the dividends and the RC of the beneficial owner can be applied.[114]

The concept of beneficial owner and different types of income plays out **2.152** differently depending on the type of income flows, i.e., dividends, interest, or royalties. The concept of the *beneficial owner of dividends* plays an important role in determining whether the reduced withholding tax can be actually applied under a bilateral treaty between the payer of dividends and a direct shareholder when dividends received by that direct shareholder are then re-distributed to other shareholders up the chain of controlled companies, particularly when holding companies are involved.[115] Most situations of beneficial ownership of dividends are now addressed by Art. 29 which is aimed at preventing treaty shopping.[116] In these cases the beneficial owner is the person who receives the dividends for his own use and assumes the risk or control for them.

Source countries of dividends can react to the abuse of their treaties (when **2.153** reduced withholding taxes on outbound dividends are improperly avoided) by relying on broad domestic anti-abuse rules.[117] Good examples of abusive transactions in this area are offered by a line of cases decided in Switzerland, a country that has introduced *ad hoc* rules in its treaties to contrast abuse regarding domiciliary companies.[118] Such abuses were addressed by the final report on Action 6 of the BEPS Project. As a result of that report, subparagraph a) was modified in order to restrict its application to situations

---

113 Denmark, Landsskatterett, 10-02772 / SKM No. 2012.26, 16 December 2011.

114 Germany, Bundesfinanzhof I R 74, 88/04, 31 May 2005; Switzerland, Bundesverwaltungsgericht (Federal Administrative Court), A-6537/2010, 7 March 2012. In general on case law: Avella, Francesco, 'Recent Tax Jurisprudence on the Concept of Beneficial Ownership for Tax Treaty Purposes' (2015) 55 *Eur. Tax.* 56; Brauner, Yariv, 'Beneficial Ownership In and Outside US Tax Treaties' in: Lang, Michael, et al., (eds), *Beneficial Ownership: Recent Trends* (IBFD 2013).

115 Switzerland, Commission fédérale de recours en matière de contributions (Federal Tax Appeal Commission), VPB 65.86, 28 February 2001, *Steuerrevue*, 2002, 30; Canada, Tax Court of Canada, *Prévost Car Inc. v. Her Majesty the Queen*, 22 April 2008.

116 Commentary to Art.10 § 12.5.

117 Switzerland, Commission fédérale de recours en matière de contributions, VPB 65.86, 28 February 2001.

118 Switzerland, Bundesgericht/Tribunal fédéral, A 30/83, 9 November 1984. On abuse of treaties on inbound dividends see: Argentina, Tribunal Fiscal de la Nación, Molinos Rio de la Plata S.A., 14 August 2013, *La Leyonline* AR/JUR/60751/2013; Austria, Verwaltungsgerichtshof, 97/14/0070, 26 July 2000.

where the company that receives the dividends holds directly at least 25 per cent of the capital of the company paying the dividends throughout a 365-day period that includes the day of the payment of the dividend.[119]

2.154 Another type of base companies which are not the beneficial owners are companies that accumulate undistributed profits or non-active companies.[120] A similar approach is found in the subject-to-tax approach as well as in the bona fide safeguard clauses suggested by the Commentary.[121]

2.155 Finally, other cases focus on parent-subsidiary structures devised to abuse the EU Parent-Subsidiary Directive to extract dividends from the EU avoiding withholding taxes provided for by treaties between EU Member States and non-EU countries.[122] Case law concerning the abuse of the reduced withholding treaty rate also provides indicators of genuine transactions.[123] Another case law indicator of non-abusive structure in respect of the reduced treaty withholding tax rate is the fact that the direct recipient of dividends, within the structure of a group, is an active holding.[124]

2.156 The concept of the *beneficial owner of interest* plays an important role in determining whether the reduced withholding tax can be actually applied under a bilateral treaty between the payer of interest and a direct recipient when interest received by that direct recipient is in turn paid to other recipients. The rationale of the beneficial owner concept is to prevent residents of third countries having access to the treaty benefits by ensuring that the recipient of the interest is also the beneficial owner of the interest.[125] Most situations of beneficial ownership of interest are now addressed by Art. 29 which is aimed at preventing abuses, including treaty shopping situations where the recipient is the beneficial owner of the interest.[126]

2.157 Courts have identified situations in which interest is received by a genuine beneficial owner, as well as situations in which interest is received by a conduit which is not a beneficial owner. The approach used by national courts is that the recipient is not the beneficial owner if the interest is paid on the basis of a loan arrangement that is a back-to-back loan, or the interest is redistributed.

---

119   Commentary to Art.10 § 17.
120   Switzerland, Bundesgericht/Tribunal fédéral, 2A.239/2005, 28 November 2005.
121   Switzerland, Bundesgericht/Tribunal fédéral A.87/19, 1 December 1981.
122   Spain, Tribunal Económico Administrativo Central, RG 1481/2007, 28 September 2009; Spain, Audiencia Nacional, 59/2005, 22 January 2009.
123   Germany, Finanzgericht Nordrhein-Westfalen, VI 452/77 KE, 9 February 1989.
124   Germany, Bundesfinanzhof, IR 201/82, 5 March 1986.
125   Mexico, Tribunal Fiscal de la Federación (00(20)33/97/20328/96, 24 February 1998.
126   Commentary to Art.12 § 4.4.

This approach has been applied to revolving and converted loans, to consortium financing, and to financing situations that involve interposed partnerships or intermediary branches[127] and also in the *Indofood case*.[128]

The concept of the *beneficial owner of royalties* plays an important role in **2.158** determining whether taxation in the SC is allowed under a bilateral treaty. Art. 12 § 1 provides that royalties arising in the SC shall be taxable only in the RC if they are beneficially owned by a resident of the RC. So if royalties are *not* beneficially owned by a resident of the RC, then other articles of the treaty become applicable allowing taxation in the SC, in particular the business profits article, or there can be imposition of withholding taxes.

The approach used by national courts to determine whether the recipient of **2.159** royalties is also the beneficial owner is to look at the contextual legal arrangements.[129] For example an entity interposed in the flow of royalties and receiving a collection or handling fee has not been deemed to be a mere conduit.[130] The effective taxation of royalties in the hands of the recipient partners of a partnership resident of the same country of the partnership is similarly an indicator that the partnership is not a conduit. National courts have identified situations in which royalties are received by a conduit which is not a beneficial owner, particularly when there is no effective taxation of royalties in the hands of the recipient partners of a partnership. A similar

---

127 Denmark, Landsskatteretten, 09-01483, 1 November 2009, *Tidsskrift for Skatter og Afgifter*, 2010, 502; Denmark, Landsskatteretten, SKM 2010.729 LSR, 17 November 2010, *Tidsskrift for Skatter og Afgifter*, 2010, 974; Indonesia, Pengadilan Pajak, Put-13602/PP/M.I/13/200814 March 2008; Brazil, Superior Tribunal de Justiça, 457.228, 18 March 2009; Denmark, Landsskatteretten, 09-00064 / SKM No. 2011.57, 22 December 2010; Denmark, Landsskatteretten, 09-03189 / SKM No. 2011.485, 25 May 2011; United States, US Tax Court, *Aiken Industries, Inc. v. Commissioner of Internal Revenue*, 5 August 1971; Denmark, Landsskatteretten, 11-00210 / SKM2012.409LSR, 31 January 2012; United States, US Court of Appeals for the Fifth Circuit, *New York Guangdong Finance Inc. v. Commission of Internal Revenue*, 20 November 2009. See also: Guttman, Daniel, 'Beneficial Ownership as Anti-Abuse Provision: The *Bank of Scotland* Case' in: Lang, Michael, et al., (eds), *Beneficial Ownership: Recent Trends* (IBFD 2013); Shapiro, Daniel, 'OECD Tax Treaties: Who Beneficially Owns Dividends in a Total Return Swap?' (2009) 27 *Taxation of Investment J.* 325; Bundgaard, Jakob and Winther-Sørensen, Niels, 'Beneficial Ownership in International Financing Structures' (2008) 50 *Tax Notes Int.* 587.
128 United Kingdom, High Court of England and Wales, *Indofood International Finance Ltd. v. JPMorgan Chase Bank NA, London Branch*, [2006] STC 192, (2005) 8 ITLR 236; Baker, Philip, 'United Kingdom: Indofood International Finance Ltd v. JP Morgan Chase Bank NA' in: Lang, Michael, et al., (eds), *Beneficial Ownership: Recent Trends* (IBFD 2013); Baker, Philip, 'Beneficial Ownership: after Indofood' (2007) 4 *Gray's Inn Tax Chamber Rev.* 23; Oliver, David and Fraser, Ross, 'Beneficial Ownership: HMRC's Draft Guidance on Interpretation of the Indofood Decision' (2007) 52 *Brit. Tax Rev.* 139; Oliver, David and Fraser, Ross, 'Treaty Shopping and Beneficial Ownership: Indofood International Finance Ltd v JP Morgan Chase Bank NA London branch' (2006) 51 *Brit. Tax Rev.* 422.
129 Canada, Tax Court of Canada, *Velcro Canada v. The Queen*, 24 February 2012, 2012 TCC 57.
130 France, Conseil d'État 191191, 13 October 1999.

method is found in the subject-to-tax approach by the Commentary.[131] In other cases courts have respected the legal form of the sale transactions.[132]

2.160 The 'beneficial owner' concept has been extended from typical cases involving interest, dividends or royalties to transactions concerning the sale of shares. In these situations the problem addressed by case law is whether an intermediate entity selling the shares (for example a holding company or a trust) is in fact the beneficial owner of capital gains.[133] In most cases courts have respected the legal form of the sale transactions.[134] A SC may however retain its power to tax gains from sales of shares by non-resident persons by relying on domestic anti-abuse rules even if no mention of them (except for PE-related transactions) is made in the Commentary.[135]

2.161 Art. 17 § 2 provides that *if* income in respect of personal activities exercised by an entertainer/sportsperson in his capacity as such accrues not to the entertainer/sportsperson himself but to another person, *then* that income may, notwithstanding Art. 7 and 15, be taxed in the SC (the CS in which the activities of the entertainer/sportsperson are exercised). Art. 17 § 2 differs, however, from the beneficial ownership principle. The rationale of the beneficial ownership principle is to prevent residents of third countries having access to the treaty benefits by ensuring that the recipient of income (dividends, interest or royalties) is also the beneficial owner of that income. By contrast, the rationale of Art. 17 § 2 is to prevent entertainers and sportspersons obtaining an inappropriate exemption by transforming their remuneration into business profits of a third party (not subject to tax in the SC).

E.   Double treaty exemption

2.162 Tax treaty analysis has traditionally accepted a principle according to which the RC is obliged to give relief (exemption or credit) if the SC 'may tax'. In fact the Commentary establishes a general principle according to which *if* the SC *may tax, then* the RC *must* give relief (exemption or credit), clarifying that the RC has the *obligation* to apply the exemption or the credit in relation to an item of income (or capital) where the Convention authorizes taxation of that

---

131   Germany, Finanzgericht Nordrhein-Westfalen, 2 K 7574/96, 28 December 1998; Spain, Tribunal Económico Administrativo Central, RG 6294/1996, 22 September 2000.
132   Canada, Tax Court of Canada, *Mil Investments S.A. v. Her Majesty the Queen*, 18 August 2006.
133   Australia, Federal Court of Australia, *Resource Capital Fund III LP v. Commissioner of Taxation*, 26 April 2013.
134   Canada, Federal Court of Appeal, *Peter Sommerer v. Revenue Agency*, 13 July 2012.
135   South Korea, Supreme Court, 2010 du 11948, 26 April 2012.

item by the SC.[136] Relief *must* be provided by the RC regardless of when the tax is levied by the SC. So the RC must provide relief of double taxation with respect to an item of income even though the SC taxes it in an earlier or later year.[137]

In a normal situation in which the SC not only 'may tax' but also effectively **2.163** taxes the *double taxation* that arises from the concurring taxing powers of the RC and the SC is relieved by the RC through the exemption or the credit (single taxation). However, there are situations in which the SC, although it 'may tax', does *not* effectively tax, with the result that double taxation does not even arise because there is taxation in only one CS, the RC (single taxation principle). The problem here is that if neither the SC nor the RC taxes, then there is *double non-taxation*. The Commentary analyses in two different parts[138] whether the RC is obliged to provide relief (exemption or credit): first, with regard to situations of double taxation, and second, with regard to situations of double non-taxation.

It is double non-taxation that poses challenging issues because it can generate **2.164** income that is not subject to tax in either CS. In fact, Art. 23A § 4 provides that Art. 23A § 1 (i.e., the exemption in the RC) shall not apply to income derived from, or capital owned by, a resident of the RC where the SC applies the provisions of the Convention to exempt such income or capital from tax or applies Art. 10 or 11 § 2 to that income (those provisions allow the SC to levy a withholding tax).[139] So there can be a situation in which both the RC and the SC do not effectively tax the income, or a situation in which the SC does not effectively tax and yet the RC provides relief as if the SC had taxed. This double non-taxation can be the result of: (i) a qualification of the transaction on the basis of the domestic laws of the RC and the SC (a 'conflict of qualifications'); or (ii) different interpretations of the Convention by the RC and in the SC (a 'different treaty interpretation').

A *conflict of qualifications* arises when the SC exempts income earned in the SC **2.165** by a taxpayer resident of the RC because of the Convention between the SC and the RC. In this situation, the SC, *on the basis of the treaty*, is of the opinion that it may *not* tax income earned in the SC by a taxpayer resident of the RC, but the RC disagrees. In that case the RC must tax the income earned

---

136 Commentary to Art. 23A–23B § 32.1.
137 Commentary to Art. 23A–23B § 32.8.
138 Commentary to Art. 23A–23B § 32.1–32.6. (Conflict of qualifications in the preliminary remarks common to the exemption and the credit) and Commentary to Art. 23A–23B §§ 56.1–66.3 (Commentary to Art. 23A § 4 – Exemption).
139 Commentary to Art. 23A–23B § 56.1, first statement.

in the SC by the taxpayer resident of the RC.[140] In practice, if the SC decides not to tax and the RC disagrees then the RC (and not the SC) has a *unilateral obligation to prevent double non-taxation* by taxing the income.

2.166 *Different interpretation* arises when the SC exempts income earned in the SC by a taxpayer resident of the RC because of its own domestic laws, but the RC disagrees *under its own domestic laws*. In that situation the RC can exempt the income earned in the SC by the taxpayer resident of the RC.[141]

2.167 This traditional analysis of double exemption under the treaties before the changes made to Model 2017 in practice legitimated double exemption in this latter case of different interpretations of the Convention by the RC and the SC, a situation that often occurred in hybrid mismatches and in other circumstances. Now in the Model 2017 the preamble expressly includes among the goals of the Convention the prevention of *opportunities for non-taxation or reduced taxation through tax evasion or avoidance*. These changes were made to expressly recognize that the purposes of the Convention are not limited to the elimination of double taxation and that the CSs do not intend the provisions of the Convention to create opportunities for non-taxation or reduced taxation through tax evasion and avoidance.

2.168 The Commentary now expressly affirms that 'since the title and preamble form part of the context of the Convention and constitute a general statement of the object and purpose of the Convention'. These words should play an important role in the interpretation of the provisions of the Convention, and thus one can conclude that different interpretations of the Convention by the RC and in the SC no longer constitute a basis to secure double exemption.[142] Additionally Art. 29 applies now to double-exemption as a type of abuse. These changes ultimately derive from the recommendations of Action 2 on hybrid mismatches. Action 2 targets deduction/no inclusion ('D/NI') mismatches and double deduction ('DD') mismatches allowed by domestic laws. For D/NI mismatches Action 2 requests that domestic laws deny a dividend exemption in respect of payments that are deductible in the country of residence of the payer. For DD mismatches Action 2 prevents taxpayers from duplicate credits or deductions generated in source-countries.

2.169 Action 2 is reflected in Art. 5 MLI, which deals with the problem of double exemption in a more detailed manner than the Model/Commentary 2017.

---

140 Commentary to Art. 23A–23B § 56.1.
141 Commentary to Art. 23A–23B § 56.1.
142 Commentary, Introduction § 16.2.

Art. 5 MLI describes three alternative ways in which countries may address problems arising from application of the exemption method, which may lead to the risk that certain incomes remain untaxed: option A expressly prohibits double-exemption; option B provides that the dividend treated as deductible in the SC may not be exempted in the RC (option C addresses abuses of the foreign tax credit which are also addressed by Art. 23A of the Model 2017 in its last statement). Moreover Art. 10 of the MLI includes an anti-abuse rule for PE in third jurisdictions: treaty benefits are denied with respect to income that the RC of the taxpayer attributes to a low-taxed PE of the taxpayer in a third jurisdiction, unless an active trade or business is carried out in that PE.

Like double-exemption, double taxation also may result from either: **2.170** (i) *conflicts of qualifications in the domestic laws* of the RC and the SC; or (ii) *different interpretations of the Convention* by the RC and in the SC. When double taxation results from a conflict of qualifications of domestic laws, the RC has a unilateral obligation to prevent double taxation and must grant relief from double taxation (exemption or credit): the result is that when relief is granted there is single taxation, but there is no double-exemption.[143]

By contrast, when double taxation results from different interpretations of the **2.171** treaty by the RC and by the SC, the RC does not have a duty to eliminate double taxation: the result is that if relief is granted by the RC there is single taxation, if relief is not granted by the RC there is double-taxation but obviously there is no double-exemption.[144] So differently from the cases in which the RC adopts the exemption as a method to eliminate double taxation which can lead to double-exemption, the cases in which the RC adopts the credit as a method to eliminate double taxation do not lead to double-exemption. The corollary is that using the foreign credit is a unilateral backstop to potential double exemption.

---

143   Of course if the SC's qualification of the income is consistent with that of the RC, there is no double taxation, and the RC does not have to give relief under Art. 23A or Art. 23B. Belgium, Hof van Cassatie/Court de Cassation (Supreme Court), F030006F, 2 December 2004, *Tijdschrift voor Fiscaal Recht* issue no. 304.

144   Commentary to Art. 23A–23B § 32.5. See in general, before the BEPS Project: IFA, '2008 OECD-Model: Conflicts of Qualification and Double Non-Taxation' (2009) *IBFD Bull.* 204; Van Raad, Kees, 'Conflicts of Qualification: The Discussion is not Finished' (2003) 57 *Bull. Intl. Fisc. Doc.* 41; IFA, 'Double Non-Taxation' (2004) 89a *Cahiers Droit Fisc. Intl;* Lang, Michael, 'Austria: Exemption Method and Progression' in: Lang, Michael, et al., (eds), *Tax Treaty Case Law around the Globe 2011* (Linde 2011); Lang, Michael, 'Double Non-Taxation-General Report in IFA' (2004) 89a *Cathiers de Droit Fiscal International.*

V. TREATY ENTITLEMENT AND NON-DISCRIMINATION

2.172 If a person has met all the applicable tests for the entitlement to tax treaties (i.e., the person is resident, and meets the LOB rule test and/or the PPT test), such a person can be protected by Art. 24 that prohibits discrimination. The principle adopted by Art. 24 is that discrimination on the grounds of nationality is forbidden: nationals of the RC may not be treated less favourably, i.e., a 'more burdensome' tax treatment cannot be imposed in the SC on nationals of the RC if they are in the 'same circumstances'.[145] This principle is typically applied in *inbound situations*, in which it protects in the SC nationals vs non-nationals.[146]

2.173 Art. 24 § 5 provides that the scope of Art. 24 is not restricted by Art. 2. Art. 24 therefore applies to taxes of every kind and description levied by, or on behalf of, the state, its political subdivisions or local authorities.[147] Art. 24 takes the form of five different specific non-discrimination clauses that will be analysed below:

1.   the nationality non-discrimination clause (Art. 24 § 1);
2.   the stateless persons non-discrimination clause (Art. 24 § 2);
3.   the PE non-discrimination clause (Art. 24 § 3);
4.   the deduction non-discrimination clause (Art. 24 § 4); and
5.   the foreign-shareholder non-discrimination clause (Art. 24 § 5).

2.174 The different specific non-discrimination clauses will be analysed elsewhere, but it is the nationality non-discrimination clause (Art. 24 § 1) that operates as the general safeguard for foreign investors in the treaty SC. Art. 24 § 1 provides that nationals of the RC or the SC shall not be subjected in the other CS (RC or SC) to any taxation or any requirement connected therewith, which is other or more burdensome than the taxation or any connected requirements to which nationals of that other state in the same circumstances, in particular with respect to residence. This provision, notwithstanding Art. 1, also applies to persons who are not residents of one or both of the CSs (i.e., persons who are resident of a third country).

2.175 So Art. 24 § 1 contains an equal treatment clause that compares nationals of the RC to nationals of the SC in inbound transactions. This clause has a

---

145   Commentary to Art. 24 §§ 15–16.
146   Spain, Tribunal Supremo 2598/2010, 25 March 2010.
147   The Netherlands, Hoge Raad der Nederlanden, 35.398, 1 November 2000; Germany, Bundesfinanzhof, II R 51/03, 10 March 2005.

specific scope of application defined by *subjective requirements* (nationals of the RC, of the SC, the third country) and by *objective requirements* (the comparable situations, in short the 'comparables').

The term 'national', for the purposes of Art. 24 § 1 covers individuals, legal persons and partnerships and refers to the concept of 'national' as defined by Art. 3 § 1 g).[148] Art. 24 § 1 typically applies to nationals who are also tax-residents of a CS. The application of Art. 24 § 1 however is not restricted by Art. 1 solely to nationals who are residents of a CS, but extends to all nationals of each CS, whether or not they are residents of one CS. **2.176**

So Art. 24 § 1 applies only to nationals of the CSs (the RC or the SC), but not to nationals of a third country even if they are resident of the CSs (the RC or the SC). This tenet which excludes nationals of a third country is usually enforced by national courts. By contrast, when nationals of the CSs (the RC or the SC) are involved, then Art. 24 § 1 applies irrespective of that residence.[149] **2.177**

Art. 24 § 1 specifically focuses on equal treatment of nationals vs non-nationals in order not to intrude in an area which constitutes a crucial feature of domestic tax systems and of treaties: the different treatment of residents and non-residents. So, as mentioned above, Art. 24 covers only discrimination based on nationality, and does not cover discrimination based on residence. The Commentary emphasizes this aspect: 'residence of taxpayers is one of the factors relevant in determining whether taxpayers are in similar circumstances'[150] and 'the expression "in the same circumstances" would be sufficient by itself to establish that a taxpayer who is a resident of a CS and a taxpayer who is not a resident of that state are not in the same circumstances'.[151] The Commentary also observes that 'a different treatment of residents and non-residents is a crucial feature of domestic tax systems and of treaties'. **2.178**

So Art. 24 § 1 prevents a different treatment based on nationality but only with respect to persons or entities 'in the same circumstances, in particular with respect to residence', so that it is important to distinguish a different treatment that is solely based on nationality from a different treatment that relates to other circumstances and, in particular, to residence.[152] National courts have **2.179**

---

148 Commentary to Art. 24 § 17.
149 France, Court Administrative d'Appel Marseille, 98MA01682, 8 February 2000.
150 Commentary to Art. 24 § 7-2.
151 Commentary to Art. 24 § 7.
152 Commentary to Art. 24 § 7.2-3.

enforced the principle that Art. 24 § 1 only prohibits discrimination based on nationality, but does not prohibit discrimination based on residence.[153]

2.180 Art. 24 § 1 has an objective scope that is identified through comparables: two situations are comparable if the taxpayers are 'in the same circumstances' from the point of view of the application of domestic laws. The term is defined by the Commentary as in 'substantially similar circumstances both in law and in fact'.[154] The term 'in the same circumstances' includes the global tax situation of the taxpayer, so it can refer to a person's tax situation, when for example, a country (such as the US) subjects its nationals to a more comprehensive tax liability than non-nationals.

2.181 A prerequisite for the application of Art. 24 § 1 is that the comparable situations or 'comparables' are identified, and this is what courts do when non-discrimination cases are litigated.[155] By contrast, if situations are not comparable, then the nationality non-discrimination clause is not applied by courts.[156] Obviously the fact that the comparable situations involve nationals of the CSs (the RC or the SC) does not necessarily imply that there is discrimination, because comparable situations may be treated equally under the treaty.[157]

2.182 The basic inbound nationality non-discrimination clause of Art. 24 § 1 is to be distinguished from the foreign-shareholder non-discrimination clause of Art. 24 § 5, a different kind of inbound test.[158] National courts have also created a 'notional inbound comparable' that is based on a hypothetical situation, rather than on a straightforward inbound test based on real comparables.[159]

---

153   See: United States, US Court of Appeals for the Seventh Circuit, *Square D Company and Subsidiaries v. Commissioner of Internal Revenue*, 13 February 2006; Mexico, Tribunal Fiscal de la Federación, 12666/98-11_06–3/99-S2-06-02, 7 September 1999.

154   Commentary to Art. 24 § 7. See: Italy, Corte Suprema di Cassazione 8717, 26 June 2001.

155   United States, US Court of Appeals for the Ninth Circuit, *UnionBanCal Corp. v. Commissioner of Internal Revenue*, 18 September 2002; Germany, Finanzgericht Rheinland-Pfalz 4 K 2730/00, 20 November 2003; France, Conseil d'État 249801, 15 July 2004.

156   The Netherlands, Hoge Raad der Nederlanden, 08/01919, 20 November 2009; France, Court Administrative d'Appel Nancy, 98-1741, 10 October 2002; France, Court Administrative d'Appel Nantes, 97NT01922, 13 March 2001; France, Conseil d'État, 233894, 14 November 2001; Mexico, Tribunal Fiscal de la Federación, 12666/98-11_06–3/99-S2-06-02, 7 September 1999.

157   Germany, Finanzgericht Bayern, 13 V 2774/03, 22 September 2003.

158   United Kingdom, High Court of Justice of England and Wales, *NEC Semi-Conductors Ltd. v. Commissioners of Inland Revenue*, 24 November 2003.

159   France, Conseil d'État, 233894, 14 November 2001; United Kingdom, High Court of Justice of England and Wales, *Commerzbank AG v. Inland Revenue Commissioners*, 31 March 1995.

The phrase in Art. 24 § 1 'shall not be subjected ... to any taxation or any **2.183** requirement connected therewith which is other or more burdensome' means that when a tax is imposed on nationals and foreigners in the same circumstances, it must be in the same form as regards basis of charge, method of assessment, rate, and formalities connected with the taxation (returns, payment, prescribed times, etc.). This implies a substantive analysis that may lead to the conclusion that one of the comparable taxpayers is subject to a more burdensome treatment.[160] Judicial applications of comparability have looked at personal allowances, generally finding no equal treatment problem.[161] Another area in which comparability analysis is applied are sales of immovable property by non-residents.[162] By contrast, a not-more burdensome treatment has been found to occur in various situations.[163]

The principle of non-discrimination of Art. 24 is not meant to have the **2.184** far-reaching application afforded by other clauses of equal treatment found in international law (MFN clause in the WTO) or in EU law (Art. 18 of the EU Treaty), so the essential feature of this treaty clause is what it does not achieve, rather than what it could possibly achieve. In summary, Art. 24 *does not:* provide a broad equal protection clause or a broad definition of discrimination; cover discrimination based on residence; prevent reverse discrimination; provide MFN treatment; eliminate all differentiated treatments imposed by treaty; or prevent differentiated treatments for public bodies or not profit organizations.

Art. 24 does not provide a broad equal protection clause because it achieves **2.185** the elimination of tax discrimination only in precise circumstances.[164] Tax

---

160 Sweden, Regeringsrätten, 2772-1999, 23 November 1999.

161 Belgium, Hof van Beroep Antwerpen, 2008/AR/3170, 2 February 2010; Switzerland, Bundesgericht/Tribunal fédéral 2P.145.1999/2A.216/1999, 31 January 2000; United States, US Tax Court, *Karl Hofstetter v. Commissioner of Internal Revenue*, 29 June 1992.

162 France, Conseil d'État, 257337, 15 December 2004; Switzerland, Bundesgericht/Tribunal fédéral, 2A.416/2005 /svc, 4 April 2006.

163 Finland, Keskusverolautakunta, KVL 14/2012, 14 March 2012; Germany, Bundesfinanzhof, I R 7/12, 29 August 2012; France, Conseil d'État, 331071, 24 January 2014.

164 In general on non-discrimination in tax treaties: Gouthiere, Bruno, 'De La Portee Du Principe De Non-Discrimination Inclus Dans Les Conventions Fiscales', (1988) *Revue de Droit des Affaires Internationales* 2; Hinnekens, Philippe, 'Non Discrimination Art. in OECD Model Convention Needs Fundamental Review' (2008) 17 *EC Tax Rev.* 248; Hughes, David, 'Non-discrimination: A Consideration of Art. 24(5) OECD Model Convention' (1996) 50 *Bull. Intl. Fisc. Doc.* 390; O'Brien, James G., 'The Non Discrimination Art. in Tax Treaties' (1978) 10 *Law and Policy in International Business* 545; Peters, Cees and Snellaars, Margreet, 'Non-discrimination and Tax Law: Structure and Comparison of the Various Non-Discrimination Clauses' (2001) 10 *EC Tax Rev* 13; Rust, Alexander, 'International Tax Neutrality and Non Discrimination: A Legal Perspective' in: Lang, Michael, et al., (eds), *Tax Treaties: Building Bridges between Law and Economics* (IBDF 2010); Van Raad, Kees, *Non-Discrimination in International Tax Law: with Special Reference to the Netherlands and The United States* (Kluwer Deventer 1986); Avery Jones, John F. et al., 'The Non Discrimination Art. in Tax Treaties' (1991) 31 *Eur. Tax.* 310; Avery Jones, John F., and Caterine

systems often rely on legitimate distinctions based on differences in ability to pay, so that the non-discrimination provisions of Art. 24 need to prevent unjustified discrimination but also take account of legitimate distinctions. Art. 24 does not provide a broad definition of discrimination because discrimination is restrictively defined by specific features. Art. 24 prevents differences in tax treatment that are solely based on certain specific grounds (e.g., nationality, in the case of Art. 24 § 1), but is not intended to provide an equal tax treatment in all situations.[165]

2.186 Art. 24 does not cover discrimination based on residence because it covers only discrimination based on nationality. So Art. 24 § 1 prevents a different treatment of certain comparable situations, i.e., discrimination based on nationality, for example, a different treatment of individuals based on whether or not they hold a passport issued by the state. However, Art. 24 § 1 does *not* prevent different treatment of resident taxpayers vs non-resident taxpayers who are not nationals of that state, for example, different treatment of two comparable individuals is allowed if one is resident for tax purposes in the RC and the other in the SC. This implies that different treatment based on residence is *not* a discrimination based on nationality, or in other terms, that it is possible to treat residents and non-residents differently for tax purposes. The result is that often national courts protect domestic laws.[166]

2.187 Art. 24 does not prevent reverse discrimination (i.e., when taxpayers are treated more favourably than others) because it prevents only outright discrimination. Art. 24 § 1 is deliberately framed in a negative form (i.e., it provides that a preferential tax regime is *not* available to non-residents), because its main goal is to forbid discrimination in CS1 *against* the nationals of CS2. This implies that it is possible for the SC to grant to non-nationals concessions which are not available to its own nationals.

2.188 The most-favoured nation treatment (MFN treatment) extends to persons of Country C the treatment already accorded by Country A to persons of

---

Bobbett, 'Interpretation of the Non-discrimination Article of the OECD Model' (2008) 62 *Bull. Intl. Fisc. Doc.* 50; Avery Jones, John F., et al., 'The Non Discrimination Art. in Tax Treaties' (1991) 36 *Brit. Tax Rev.* 421; Bennett, Mary C., 'Non-discrimination in International Tax Law: A Concept in Search of a Principle', (2006) 26 *Tax Law Rev.* 439.

165   Commentary to Art. 24 §§ 3 and 7. See: Canada, Tax Court of Canada, *Specialty Manufacturing Ltd. v. Her Majesty the Queen*, 25 August 1997.

166   Germany, Bundesfinanzhof, V B 123/03, 8 April 2005; Canada, Tax Court of Canada, *Saipem UK Ltd. v. Her Majesty the Queen*, 14 January 2011; Austria, Verwaltungsgerichtshof, 92/13/0306, 24 January 1996.

Country B. Art. 24 does not provide MFN treatment because it only provides a bilateral test applicable to the two CSs of a specific bilateral treaty. As double taxation treaties are based on the principle of reciprocity, a tax treatment that is granted by CS1 under a Convention to a resident or national of CS2 by reason of the specific relationship between those CSs may *not* be extended to a resident or national of a third country under the non-discrimination provision of the Convention between CS1 and CS2.

Art. 24 provides only (i) an inbound test applicable in the SC of reference **2.189** to nationals vs non-nationals on inbound transactions in that country, and (ii) an outbound equal treatment test applicable to nationals vs nationals of that country on outbound transactions operating domestically or abroad, but it does *not* provide full reciprocity, i.e., a situation in which the other country is in all cases also obliged to provide the same inbound/outbound equal treatment.[167]

Art. 24 does not eliminate all differentiated treatments imposed by treaty. **2.190** Art. 24 is in fact a provision that in theory ensures equal treatment, but is applied in the context of the other articles of the Convention, so that measures that are mandated or expressly authorized by these articles cannot be considered to violate Art. 24 even if they only apply, for example, as regards payments to non-residents.[168] By contrast, the fact that a particular measure does not constitute a violation of Art. 24 does not mean that it is authorized by the Convention, since that measure could violate other articles of the Convention.[169]

Finally, Art. 24 § 1 should *not* be construed as obliging a CS which accords **2.191** special taxation privileges to its own public bodies or not-for-profit entities, to extend the same privileges to similar entities of the other CS. In other words, immunity is justified because the circumstances may not be comparable to those of the public bodies and services of the other state.[170] The Commentary goes on by noting that Art. 24 § 3 should not be construed as obliging CS1 which accords special taxation privileges to non-profit institutions whose activities are performed for purposes of public benefit that are

---

167 The Netherlands, Hoge Raad der Nederlanden, 08/01919, 20 November 2009.
168 Commentary to Art. 24 § 4.
169 United States, US Tax Court, *LeTourneau Christina Jeannine v. Commissioner of Internal Revenue*, 21 February 2012.
170 Commentary to Art. 24 §§ 10–12.

specific to that CS1, to extend the same privileges to PEs of similar institutions of CS2 whose activities are not exclusively for the public benefit of the CS1.[171]

---

171 Commentary to Art. 24 § 33-22. See: France, Court Administrative d'Appel Paris, 06PA03370, 6 December 2007; France, Court Administrative d'Appel, 06PA03371, 6 December 2007.

3

OPERATING THROUGH CORPORATE
VEHICLES

A foreign investor can decide to operate in the country of destination through **3.01** a separate corporate vehicle, a controlled company or as a subsidiary. The *'separate unity principle'* recognizes the separate nature of the controlled company or subsidiary and thus profits or losses of such company cannot be attributed to the controlling or parent company. This is confirmed by Art. 7 § 1 of the Model.

This chapter focuses on the the main treaty aspects that need to be considered **3.02** when doing business in a CS through corporate vehicles, first by looking at the foreign-shareholder and the subsidiary-PE non-discrimination clauses (section I), and then discussing remuneration on corporate equity investments, debt and intangibles as well as remuneration in the form of capital gains (sections II–V).

I. THE FOREIGN-SHAREHOLDER AND THE SUBSIDIARY-PE NON-DISCRIMINATION CLAUSES

3.03 The existence of a subsidiary company does not, of itself, constitute that company a PE of its parent company because the subsidiary company is an independent legal entity.[1] Moreover the fact that the trade or business carried on by the subsidiary company is managed by the parent company does not constitute the subsidiary company a PE of the parent company. The Commentary defines subsidiary's independence as follows:

> Control which a parent company exercises over its subsidiary in its capacity as shareholder is not relevant in a consideration of the dependence or otherwise of the subsidiary in its capacity as an agent for the parent ... But, subsidiary may be considered a dependent agent by application of the same tests applied to unrelated companies.[2]

3.04 A subsidiary can be re-characterized as a PE under certain circumstances. This re-characterization can be of two types: a subsidiary is re-characterized as material-PE, or a subsidiary is re-characterized as agency-PE. Any space or premises belonging to the subsidiary at the disposal of the parent company constitutes a fixed place of business through which the parent carries on its own business (material-PE).[3] Moreover, on the basis of Art. 5 § 5, a parent is deemed to have a PE in a state in respect of any activities that its subsidiary undertakes for it, if the subsidiary has, and habitually exercises, in that state an authority to conclude contracts in the name of parent (agency-PE) unless activities are limited to those referred to in Art. 5 § 4, or the subsidiary acts in the ordinary course of business as an independent agent (Art. 5 § 6).[4]

3.05 The Commentary makes it clear that a sub-material-PE or a sub-agency-PE approach applies to any individual company forming part of a multinational group, and must be done separately for each company of the group, so that the existence in one state of a PE of one company of the group will not have any relevance as to whether another company of the group has itself a PE in that state.[5] A company member of a multinational group which provides services (e.g., management services) to another company of the group as part of its own

---

1 Commentary to Art. 5 § 115.
2 Commentary to Art. 5 § 105. See: Italy, Corte Suprema di Cassazione, 7682, 25 May 2002; Italy, Corte Suprema di Cassazione, 13579, 11 June 2007.
3 See: Switzerland, Bundesgericht/Tribunal fédéral, 102 ATF 264, 17 September 1977; India, Income Tax Appellate Tribunal Delhi, *Perfetti SPA v. ACIT*, 31 October 2007.
4 See §§ 32, 33 and 34 Commentary to Art. 5. United States, US Tax Court, *Inverworld Inc. v. Commissioner*, 12 May 1997, 73 T.C.M. 2777; France, Conseil d'État), 224407, 20 June 2003.
5 Commentary to Art. 5 § 117.

business carried on in premises that are not those of that other company, and using its own personnel, is not a PE of the recipient company, on the condition that the place where those services are provided is not: (i) at the disposal of the recipient company; or (ii) is not the business of the recipient company that is carried on through that place.[6]

Art. 24 § 5 (the foreign-shareholder non-discrimination clause) is one of the **3.06** non-discrimination clauses of Art. 24 which can protect a corporate entity doing business in the destination country. Art. 24 § 5 provides in fact that enterprises of CS1, the capital of which is wholly or partly owned or controlled, directly or indirectly, by one or more residents of CS2, shall not be subjected in CS1 to any taxation or requirement connected therewith which is other or more burdensome than the taxation or connected requirements to which other similar enterprises of CS1 are or may be subjected. This provision establishes a comparable between a resident company with domestic share-holders and a resident company with foreign shareholders and establishes an equal treatment clause which in principle fully implies inbound equal treat-ment in the SC of companies irrespective of the location of their shareholders.

The Commentary however observes that Art. 24 § 5 does *not* extend to **3.07** non-resident taxpayers the benefits of rules that take account of the relation-ship between a resident enterprise and other resident enterprises (e.g., rules that allow consolidation, transfer of losses or tax-free transfer of property between companies under common ownership).[7] For example, if domestic laws of one state allow a resident company to consolidate its income with that of another resident parent company, Art. 24 § 5 cannot have the effect to force the state to allow such a consolidation between a resident company and a non-resident parent company.[8] National courts have taken differing views: one judicial approach tends to bar domestic consolidation rules that adversely ring fence foreign companies, while an opposing approach protects domestic consolidation rules.[9]

---

6 Commentary to Art. 5 § 118.
7 Commentary to Art. 24 § 77.1. See in general: Avery Jones, John F. et al., 'Art. 24(5) of the OECD Model in Relation to Intra-Group Transfers of Assets and Profits and Losses' (2011) 3 *World Tax. J.* 179; Van Raad, Kees, 'Non Discrimination Under Tax Treaties Regarding Groups of Companies' in: Maisto, Guglielmo, (ed.), *International and EC Tax Aspects of Groups of Companies* (IBFD 2008), 157.
8 Commentary to Art. 24 § 77.2.
9 Finland, Korkein Hallinto-oikeus, 2004:65, 22 June 2004; United Kingdom, High Court of Justice of England and Wales, *NEC Semi-Conductors Ltd. v. Commissioners of Inland Revenue*, 24 November 2003; United Kingdom, Court of Appeal of England and Wales (Civil Division), *R&CC v. FCA Bank*, [2012]; Germany, Bundesfinanzhof, I R 6/99, 29 January 2003; Germany, Bundesfinanzhof, I R 54/10, 9 February 2011; The Netherlands, Hoge Raad der Nederlanden, 27764, 16 March 1994.

3.08 Moreover Art. 24 § 5 is aimed at ensuring that all resident companies are treated equally regardless of who owns or controls their capital, but does not seek to ensure that distributions to residents and non-residents are treated in the same way.[10] As a consequence withholding tax obligations that are imposed on a resident company with respect to dividends paid to non-resident shareholders but not with respect to dividends paid to resident shareholders do not violate Art. 24 § 5.[11] An opposing view is taken in other judicial decisions which deem that a withholding tax on outbound dividends falls under the scope of Art. 24 § 5.[12]

3.09 Domestic rules often provide that a seller (which has shareholders resident in the same country) can defer taxation on the capital gains realized upon the sale of participations upon the condition that the purchaser also has shareholders who are resident of the same country as the seller (or is resident of the same country as the seller). This limitation is established to prevent a situation in which gains are eventually realized by the shareholders of the purchaser outside the tax reach of the country of residence of the seller. Similar rules are found in reorganizations based on the rollover relief. The Commentary does not take a position on this issue, and national courts come to different conclusions.[13]

3.10 The Commentary takes the position that compensatory corporate taxes (such as the ACT levied in the UK) fall outside the scope of Art. 24 § 5 and observes that there is no discrimination if capital of the company is owned or controlled by non-residents but dividends paid to non-residents are taxed differently.[14]

II. REMUNERATION ON CORPORATE EQUITY INVESTMENTS

A. Protecting the interests of the SC: the holding requirement

3.11 When a foreign person conducts business through a corporate entity (a controlled company, a subsidiary or a participated company) in the destination country, the remuneration of the investment is usually in the form of

---

10 Commentary to Art. 24 § 76.
11 Commentary to Art. 24 § 62–66. See: France, Court Administrative d'Appel Nantes, 97NT01922, 13 March 2001. See also: Vanistendael, Frans, 'Taxation and Non-discrimination, A Reconsideration of Withholding Taxes in the OECD' (2010) 2 *World Tax J.* 175.
12 Spain, Audiencia Nacional, 418/1997, 8 June 2000; Zimbabwe, High Court of Zimbabwe, *British American Tobacco v. Commissioner for Taxes*, 14 December 1994.
13 Sweden, Regeringsrätten, 2225-1987, 19 November 1987; Luxembourg, Tribunal Administratif, 10473, 5 April 2000.
14 Commentary to Art. 24 § 78.2–3.

dividends. A 'dividend' is a distribution of profits to shareholders by: 'corporations'; companies limited by shares; limited partnerships with share capital; limited liability companies; and by other joint stock companies. Such legal entities with a separate juridical personality distinct from their shareholders differ from partnerships (which do not have juridical personality). In fact, in respect of profits of a business carried on by a partnership, a partner is taxed personally on her/his share of partnership capital and partnership profits, while in respect of profits of a business carried on by a corporation, a shareholder is taxable only on those profits distributed by the company.[15]

Art. 10 § 1 does not prescribe the principle of taxation of dividends either **3.12** exclusively in the RC (state of the beneficiary's residence) or in the SC (the CS where the payer of the dividends is resident). Exclusive allocation of taxing rights in the RC, notes the Commentary, is not feasible as a general rule; moreover, it would unrealistic to suppose that all taxation of dividends at source be relinquished.[16] By contrast, exclusive taxation of dividends in the SC would not be acceptable as a general rule because some states do not tax dividends at source and all states tax residents in respect of dividends they receive from non-resident companies. So Art. 10 § 1 introduces concurrent taxation in the RC and the SC and provides that dividends *may be taxed* in the RC.[17]

The term *'dividends paid'* used by Art. 10 has a wide meaning as fulfilment of **3.13** an obligation to put funds at the disposal of the shareholder in a manner required by contract or by custom.[18] The Commentary also defines the *scope of Art. 10.* Art. 10 applies only to dividends paid by a company which is a resident of the SC to a resident of the RC, but does not apply to dividends paid by a company to a resident of a third country, or to dividends paid by a company which is a resident of the SC (of dividends) which are attributable to a PE which an enterprise of the RC has in the SC.[19]

---

15 Commentary to Art. 10 § 1–3.
16 See in general: Maisto, Guglielmo, *Taxation of Intercompany Dividends Under Tax Treaties and EU Law* (IBFD 2012); Graetz, Michael J. and Warren, Alvin C. Jr, Dividend Taxation in Europe: When the ECJ Makes Tax Policy (2007) 44 *Common Mkt Law Rev.* 1577; Maisto, Guglielmo, *International and EC Tax Aspects of Groups of Companies* (IBFD 2008); Dahlberg, Mattias and Wiman, Bertil, 'General Report' in: IFA, 'The Taxation of Foreign Passive Income for Groups of Companies' *Cahiers Droit Fisc. Intl.* (2013) 98a.
17 Commentary to Art. 10 § 4–6.
18 Commentary to Art. 10 § 7. See: Canada, Tax Court of Canada, *Florsheim Inc. v. Her Majesty the Queen*, 22 July 1994; Germany, Bundesfinanzhof, I R 69/93, 6 October 1993.
19 Commentary to Art. 10 § 8.

3.14 Art. 10 does not serve the purpose of reducing or eliminating economic double taxation on distributed dividends (i.e., simultaneous taxation of a company's profits at the level of the company and of the dividends at the level of the shareholder) that arises in connection with cross-border distributions of dividends. The Commentary indeed devotes attention to the effects of special features of the domestic laws of certain countries discussing briefly how certain countries' laws seek to avoid or mitigate economic double taxation. There are various ways of achieving this: 1) corporation tax in respect of distributed profits may be charged at a lower rate than that on retained profits; 2) relief may be granted in computing a shareholder's personal tax; or 3) dividends may bear only one tax, distributed profits not being taxed at the level of the company. The Commentary discusses how economic double taxation can be eliminated on dividends distributed to individuals,[20] as well as on dividends distributed to companies.[21]

3.15 Art. 10 § 2 a) has been modified by Model 2017 as a result of Action 6. Previously, Art. 10 § 2 a) reserved a right to tax the SC on dividends (i.e., the state of which the company paying the dividends was a resident) and the rate of tax was limited to 5 per cent of the gross amount of the dividends if the beneficial owner was a company (other than a partnership) that held directly at least 25 per cent of the capital of the company paying the dividends.

3.16 Before 2017 there were no time participation requirements for the reduced treaty withholding tax to apply. However, the Commentary stated that when a minimum participation was established the reduced withholding tax should not be granted in cases of abuse of this provision, for example, when a company with participations of less than 25 per cent has, shortly before the dividends become payable, increased its participations primarily for the purpose of securing the benefits of a lower withholding tax, or when qualifying participations are arranged primarily in order to obtain lower withholding tax.[22] Such abuses are now addressed by Action 6 of the BEPS Project and so subparagraph a) is now modified to restrict its application to situations where

---

20   The Commentary describes the classical system (Commentary to Art.10 § 42), the split rate corporate tax (Commentary to Art.10 § 43), and the relief at shareholder level (Commentary to Art. 10 §§ 47–55). See in general: IFA, Trends in Company Shareholder Taxation. Single or Double Taxation? *Cahiers Droit Fisc. Intl.* (2003) 88a; Lodin, Sven-Olof, 'The Imputation Systems and Cross-Border Dividends – The Need for New Solutions (1998) 7 *EC Tax Rev.* 229; McDaniel, Paul, 'Integration in the International Context: Identifying Principles for Unilateral and Bilateral Approaches' (1991) 47 *Tax Law Rev.* 609; Warren, Alvin C., 'Alternatives for International Corporate Tax Reform' (1993) 49 *Tax Law Rev.* 599.

21   The Commentary describes the application of the classical system (Commentary to Art.10 §§ 59–62), of the split-rate (Commentary to Art. 10 § 64), and of the imputation system (Commentary to Art. 10 § 65).

22   Commentary 2014 to Art. 10 § 16 was deleted in Commentary 2017. See: Blessing, Peter H., 'Domestic and Treaty Anti-Abuse Rules as Applied to Dividends' in: Maisto, Guglielmo, (ed), *Taxation of Intercompany Dividends under Tax Treaties and EU Law* (IBFD 2012).

the company that receives the dividend holds directly at least 25 per cent of the capital of the company paying the dividends throughout a 365-day period that includes the day of the payment of the dividend.

Art. 10 § 2 a) now provides that the 5 per cent cap is applied if an additional **3.17** condition is met, i.e., if the 25 per cent participation is held throughout a 365-day period that includes the day of the payment of the dividend. That same provision also clarifies that for the purpose of computing that period, no account shall be taken of changes of ownership that directly result from a corporate reorganization, such as a merger or divisive reorganization, of the company that holds the shares or that pays the dividend. Art. 8 of the MLI is a similar provision.

Before 2017, Art. 10 § 2 a) referred to a company 'other than a partnership', **3.18** but Model 2017 has deleted this reference; as a result if a partnership is treated as a company for tax purposes by the CS in which it is established, the other state must grant the benefits of subparagraph a) to that partnership. Indeed, an entity or arrangement (i.e., a partnership) that is treated as a company for tax purposes qualifies as a company under the definition in subparagraph b) of § 1 of Art. 3 and therefore, if resident of a CS, is entitled to the benefits of subparagraph a) of § 2 with respect to dividends paid by a company resident of the other state, as long as it holds directly at least 25 per cent of the capital of that company. The Commentary clarifies that this conclusion holds true regardless of the fact that the state of source of the dividends may regard that entity or arrangement as fiscally transparent (and that is confirmed by the provision on fiscally transparent entities in Art. 1 § 2).[23]

Under the domestic law of some states, it is possible to make portfolio **3.19** investments in shares of companies of that state through certain collective investment vehicles (CIVs) established in that state which do not pay tax on their investment income. In such cases, a non-resident company that would own at least 25 per cent of the capital of such a vehicle could be able to access the lower rate provided by subparagraph a) with respect to dividends paid by that vehicle even though the vehicle did not own at least 25 per cent of the capital of any company from which it received dividends.[24]

The withholding cap is a 'reasonable maximum figure' and a higher rate would **3.20** not be justified since the SC can already tax the profits of the distributing company, while the lower rate (5 per cent) is provided for dividends paid by a

---

23 Commentary to Art. 10 § 11.
24 Commentary to Art. 10 § 17.

subsidiary company to its parent company. The reduction of rates provided for in Art. 10 § 2 refers solely to the taxation of dividends and not to the taxation of profits of the company paying the dividends and is based on the idea that it is reasonable that payments of profits by the subsidiary to the foreign parent company should be taxed less heavily to avoid economic double taxation.[25]

3.21 The treaty withholding taxes are maximum rates but the CSs may agree lower rates, or even taxation exclusively in the state of the beneficiary's residence.[26] Moreover CSs may exempt from withholding tax certain outbound dividends if there is a preferential tax regime in the RC, for example when dividends are derived from pension funds resident of another state, or paid to other states and some of their wholly-owned entities to the extent that such dividends derived from activities of a governmental nature. This is to ensure equal treatment of domestic and foreign investments by these entities.[27] The Commentary 2017 has introduced an important reference to address abusive situations in which the beneficial owner of the dividends arising in a CS is a company resident of the other CS which enjoys preferential taxation treatment, all or part of its capital is held by shareholders resident outside that other state and which does not distribute its profits as dividends. The Commentary clarifies that Art. 29 applies, but also that provisions such as those described in §§ 82–100 of the Commentary on Art. 1 can be introduced.[28]

3.22 The concept of the beneficial owner of dividends plays an important role in determining whether the reduced withholding tax can be actually applied under a bilateral treaty between the payer of dividends and a direct shareholder when dividends received by that direct shareholder are then re-distributed to other shareholders up the chain of controlled companies, particularly when holding companies are involved. Moreover, source countries of dividends can react to the abuse of their treaties by relying on broad domestic anti-abuse rules. For details about the indicators of beneficial ownerships developed by national courts and the recourse to anti-abuse rules see Chapter 2.III and 2.IV.

3.23 Distributions of profits by partnerships are not dividends within the meaning of the standard definition, unless partnerships are subject, in the state where their place of effective place of management is situated, to a fiscal treatment substantially similar to that applied to companies limited by shares. So clarifications in treaties may be necessary in cases where the domestic law of a

---

25   Commentary to Art. 10 §§ 9–10.
26   Commentary to Art. 10 § 13.
27   Commentary to Art. 10 § 13.1–13.2.
28   Commentary to Art. 10 § 22.

CS gives the owner of participations in a company a right to opt for being taxed as a partner of a partnership, or gives the partner of a partnership the right to elect for taxation as owner of participations in a company.[29] This situation is exemplified by a series of cases concerning the so-called 'S-Corporations'.[30]

Since the treaty prevails over domestic laws the reduced treaty withholding tax applies directly, but Art. 10 § 2 lays down nothing about the mode of taxation in the SC. So states are free to apply their own laws and, in particular, to levy taxes either by deduction at source or by individual assessment. As Art. 10 § 2 does not settle procedural questions each state applying the reduced withholding tax of Art. 10 § 2 can resort to procedures provided in domestic laws, i.e., the SC can initially levy the full withholding tax and then make a refund.[31] So traditionally at judicial level it has been confirmed that the application of the reduced withholding tax rate on outbound dividends does not imply that procedures established by domestic laws can be bypassed.[32] **3.24**

Art. 10 § 2 does not specify whether relief in the SC should be conditional upon the dividends being subject to tax in the RC.[33] This is an important aspect which has been brought to the attention of courts. There are two main approaches. According to the first approach the reduced treaty withholding tax rate applies if the dividends are taxable in the other CS regardless of whether any tax is actually paid on the dividends in the other CS (*subjective tax liability*). According to the second approach the treaty rate can apply only if the taxpayer proves that he or she is the beneficial owner of the dividends and has paid taxes on them in his RC (*objective tax liability*).[34] **3.25**

---

29 Commentary to Art. 10 § 27.
30 Germany, Bundesfinanzhof, I R 48/12, 26 June 2013; Germany, Bundesfinanzhof, I R 39/07, 20 August 2008; Germany, Finanzgericht Nordrhein-Westfalen (Köln), 2 K 2100/03, 16 February 2006.
31 Commentary to Art. 10 §§ 18–20.
32 Netherlands, Hoge Raad der Nederlanden), 38.191, 6 February 2004; Spain, Tribunal Supremo, 2789/1995, 26 January 2000; Italy, Corte Suprema di Cassazione, 6583, 22 March 2011.
33 Commentary to Art. 10 § 20.
34 Italy, Corte Suprema di Cassazione, 2348, 17 February 2001; Italy, Corte Suprema di Cassazione, 2532, 21 February 2001; Italy, Corte Suprema di Cassazione, 1231, 29 January 2001; Italy, Corte Suprema di Cassazione, 12458, 10 November 1999; Germany, Bundesfinanzhof, I R 106/87, 7 February 1990. See also: Burgstaller, Eva and Schilcher, Michael, 'Subject-to-tax Clauses in Tax Treaties' (2004) 44 *Eur. Tax.* 266; Chen, His-Hsiang, 'Interpretation of Subject-to-Tax Clauses' in: Schilcher, Michael and Weninger, Patrick, (eds), *Fundamental Issues and Practical Problems in Tax Treaty Interpretation* (Linde 2008); Galea, Rachel, 'The Meaning of Liable to Tax and the OECD Reports: their Interpretation and Ambiguous Interpretation' (2012) 66 *Bull. Intl. Tax.* 6; Lampe, Marc, 'General Subject-To-Tax Clauses in Recent Tax Treaties' (1999) 39 *Eur. Tax* 189.

B. The treaty definition of 'dividends': a moving target

3.26 The Commentary realistically assumes that in light of the great differences between the laws of OECD Member Countries it is impossible to work out an autonomous definition of dividends that would be independent of domestic laws and thus acknowledges that it is open to CSs to make allowance for peculiarities of their laws.[35] This approach has led, on the one hand, to the acceptance of the principle that characterization of dividends is based on domestic laws of the SC, and, on the other hand, to judicial adaptations of the concept of 'dividends' at the local level.[36]

3.27 Reliance on domestic laws of the SCs has led to interesting results.[37] Local judicial practice has mainly used characterization of dividends based on domestic laws of the SC with respect to hybrid financial instruments, redemption of shares and hidden profits distributions. An active area of judicial elaboration focuses on hybrid situations that straddle the border of remuneration from equity or debt in legal arrangements variously denominated as profit participating loans, silent partnerships and *'jouissance'* shares.

3.28 Dividends occur typically in distributions of profits whose legal title is straightforward shares, but also in relation to securities issued by companies which carry a right to participate in the companies' profits without being debt-claims, as it occurs in *'jouissance'* shares, founders' shares or other rights participating in profits.[38] In the treaties this enumeration may be adapted to the legal situation in the CSs concerned, so that certain payments may not be

---

35 Commentary to Art. 10 § 23. See: Avery Jones, John F., et al., 'The Definitions of Dividends and Interest in the OECD Model: Something Lost in Translation?' (2009) 1 *World Tax. J.* 5; Helminen, Marjaana, *The International Tax Law Concept of Dividend* (Kluwer Law International 2010); Sasseville, Jacques, 'The Definition of 'Dividends' in the OECD Model Tax Convention', in: Maisto, Guglielmo, (ed.), Taxation of Intercompany Dividends under Tax Treaties and EU Law (IBFD 2012); van Weeghel, Stef, 'Dividends (Art. 10 OECD Model Convention)' in: Lang, Michael, et al., (eds), *Source versus Residence. Problems Arising from the Allocation of Taxing Rights in Tax Treaty Law and Possible Alternatives* (Kluwer Law International 2008); Kemmeren, Eric, 'Preface to Artt. 10–12' in: Reimer, Ekkehart and Rust, Alexander, (eds), *Klaus Vogel on Double Taxation Conventions.* (Kluwer Law International 2015); Giuliani, Federico, 'Art.10 al.3 of the OECD Model and Borderline Cases of Corporate Disributions' (2002) 1 *Eur. Tax.* 11.

36 United Kingdom, Court of Appeal of England and Wales, *Memec plc v. Commissioners of Inland Revenue*, 9 June 1998; Netherlands, Hoge Raad der Nederlandend, 29 296, 15 December 1993.

37 Germany, Bundesfinanzhof, I R 44/03, 25 February 2004; Netherlands, Hoge Raad der Nederlanden, 38.461, 12 December 2003.

38 Commentary to Art. 10 § 24. See also: Bärsch, Sven Eric, *Taxation of Hybrid Financial Instruments and the Remuneration Derived Therefrom in an International and Cross-border Context* (Springer-Verlag 2013); IFA, The Tax Treatment of Hybrid Financial Instruments in Cross-Border Transactions *Cahiers Droit Fisc. Intl.* (2000) 85.

characterized as dividends in so far as they arise from debt-claims participating in profits or interest.[39]

The *remuneration arising from conversion debt into equity* may not be character- **3.29** ized as dividends but as interest. If a company is 'thinly capitalized', income arising from such capital is often treated as a dividend, rather than as interest.[40] Art. 10 deals with interest on loans in another hybrid situation at the intersection of remuneration of debt and equity, when the lender effectively shares risks run by the company, i.e., when repayment depends largely on the success or otherwise of the enterprise's business. This type of interest is treated as dividends under the national rules on thin cap applied in the borrower's country if certain circumstances for such re-characterization occur (i.e., the loan outweighs any other contribution to the enterprise's capital; creditor shares profits of the company; repayment of a loan is subordinated to claims of other creditors or to payment of dividends; the level or payment of interest depends on the profits of the company; the loan contract contains no fixed provisions for repayment by a definite date).[41]

Dividends are distinguished from reimbursements of capital, because divi- **3.30** dends include distributions of profits decided by annual general meetings of shareholders, other benefits in money or money's worth, such as bonus shares, bonuses, profits on a liquidation and disguised distributions of profits, and it is immaterial whether such benefits are paid out of current profits made by a company derived from reserves, i.e., profits of previous financial years.

The Commentary to Art. 10 also clarifies that the concept of dividends does **3.31** not include distributions by a company which have the effect of reducing membership rights, and refund of capital in any form,[42] but it does not explicitly mention *redemptions or repurchases of shares*. It is actually the Commentary to Art. 13 that provides a guideline for the redemption of securities according to which the difference between selling price and the par value of the shares sold by a shareholder to the issuing company in connection with the liquidation of such company or the reduction of its paid-up capital, may be treated in the state of which the company is a resident as a distribution of accumulated profits and not as a capital gain,[43] specifying that Art. 13 does

---

39 Commentary to Art. 10 § 25. See: Germany, Finanzgericht Hessen, 4 K 199/87, 27 April 1990; Canada, Tax Court of Canada, *Prévost Car Inc. v. Her Majesty the Queen*, 22 April 2008; France, Conseil d'État, 356878, 10 October 2014.
40 Commentary to Art. 10 § 15.
41 Czech Republic, Nejvyšší Správní Soud, 2Afs 108/2004-106, 10 February 2005.
42 Commentary to Art. 10 § 28.
43 Commentary to Art. 10 § 31.

not prevent the RC of the company from taxing such distributions at the rates provided for in Art. 10.[44]

3.32 Another aspect on which judicial practice at local level has focused are *hidden* or constructive dividends arising from persons who are shareholders but receive hidden benefits, or who are not shareholders if the legal relations between them and the company can be assimilated to a participation in a company ('concealed participations'). Essentially in these cases the issues are whether a hidden distribution can be characterized as a dividend under the treaty for the purpose of withholding tax.[45] The concept of hidden profit distributions also captures persons receiving such benefits who are closely connected with a shareholder (such as a relative of shareholder or a company belonging to same group as the company owning shares).[46] With few exceptions[47] courts adopt a substance over form approach to hidden profit distributions.[48]

C. Prohibition of extraterritorial taxation

3.33 Art. 10 deals only with dividends paid by a company which is a resident of the SC of dividends (here the SC of dividends is the country of residence of the payer of dividends) to a resident of the RC (here the RC is the country of residence of the recipient of dividends). Certain SCs, however, tax not only dividends distributed by companies resident in that state drawn from corporate profits generated in that same country, but also dividends distributed by those companies resident in the SC drawn from corporate profits effectively generated through a PE located in a different country. Such a country economically is the country of source of the business profits from which dividends are then paid to shareholders by the distributing company (hereinafter 'the SCP': country of source of corporate profits).

3.34 This situation typically occurs when dividends paid out by a company resident of the SC of dividends arise from profits of its PE in the SCP. In this respect

---

44 See Commentary to Art. 10 § 3. and § 28. See: Netherlands, Hoge Raad der Nederlanden, 36.773, 6 December 2002; The Netherlands, Hoge Raad der Nederlanden, 29.531, 15 March 1995; The Netherlands, Hoge Raad der Nederlanden, 29 296, 15 December 1993; The Netherlands, Hoge Raad der Nederlandend, 38.461, 12 December 2003.

45 Switzerland, Eidgenössische Steuerrekurskommission, SRK 2002-032, 7 June 2004.

46 Commentary to Art. 10 § 29. See: United States, US Tax Court, *Framatome Connectors USA Inc. and Subsidiaries v. Commissioner of Internal Revenue*, 5030-98, 9160-99, 16 January 2002, 118 T.C. 32 (2002); Czech Republic, Nejvyšší Správní Soud, No. 5 Afs 42/2005-102, 30 November 2006.

47 France, Court Administrative d'Appel Paris (Administrative Court of Appeal Paris), 93PA00572, 8 July 2001.

48 Switzerland, Eidgenössische Steuerrekurskommission, VPB 64.79, 22 February 2000.

the Commentary clarifies that Art. 10 § 5 deals with extraterritorial taxation of dividends from the perspective of the state where the company which pays the dividends is resident.[49] The Commentary establishes that there is a prohibition of extraterritorial taxation on dividends distributed by a company which are drawn from profits generated in another country, the SCP, but also provides exceptions to this prohibition.[50]

Art. 10 § 5 provides that *if* a company resident of the SC of dividends derives **3.35** profits or income from the SCP (i.e., through a PE), *then* the SC of dividends may *not* impose any tax on the dividends paid by the company resident of that country, *except* in two situations: a) the case in which the dividends paid by that company are received by a resident of the SC (in-coming dividends in the SC), or b) the participation in respect of which the outbound dividends are paid is effectively connected with a PE situated in the SCP.[51]

Art. 10 § 5 should be interpreted in the sense that if a company resident of the **3.36** SC derives profits or income from the SCP, then the country of residence of the controlling company may subject the *undistributed profits* of the company resident of the SC to a tax on the company's undistributed profits.[52] The prohibition of extraterritorial taxation provided by Art. 10 § 5 does not imply a broader prohibition for a country of extraterritorial taxation on undistributed dividends of controlled companies resident of another country.[53] In practice the country of the controlling company is allowed under the treaty to unilaterally enact CFC rules because such a situation is not covered by Art. 10 § 5 (which does not constitute a prohibition of CFC rules).[54]

III. REMUNERATION ON DEBT

A. Abusive structures that extract interest

When a foreign person conducts business through a corporate entity (a **3.37** controlled company, a subsidiary or a participated company) in the destination country, the remuneration of the investment can also be in the form of interest that is 'extracted' from the SC either from the controlled company, a

---

49 Commentary to Art. 10 § 34.1.
50 The Netherlands, Hoge Raad der Nederlanden, 27.252, 2 September 1992, 9; Germany, Finanzgericht 6 K 3079/90, 9 May 1996.
51 Commentary to Art. 10 § 34.
52 Commentary to Art. 10 § 36.
53 Commentary to Art. 10 § 37.
54 Commentary to Art. 10 § 39.1–2. See: Germany, Bundesfinanzhof, I R 46/85, 12 July 1989.

subsidiary or a participated company or from third parties. 'Interest' is the remuneration on money lent, so, like dividends, it is 'income from movable capital'.[55] Unlike dividends, interest does not suffer economic double taxation, because it is not taxed both in the hands of the payer and the recipient.[56] By contrast, as for dividends, the tax charged on interest by deduction at source is taxed twice – by the SC and by the RC – and this hinders the movement of capital and of international investment.[57]

3.38 It is unlikely that exclusive taxation of interest in one state (the RC or the SC) receives general approval, so that an intermediate approach has been adopted, according to which interest *may be taxed* in the RC, but the SC maintains the right to impose a tax. The SC is however free to give up all taxation on interest paid to non-residents, but if the SC decides to tax outbound interest, its exercise of this right is limited by a capped relief to be attributed by the RC for the tax charged in the SC (see Art. 23A or 23B).[58] So Art. 11 § 1 lays down the principle that interest arising in a CS and paid to a resident of the other CS may be taxed in the latter but does not stipulate an exclusive right to tax in favour of the RC.

3.39 Certain countries do not allow interest paid to be deducted for the purposes of the payer's tax *unless* the recipient also resides in the same state or is taxable in that state, so the issue arises whether the deduction should also be allowed in cases where the interest is paid by a resident of a CS to a resident of the other state; this problem is covered by Art. 24 § 4.

3.40 The term 'paid' in respect to interest denotes the fulfilment of the obligation to put funds at the disposal of the creditor in the manner required by contract or by custom.[59] Problems arose as to whether a 'notional interest' should be deemed as not paid.[60] The Commentary also defines the *scope of Art. 11*. Art. 11 applies only to interest paid by a company which is a resident of the SC to a resident of the RC, but does not apply to interest paid by a company which is a resident of a third country, or interest paid by a company which is a

---

55   Commentary to Art. 11 § 1.

56   Commentary to Art. 11 § 2.

57   See in general: Danon, Robert, 'Interest (Art. 11 OECD Model Convention)' in: Lang, Michael, et al., (eds), *Source versus Residence. Problems Arising from the Allocation of Taxing Rights in Tax Treaty Law and Possible Alternatives* (Kluwer Law International 2008); IFA, The Tax Treatment of Interest in International Economic Transactions (General report) *Cahiers Droit Fisc. Intl.* (1982) 67a.

58   Commentary to Art. 11 § 3.

59   Commentary to Art. 11 § 5.2.

60   The Netherlands, Hoge Raad der Nederlanden, 18 June 2004, 39.385; United States, US Tax Court, *Morgan Pacific Corp. v. Commissioner of Internal Revenue*, 28 August 1995.

resident in the RC which is attributable to a PE which an enterprise of the RC has in the SC (see §§ 4–6 of the Commentary to Art. 21).

Art. 11 § 2 reserves a right to tax the SC of interest (i.e. to the state of which **3.41** the payer is a resident) and the rate of tax limited to 10 per cent. The treaty withholding tax is at maximum rates but the CSs may agree lower rates, or even taxation exclusively in the state of the beneficiary's residence.[61]

In the past the Commentary focused on the fact that in certain cases, the **3.42** approach of Art. 11 § 2 can be an obstacle to international trade because under that treaty rule a tax in the SC can be levied on the gross amount of interest regardless of expenses incurred to earn such interest, and thus the creditor may decide to shift to the debtor (i.e., the investor) the burden of the tax levied by the SC on the interest. This shifting of the tax on the outbound interest therefore increases the rate of interest charged to the debtor, whose financial burden is in turn increased by an amount corresponding to the tax payable to the SC.[62] To prevent this cascading effect the Commentary advances an additional clause preserving exclusive taxation in the RC. The categories of interest which may fall under the rule of exclusive taxation in the RC are: interest paid to a state, its political subdivisions or local authorities and to central banks; interest paid by a state or its political subdivisions; interest paid pursuant to export financing programmes; interest paid to financial institutions; interest on sales on credit; and interest paid to some tax-exempt entities (e.g., pension funds).[63]

The reduction of taxes in the SC of interest however has created the potential **3.43** for abusive transactions: in fact when the beneficial owner of interest arising in the SC is a company resident of the RC, interest is then transferred to a beneficial owner which is resident in a third country where it enjoys a preferential tax regime. The issue is whether, in terms of policy, it is justifiable to allow in the SC of the interest the limitation of tax which is provided by Art. 11 § 2.

The Commentary 2017 has introduced an important reference to address **3.44** these abusive situations. The Commentary clarifies that Art. 29 applies, but also that provisions such as those described in §§ 82–100 of the Commentary on Art. 1 can be introduced.[64] Moreover the concept of the beneficial owner of

---

61 Commentary to Art. 11 § 7.10.
62 Commentary to Art. 11 § 7.2.
63 Details about these categories on interest are found in §§ 7.4–7.10.
64 Commentary to Art. 11 § 7.11 and 8.

interest plays an important role in determining whether the reduced with-holding tax can be actually applied under a bilateral treaty between the payer of interest and a direct recipient when interest received by that direct recipient is in turn paid to other recipients.

3.45 As Art. 11 § 2 does not settle procedural questions each state applying the reduced withholding tax of Art. 11 § 2 can resort to procedures provided in domestic laws.[65] Art. 11 § 2 neither specifies whether relief in the SC is conditional upon the interest being subject to tax in the RC, nor contains provisions as to how the RC should provide relief for taxation in the SC of interest, so Art. 23A and 23B should be applied.

B. 'Interest' and hybrid instruments

3.46 Under Art. 11 § 3 'interest' is defined as income from *debt-claims* of every kind, whether or not secured by mortgage and whether or not carrying a right to participate in profits, which includes cash deposits and security in the form of money, government securities, bonds and debentures, and mortgage inter-est.[66] Debt-claims, and bonds and debentures, which carry a right to partici-pate in the debtor's profits, are regarded as loans if the contract clearly evidences a loan at interest.[67] The Commentary observes that the definition of interest in the first sentence of Art. 11 § 3 is exhaustive and that it is preferable not to include a subsidiary reference to domestic laws in the text in so far as the definition covers all the kinds of income which are regarded as interest in the various domestic laws and ensures that treaties are unaffected by future changes in any country's domestic laws.

3.47 When interest yielded by a loan security taxed in the SC and the payment made by institution issuing the loan exceeds the amount paid by the sub-scriber, the interest accruing together with the premium paid at issue and at redemption is taxable.[68] The definition of interest in the first sentence of Art. 11 § 3 does not apply to payments made under certain kinds of non-traditional financial instruments where there is no underlying debt (for example, interest rate swaps), but applies to the extent that a loan is considered to exist under a 'substance over form' rule, an 'abuse of rights' principle, or any similar doctrine.[69]

---

65 Italy, Corte Suprema di Cassazione, 5927, 21 April 2001.
66 Commentary to Art. 11 § 18.2.
67 Commentary to Art. 11 § 18.
68 Commentary to Art. 11 § 20.2.
69 Commentary to Art. 11 § 21.1.

Various criteria are used to distinguish remuneration from debt versus **3.48**
remuneration from equity when so-called 'hybrid instruments' are used. For
example interest participating bonds should be considered as dividends rather
than as interest,[70] while interest on convertible bonds should not be considered as dividends until bonds are converted into shares or if the creditor
effectively shares the risks run by the debtor company.[71] In situations of thin
cap, it may be difficult to distinguish between dividends and interest so a
potential overlap between Art. 10 and Art. 11 may be an issue. Premiums or
prizes, government securities, and bonds and debentures constitute interest.[72]

Penalty charges payable for late payment (referred to in the second sentence of **3.49**
Art. 11 § 3) are excluded from the definition of interest because they are
special forms of compensation for the loss suffered by the creditor through the
debtor's delay in meeting his obligations.[73] However, considerations of legal
security and practical convenience make it advisable to place all penalty
charges of this kind, in whatever form they are paid, on the same footing for
the purposes of their taxation treatment.[74]

Annuities are not assimilated to interest. With regard to instalments of **3.50**
purchased annuities that include an interest element on the purchase capital as
well as return of capital (*'fruits civils'* which accrue from day to day) it is often
difficult to make a distinction between the element representing income from
capital and the element representing a return of capital. Taxation laws often
contain special provisions classifying annuities in the category of salaries,
wages and pensions, and taxing them accordingly.[75]

National courts have applied the 'restricted force of attraction of PE' to **3.51**
determine, on the basis of the OECD guidelines, in which cases interest is
attracted and therefore subject to isolated treaty treatment and in which
cases it is attracted and subject to the business profits article (see *supra*
Chapter 1.II).

---

70 Commentary to Art. 11 § 19.
71 United States, US Tax Court, *Morgan Pacific Corp. v. Commissioner of Internal Revenue*, 28 August 1995, 70
    T.C.M. (CCH) 540; Australia, Federal Court of Australia – Full Court, *Deutsche Asia Pacific Finance Inc. v.
    Federal Commissioner of Taxation*, 22 October 2008.
72 Commentary to Art. 11 § 20.1.
73 Commentary to Art. 11 § 22.
74 France, Conseil d'État, 215124, 27 July 2001.
75 Commentary to Art. 11 § 22.

IV. REMUNERATION ON INTANGIBLES

A. Allocation rule

3.52 When a foreign person conducts business through a corporate entity (a controlled company, a subsidiary or a participated company) in the destination country, the remuneration of the investment can also be in the form of royalties that are 'extracted' from the SC either from the controlled company, a subsidiary or a participated company or from third parties. Art. 12 § 1 provides that the royalties arising in the SC and beneficially owned by a resident of the RC shall be taxable only in the RC. The Model adopts the principle of exclusive taxation of royalties in the state of the beneficial owner's residence and admits only one exception at Art. 12 § 3 with respect to the force of attraction on outbound royalties effectively connected to a PE.[76] This is one of the few situations in which the Model prevents double taxation by attributing an exclusive right to tax to only one of the CSs, by using the expression royalties *'shall be taxable only'* in the RC, thereby precluding the other CS from taxing.

3.53 In spite of the principle of exclusive taxation of royalties in the RC adopted in the Model, many countries adopt a treaty clause (similar to that adopted for dividends and interest by the Model) that also attributes taxing rights to the SC, so that an intermediate approach has been adopted, according to which royalties *may be taxed* in the RC, but the SC maintains the right to impose a tax.[77] The SC is, however, free to give up all taxation on royalties paid to non-residents, but if the SC decides to tax outbound royalties its exercise of this right is limited by a capped relief to be attributed by the RC for the tax charged in the SC (see Art. 23A or 23B). So in existing treaties the royalties article often provides that royalties arising in a CS and paid to a resident of the other CS may be taxed in the latter but does not stipulate an exclusive right to tax in favour of the RC.

3.54 The attribution of taxing rights to the SC on outbound royalties in those treaties and the concurrent taxation of those royalties in the RC has created issues that have been addressed by national courts. So there are withholding tax issues similar to those of outbound dividends and interest, such as the extent of the exercise of the right to tax in the SC (in particular if the

---

76 Commentary to Art. 12 § 3.
77 Meloni, Eduardo O., 'Taxation of Royalties under Treaty Law: How Far Can a Source State Go?' (2010) 64 *Bull. Intl. Tax.* 315.

non-resident recipient of royalties does not have a PE in the SC), and how and if withholding tax refunds should be effected in the SC.

When the SC has a right to tax outbound royalties, national courts have often **3.55** considered the reduced treaty withholding tax rate as a limit to domestic laws which may impose a higher withholding tax.[78] The attribution of taxing rights to the SC on outbound royalties also poses the issue of how withholding tax refunds should be effected in the SC.[79]

The attribution of taxing rights to the SC on outbound royalties has created a **3.56** major issue with respect to the scope of taxing rights of the SC in those cases in which the payments were to non-residents who did not have a PE in the SC. The position of tax authorities of the SCs is that the SC has a right to tax those outbound royalties if a non-resident recipient has a PE or a fixed base in the SC.[80]

Art. 12 § 1 provides that royalties arising in the SC shall be taxable only in the **3.57** RC if they are *beneficially owned* by a resident of the RC. So if royalties are *not* beneficially owned by a resident of the RC, then other articles of the treaty become applicable allowing taxation in the SC, in particular the business profits article. The concept of the beneficial owner of royalties thus plays an important role in determining whether taxation in the SC is allowed under a bilateral treaty between the payer of royalties and a direct recipient when royalties received by that direct recipient are in turn paid to other recipients. These structures are also targeted by Art. 29.

Art. 12 only applies to royalties paid by a company which is a resident of the **3.58** SC to a resident of the RC, but does not apply to royalties paid by a company which is a resident of a third country, or royalties paid by a company which is a resident of the RC which are attributable to a PE which an enterprise of the RC has in the SC (§§ 4–6 of the Commentary to Art. 21).[81] Procedural questions should be addressed by domestic laws and specific questions arise

---

78 Italy, Corte Suprema di Cassazione, 3251, 20 March 2000; Italy, Corte Suprema di Cassazione, 3414, 21 February 2005; Italy, Corte Suprema di Cassazione, 1768, 30 January 2004.

79 Austria, Verwaltungsgerichtshof (Supreme Administrative Court), 99/13/0036, 17 December 2003, Germany, Bundesfinanzhof, I R 41/92, 5 November 1992.

80 According to Art. 7 royalties received by a resident of one of the CSs were exempt from tax in the other CS provided the resident did not have a PE in the other CS. See: United States, US Tax Court, *Georges Simenon v. Commissioner of Internal Revenue*, 29 September 1965; United States, US Tax Court, *Jules Samann v. Commissioner of Internal Revenue*, 14 September 1961; Italy, Corte Suprema di Cassazione, 3931, 15 January 1981; Italy, Corte Suprema di Cassazione, 3931, 15 January 1981; Italy, Corte Suprema di Cassazione, 14253, 28 October 2000; Australia, Supreme Court of New South Wales, *Unisys Corporation v. Federal Commissioner of Taxation*, [2002].

81 Commentary to Art. 12 § 5.

with triangular cases involving non-discrimination issues, that are discussed at the Commentary to Art. 24 § 71.

B. Definition of 'royalties'

3.59 Art. 12 § 3 provides that the term 'royalties' as used in that article means payments of any kind received as a consideration for the use of, or the right to use, any copyright of literary, artistic or scientific work including cinematograph films, any patent, trade mark, design or model, plan, secret formula or process, or for information concerning industrial, commercial or scientific experience. This general definition of the term 'royalties' raises several legal issues addressed in the Commentary, which essentially defines four major areas: (i) payments that are not considered royalties, but business profits; (ii) payments for know-how (which are generally royalties unless new knowledge is created); (iii) payments for computer software (which are generally royalties under a copyright concept); and (iv) payments for mixed contracts (which are often governed by treaty provisions different from the royalties article).[82]

3.60 The Commentary addresses the problem of the definition of the term 'royalties' by relying on a basic distinction between payments for the *use of rights* (which are generally royalties) and payments for the *transfer of intangible property* (which are generally not royalties), and then provides a set of criteria to determine whether a transfer of rights effectively occurs, concluding with a discussion about hybrid situations. The Commentary also notes that the term 'paid' used by Art. 12 denotes the fulfilment of the obligation to put funds at the disposal of the creditor in the manner required by contract or by custom.[83]

3.61 The Commentary emphasizes the relevance of the term 'use' of right as opposed to any other form of economic transfer of intangible property, and therefore affirms that the definition of royalties cover payments for the *use* of rights listed in Art. 12 § 3 (including the payment made for compensation for fraudulently copying or infringing the right), while the definition of royalties does *not* cover payments to a recipient who does not own the right to use, for

---

82 See in general: Bobbett, Catherine and Avery Jones, John F., 'The Treaty Definition of Royalties' (2006) 60 *Bull. Intl. Tax.* 23; IFA, 'Tax Treatment of the Importation and Exportations of Technology: Know-How, Patents, Other Intangibles and Technical Assistance' *Cahiers Droit Fisc. Intl.* (1975) 60a; Martín Jiménez, Adolfo, 'La Tributación de los Cánones o Regalías' in: José Manuel Calderón Carrero and José Ramón Ruiz García (eds), 'Comentarios a los Convenios Para Evitar la Doble Imposición y Prevenir la Evasión Fiscal Concluidos por España', (2004) *Instituto de Estudios Económicos de Galicia* 1342.

83 Commentary to Art. 12 § 8.

example payments for artistic performances.[84] There is a payment for the transfer of ownership *if* a payment is in consideration for the *transfer* of the full ownership of an element of intangible property, so that the payment is *not* in consideration 'for the use of, or the right to use' that property and cannot therefore represent a royalty.[85]

Where consideration is paid for the transfer of the *full ownership of the rights in* **3.62** *the copyright*, the payment cannot represent royalties and Art. 12 is *not* applicable.[86] In practice *if* ownership of rights is alienated, *then* consideration cannot be for the *use* of rights. The character of the transaction as an alienation cannot be altered by the form of the consideration or payment of consideration in instalments or related to a contingency. There are however difficulties when the transfer of rights involves the exclusive right of use of the copyright during a specific period or in a limited geographical area, or when additional payments are made for usage or in the form of a lump sum payment.[87]

The Commentary acknowledges that 'difficulties can arise in the case of a **3.63** transfer of rights that could be considered to form part of an element of property where these rights are transferred in a way that is presented as an alienation', for example, in a transaction structured as a sale, exclusive granting of all rights to intellectual property for a limited period, or all rights to the property in a limited geographical area. If the payment is in consideration for an alienation of rights that constitute distinct and specific property the business profits article or the capital gains article apply, rather than the royalties article.[88] *If* ownership of rights is alienated, *then* consideration is not for the use of the rights, and the character of the transaction as an alienation cannot be altered by the form of the consideration, or by the fact that additional payments are made for usage or in the form of a lump sum payment.

1. Payments that are not royalties, but business profits

The common feature of transactions that create business profits rather than **3.64** royalties is the technological or commercial structure of the transaction combined with the lack of the attribution of the use of rights under licencing agreements. On this basis, payments for the leasing of equipment, for

---

84   Commentary to Art. 12 § 8.1. See for example: United States, *US Tax Court, Boulez v. Commissionaire.*
85   Commentary to Art. 12 § 8.2-1.
86   Commentary to Art. 12 § 15.
87   Spain, Tribunal Supremo, RG núms. 6206/1995, 3 June 2000; Spain, Tribunal Supremo (Supreme Court), RG 7103/1995, 29 July 2000, *Asociación Española de Asesores Fiscales, Fiscalidad Internacional. Convenios de doble imposición – Aranzadi*, 2002, 262; Spain, Audiencia Nacional, 1995–05–16, 16 May 1995; February 1995; Spain, Audiencia Nacional, 207021/1990, 28 June 1994.
88   Commentary to Art. 12 § 8.2.

'transponder leasing' agreements, for 'roaming' agreements, for spectrum licenses, for exclusive distribution rights, for the development of a design, for rents of films as well as management fees generally fall under the ambit of the treaty business profits article. This distinction of royalties vs business profits is important in countries that levy a withholding tax on outbound royalties, because such a tax cannot be levied on business profits.

3.65 In 1963 Draft Convention and the 1977 Model payments 'for the use of, or the right to use, industrial, commercial or scientific equipment' were considered as royalties, but then that reference was eliminated.[89] In spite of this change courts still tend to characterize these payments as royalties.[90] The same approach is applied to the leasing of different equipment (phone system, TV equipment, crane, or chartering of bareboat vessels).[91] A different outcome is reached if the non-resident recipient has a PE in the SC, as in that case the payments are considered business income if effectively connected to the PE.[92]

3.66 Another situation that falls under the treaty business profits article is *payments for 'transponder leasing'* agreements in which a satellite operator allows customers to utilize the capacity of a satellite transponder to transmit over large geographical areas. Because the payments by customers are made for the use of the transponder transmitting capacity, they are, thus, *not* made in consideration for the use of, or right to use, property, or for information.[93] In most cases the customer acquires the transponder's transmission capacity (the satellite is operated by the lessor, and the lessee has no access to transponder), but does not acquire physical possession of the transponder.[94] Situations that are similar to 'transponder leasing' agreements are those that involve payments made to lease or purchase the capacity of cables for the transmission of electrical power or communications, or the capacity of pipelines for transportation of gas or oil.

3.67 A less frequent transaction is one in which the owner of the satellite leases it to another party so that the latter may operate it and either use it for its own purposes or offer its data transmission capacity to third parties: in such a

---

89 Commentary to Art. 12 § 9.
90 Spain, Audiencia Nacional, 1069/2004, 24 April 2008; Spain, Tribunal Económico Administrativo, 4085/2005, 28 February 2008.
91 Austria, Verwaltungsgerichtshof, 2003/13/0015, 31 May 2006; Spain, Audiencia Nacional, RG 590/1997, 6 April 2000; Malaysia, Commissioners for Her Majesty's Revenue and Customs, PKR 651, 30 May 1996, 752; Malaysia, High Court, 14-1-88, 22 March 1990.
92 Art. 4 § 3 b). See: Australia, Federal Court of Australia, *Mcdermott Industries v. Commissioner of Taxation of the Commonwealth of Australia*, 29 April 2005.
93 Commentary to Art. 12 § 9.1.
94 Commentary to Art. 12 § 9.2.

situation the payments made by the satellite operator to the satellite owner are payments for the leasing of industrial, commercial or scientific equipment.

Payments made for the telecommunications services provided by a foreign **3.68** network operator (so called *'roaming' agreements*) also fall under the treaty business profits article, because these payments are not made in consideration for the use of, or right to use, property, or for information, since the payments for roaming are not for the use, or the right to use, any equipment.[95] The same applies to payments to acquire part of a *radio/TV frequency spectrum* that allows the holder to transmit media content (i.e., spectrum license).[96]

Payments for the *rent of films* fall under the treaty business profits article.[97] **3.69** Courts have developed a distinction between economic exploitation of a programme by leasing it, and economic exploitation of a programme by licensing somebody to use it. Courts have held that in the first case the exploitation is a business activity within the meaning of the business profits article, whereas in the second case the exploitation implies the attribution of the use of an intellectual property right within the meaning of the royalties article.[98]

Payments for *exclusive distribution rights* generally fall under the treaty business **3.70** profits article because they are not made in consideration for the use of, or the right to use, an element of property. The Commentary provides the example of a distributor of clothes resident of the SC who pays a certain sum of money to a manufacturer of branded shirts as consideration for the exclusive right to sell in the SC the branded shirts manufactured abroad by that manufacturer, noting that the resident distributor merely obtains the exclusive right to sell the SC shirts that he will buy from the manufacturer, but does not pay for the right to use the trade name or trade mark under which the shirts are sold.[99]

Payments for the *development of a design* fall under the treaty business profits **3.71** article. These payments are for the development of a design, model or plan that does not already exist which are not made 'for the use of, or the right to use' a design, model or plan, but are made in consideration for the services that will result in the development of that design, model or plan (this will be the

---

95 Commentary to Art. 12 § 9.2.
96 Commentary to Art. 12 § 9.3.
97 Commentary to Art. 12 § 10.
98 Spain, Audiencia Nacional, RG 257/1997, 4 May 2000; Spain, Audiencia Nacional, RG 231/1996, 7 February 2000; Spain, Audiencia Nacional, RG. Núms. 171/1996, 7 February 2000; Canada, Federal Court of Appeal, *Vauban Productions v. The Queen* [1979].
99 Commentary to Art. 12 § 10.1. See: Canada, Federal Court of Appeal, *Farmparts Distributing Ltd. v. Her Majesty the Queen*, [1980] C.T.C. 20528 February 1980.

case even if the designer of the design, model or plan, e.g., an architect, retains all rights, including the copyright, in that design, model or plan). By contrast, when the owner of the copyright in previously developed plans grants a right to modify or reproduce these plans without performing any additional work, the payments received by that owner in consideration for granting the right to such use of the plans are royalties.[100]

3.72 Rights (partial or complete) in a copy of the program are generally compensated by payments that are business profits (Commentary to Art. 12, §§ 14–14.2); these payments are made for a copy or for mere distribution of software and include: (i) payments for limited rights to reproduce the program; (ii) payments for rights to make multiple copies of the program); and (iii) payments for the right to distribute copies of the program without the right to reproduce that program).

2. Payments for know-how

3.73 The Commentary provides a definition of 'know-how' and then distinguishes know-how vis-à-vis the provision of services, articulating a set of criteria for this distinction and providing relevant examples of services involving use of knowledge that are not actual transfers of know-how, including remarks on information on computer programs and payments for franchising.

3.74 The term 'know-how' denotes *undivulged information* of an industrial, commercial or scientific nature arising from previous experiences that have not been patented and do not generally fall within other categories of intellectual property rights, but which have practical application, so that the disclosure of such information creates an economic benefit. As a general principle payments for know-how are royalties.[101] Moreover in certain cases information is supplied, or the use of, or right to use, property is granted by a the person who owns that information/property who agrees not to supply or grant to anyone else that information or right: payments made as consideration for such an agreement are essentially made to secure the exclusivity of that information or exclusive right to use property, so they are also characterized as royalties.

3.75 The following are a few examples of judicial applications of this principle. Payments for intra-group services such as assistance in the field of financial planning, market research, assistance in the selection of partners and a general manager for the local operations, and services in the field of human resourcing

---

100 Commentary to Art. 12 § 10.2.
101 Commentary to Art. 12 § 11, 11.1. See: Palma, Rui, 'Income Taxation of Intellectual Property and Know-How: Conundrums in The Interpretation of Domestic and Tax Treaty Law' (2004) 44 *Eur. Tax.* 480.

such as the selection and training of the work force were considered royalties because the services include the transfer of commercial experience (know-how) and technical assistance.[102] The acquisition of 'know-how' or a secret formula can also occur in the form of a licence of software.

The Commentary distinguishes know-how vis-à-vis the provision of services. **3.76** When 'know-how' is involved, the grantor transfers to the other party special knowledge and experience which is not disclosed to the public and usually neither party participates in the use made by the recipient of this knowledge nor guarantees the result of such a use.[103] By contrast, when the provision of services is involved, the provider uses its own skills and knowledge to create an economic benefit for the recipient.[104] So the distinguishing feature is that the supplier of know-how provides information that already exists and his confidentiality is protected contractually,[105] while the supplier of services performs activities which require the use, by that supplier, of special knowledge, skill and expertise (but which do not require the transfer of such special knowledge, skill or expertise to the other party) as well as incurring costs for the performance of services.[106]

The consequence of this distinction is that payments for the supply of **3.77** know-how constitute royalties, while payments for the provision of services constitute business profits. The Commentary provides that Art. 12 does *not* apply to payments for *new information* obtained as a result of performing services at the request of the payer because know-how relates to information concerning previous experience.[107]

The Commentary provides examples of services that generate business profits, **3.78** such as after-sales service, services rendered by a seller to the purchaser under a warranty, technical assistance, the disclosure of a list as developed specifically for the payer of generally available information, an opinion given by an engineer, an advocate or an accountant, advice provided electronically, electronic communications with technicians, access through computer networks to

---

102 Malaysia, Federal Court, Civil Appeal No. 39 of 1981, 25 September 1982, [1983] 1 MLJ 74; Canada, Exchequer Court of Canada, *Western Electric Co. v. Minister of National Revenue*, 11 April 1969; Turkey, Bursa Tax Court, E.2011/777 – K.2012/328, 22 March 2012.

103 Commentary to Art. 12 § 11.1.

104 Commentary to Art. 12 § 11.2.

105 Commentary to Art. 12 § 11.3.

106 Commentary to Art. 12 § 11.4.

107 Commentary to Art. 12 § 11.2. See: Spain, Tribunal Supremo, 1804/2006, 28 December 2006; Spain, Audiencia Nacional, RG 1057/1997, 23 November 2000; Brazil, Tribunal Regional Federal da 2ª Região Rio de Janeiro, 2004.50.01.001354-5/ES, 16 March 2010.

a trouble-shooting database (software with non-confidential information in response to common problems).[108]

3.79 An example of payment that constitutes business profits received in consideration for services is the disclosure of a list developed specifically for the payer out of generally available information, while payments for the confidential list of customers to which the payee has provided a particular product or service are royalties because they are in consideration for know-how which is the commercial experience of the payee in dealing with these customers.[109]

3. Payments for computer software

3.80 One of the most complex parts of the Commentary to Art. 12 is that devoted to the treatment of payments for computer software. The Commentary defines the term 'software' making a distinction between operational and application software and then focuses on copyright protection, devoting considerable attention to the idea that software is a special kind of 'literary work' falling under copyright protection.[110]

3.81 The Commentary then provides a list of different payments that, depending on the surrounding legal arrangements, may be subject to different articles of the treaties. This list includes: payments for copyright on software; payments for copies of software; payments for limited rights to reproduce programs; payments for rights to make multiple copies of programs; payments for information about principles underlying the program (algorithms or programming languages); and payments for a right to distribute copies without a right to reproduce it. The Commentary observes that the characterization of these payments involves difficult problems which led to modifications of §§ 12–17 in 2000.

3.82 The Commentary advances a definition of software, distinguishing operational software from application software. *Operational software* is defined as a program, or series of programs, containing instructions for a computer required for the operational processes of the computer itself, while *application software* is defined as a program, or series of programs for the accomplishment of other tasks. In both cases the software can be transferred in writing or

---

108 Argentina, Tribunal Fiscal de la Nación, 21.175-I, 14 April 2010; 6; Turkey, Bursa Tax Court, E.2011/777 – K.2012/328, 22 March 2012.

109 Thailand, Supreme Court, *Hana Semiconductor (Bangkok) Co. Ltd. v. Thai Revenue Department*, 23 February 2006.

110 See in general: De Hosson, Fred, 'Taxation of Cross-Border Software Payments' (1992) 20 *Intertax* 682; IFA, Tax Treatment of Computer Software (1988) 73a *Cahiers Droit Fisc. Intl.*

electronically, on a magnetic tape or disk, or on a laser disk or CD-ROM, as part of hardware or in an independent form.

Software is a special kind of 'literary work' falling under copyright protection. **3.83** The Commentary states that rights in computer programs are a form of intellectual property and refers to the practices of OECD Member Countries which protect rights in computer programs under copyright laws.[111] A distinction should be drawn between, on the one hand, the *copyright in the program* (or in the software which incorporates a copy of the copyrighted program), and, on the other hand, the *transfers of rights on software*, in light of the fact that copies of software need often to be made to enable the actual operation of software.[112]

Art. 12 § 2 requires that software be classified as a literary, artistic or scientific **3.84** work, but also notes that none of these categories is entirely apt, and for this reason the copyright laws of many countries specifically classify software as *a literary or scientific work*.[113] Once it is accepted that software should be subject to copyright protection, a strategy that is an alternative to that of attributing copyright protection to software treating it as 'literary or scientific work', is the creation of a special category of copyright protection for software.

The Commentary provides a list of different payments that, depending on the **3.85** surrounding legal arrangements, may be subject to different parts of the treaties. There are two types of transferee's rights and related payments:[114] 1) software related payments that are royalties (for copyright software and programming languages); and 2) software related payments that are business profits (for copy or distribution of software).

When payments are made for copyright on software the transferor does not **3.86** fully alienate the copyright, but licences (i.e., authorizes) a specific use of program that, without such a license, would constitute an infringement of copyright. The consequence is that the payments are royalties (and not business profits) because they are specifically made to exploit the rights that

---

111 Commentary to Art. 12 § 12.2-1.
112 Commentary to Art. 12 § 12.2-2.
113 Commentary to Art. 12 § 12.2. See: Spain, Tribunal Económico Administrativo Central, 3604/2006, 17 April 2008; Spain, Tribunal Supremo, 2598/2010, 25 March 2010; Spain, Tribunal Supremo, 346/1996, 28 April 2001; Italy, Corte Suprema di Cassazione, 21220, 29 September 2006; Canada, Tax Court of Canada, *Angoss International Ltd. v. Her Majesty the Queen*, 4 February 1999. See: Garcia Heredia, Alejandro, 'Software Royalties in Tax Treaties: Should Copyright Rights Be Reconsidered in the OECD Commentary on Art. 12' (2005) 59 *Bull. Intl. Fisc. Doc.* 225.
114 Commentary to Art. 12 § 13.

would otherwise be the sole prerogative of the copyright holder.[115] The Commentary uses the example of licenses to reproduce and distribute to the public software incorporating the copyrighted program, and to modify and publicly display the program.[116]

3.87 The acquisition of 'know-how' or secret formulas can occur in the form of a licence of software. The Commentary takes the position that the provision of information on computer programs is know-how compensated by royalties if three requirements are met: operational software (i.e., algorithms or programming languages or techniques) is transferred rather than application software to solve specific problems; the user has a duty of non-disclosure; and the information transferred enjoys trade secret protection.[117]

3.88 Those payments are characterized as royalties to the extent that they represent consideration for the use of, or the right to use, secret formulas or for information concerning industrial, commercial or scientific experience which cannot be separately copyrighted.[118] The acquisition of 'know-how' or secret formulas in the form of software is generally compensated by payments that are royalties,[119] but payments that are consideration for the use of, or the right to use, secret formulas or for information concerning industrial, commercial or scientific experience which cannot be separately copyrighted fall under the business profits article.[120]

3.89 With regard to payments for copies for distribution of software a distinction should be made between three cases: payments for limited rights to reproduce a program (*case 1*), payments for rights to make multiple copies of a program (*case 2*), and payments for the right to distribute copies without the right to reproduce the program (*case 3*). In *case 1*, payments made for the transfer of rights which enable the user to operate the program (e.g., by attributing limited rights to reproduce the program or by transferring rights specific to the nature of computer programs) are business profits (and not royalties). The reason is that in these cases the payments are to obtain authorization to a copy of the program which is an essential technical step in utilizing it (and are not made to exploit rights on the program that would otherwise be the sole

---

115 Commentary to Art. 12 § 13.1-1.
116 Portugal, Supremo Tribunal Administrativo, 0621/09, 2 February 2011; Portugal, Supremo Tribunal Administrativo (Supreme Administrative Court), 03506/09, 3 July 2012; Poland, Wojewódzki sąd administracyjny, III SA/Wa 1092/09, 23 November 2009.
117 Commentary to Art. 12 § 11.5.
118 Commentary to Art. 12 § 14.3.
119 Ibid.
120 Ibid.

prerogative of the copyright holder).[121] In these situations the method of transferring the computer program to the transferee is not relevant.

In *case 2* the transferee obtains rights to make multiple copies of the program **3.90** for operation only within its own business ('*site licences*'), and the rights *are limited to enabling the operation of the program on the licensee's computers or network* (and are not made to exploit rights of the program that would otherwise be the sole prerogative of the copyright holder). As a result, the payments for those technical rights are business profits (and not royalties).[122]

By contrast, in *case 3* payments are for the right to simply distribute copies of a **3.91** program without the right to actually reproduce it. In these cases, the software copyright holder grants to the distribution intermediary the right to distribute copies of the program without the right to reproduce the program. These payments received by the software copyright holder are business profits (and not royalties) because the rights acquired in relation to the copyright are limited to those necessary for the intermediary to distribute copies of the software program, so that the intermediary does not to exploit any right in the software copyrights. It is irrelevant whether the distributed copies are delivered on tangible media or electronically (without the distributor having the right to reproduce the software), or whether software is subject to minor changes for its installation.[123]

Payments for mixed contracts are usually complex legal arrangements which **3.92** may include payments for software, but which are not limited to licensing such rights. Software payments may be made under mixed contracts, for example, when computer hardware is sold with built-in software or when licences of the right to use software are combined with the provision of services. The issue is whether in those cases the royalties article or the business profits article applies, and the solution is advised in terms of either apportionment of payments to each category of income, or re-characterization based on the principal purpose of the transaction.[124]

When payments for digital products (images, sounds or text) are concerned, **3.93** the same principles for software payments apply, and the tax treatment varies depending on whether the download of digital products leads to the acquisition of data (*case 1*), or to the acquisition of copyright (*case 2*).

---

121 Commentary to Art. 12 § 14.
122 Commentary to Art. 12 § 14.2. See: Finland, Korkein Hallinto-oikeus, KHO:2011:101, 12 December 2011.
123 Commentary to Art. 12 § 14.4. See; Spain, Tribunal Supremo, 2598/2010, 25 March 2010.
124 Commentary to Art. 12 § 17. See; Spain, Audiencia Nacional, RG 1057/1997, 23 November 2000.

3.94 When the download of digital products leads to acquisition of data (*case 1*), there is *a use of* copyright by the customer which is remunerated by royalties when a right to make one or more copies of the digital content is granted under the contract.[125] *If* however the customer pays consideration for something other than for the use of, or right to use, rights in the copyright (such as to acquire other types of contractual rights, data or services), and the use of copyright is limited to rights required to enable downloading, storage and operation on the customer's computer, network or other storage, performance or display device, *then* the payments are business profits or capital gains (and not royalties) for the recipient.[126] When the download of digital products leads to the acquisition of copyright (*case 2*), the granting of the right to use such copyright in a digital product is remunerated by payments of royalties and not business profits.[127]

V. CAPITAL GAINS

A. Capital gains and country of destination: a grey area

3.95 When a foreign person conducts business through a corporate entity (a controlled company, a subsidiary or a participated company) in the destination country, the remuneration of the investment can also be in the form of capital gains that are realized either from sale of participations in a controlled company, a subsidiary or other participated company, or from the sale of assets to third parties. Art. 13 does not deal with capital gains policy issues since the taxation of capital gains varies considerably from country to country, so that it is left to domestic laws to decide whether and to what extent taxation can occur, being however understood that treaties cannot be construed as giving a state the right to tax capital gains if such a right is not provided for in its domestic laws.[128] Under domestic laws capital gains are subject to a special tax on capital gains or are treated as ordinary income.[129] As a result, the issue

---

125   Commentary to Art. 12 § 17.2-1.
126   Commentary to Art. 12 § 17.2-2. See: Spain, Tribunal Económico Administrativo Central, 3730/2004, 15 February 2007.
127   Commentary to Art. 12 § 17 and 3.
128   Commentary to Art. 13 § 1–3. and on policy issues Commentary to Art. 13 §§ 4–21. See in general: Simontacchi, Stefano, *Taxation of Capital Gains under the OECD Model Convention: With Special Regard to Immovable Property* (Kluwer 2008).
129   Commentary to Art. 13 § 4.

arises in case law whether treaties apply to capital gains when domestic laws do not specify whether capital gains are treated separately or as ordinary income.[130]

A problem that is not covered by the Commentary is the relevant period of **3.96** maturation of capital gains when an asset is transferred from a country of origin to a country of destination. Gains begin to be generated at the initial moment – t1 (i.e., *date of acquisition of the asset*), may be determined in a subsequent moment – t2 (i.e., *date of a tax-relevant evaluation of the asset*, for example, when an asset enters the tax jurisdiction of a country), or realized – t3 (the *final moment of disposition*), so it is essential to determine which is the relevant date to determine the recognized tax basis.[131] Another problem is connected to the transition from an old to a new treaty when the gains accrue under both the old and the new treaties.[132]

In Art. 13 there is no detailed definition of 'alienation of property'. The **3.97** Commentary provides a broad definition of the term, which encompasses the sale or exchange of property, partial alienation, expropriation, transfer to a company in exchange for stock, sale of a right, gifts, as well as passing of property on death.[133] Domestic courts have generally adopted this broad approach.[134] A similar broad concept of 'alienation' is found in respect of redemption of shares.[135]

Art. 13 does not settle the question of exchange gains which is entirely left to **3.98** domestic laws.[136] Often exchange gains are realized in connection with immovable property but the immovable property article does not specifically mention them. The judicial approach is generally to tax those gains in the SC under the capital gains article, but sometimes the immovable property article is applied.[137]

---

130 Australia, Federal Court of Australia, *Undershaft Ltd. v. Commissioner of Taxation*, 3 February 2009; The Netherlands, Hoge Raad der Nederlanden, 32.330, 28 October 1998.

131 Canada, Federal Court of Appeal, *William F. Kubicek v. the Attorney General of Canada*, 26 September 1997; Canada, Federal Court of Appeal, *Haas v. Her Majesty the Queen*, 14 October 1999; Germany, Bundesfinanzhof, VIII R 15/94, 19 March 1996; Germany, Bundesfinanzhof, VIII R 44/90, 30 March 1993; The Netherlands, Hoge Raad der Nederlanden, 36.954, 12 July 2002.

132 Norway, Tingrett Asker og Bærum, 47–90 A, 17 March 1991.

133 Commentary to Art. 13 §§ 16–17.

134 Mexico, Tribunal Fiscal de la Federación, 12666/98-11_06-3/99-S2-06-02, 7 September 1999; Canada, Federal Court, *Gladden v. Her Majesty the Queen*, 22 January 1985.

135 See for example: Huiskes, Theodoor, 'Netherlands: Capital Gains on a Company's Repurchase on Shares', *34 Eur. Tax.* 472 (1994).

136 Commentary to Art. 13 § 16–17. See: Czech Republic, Nejvyšší Správní Soud, 5 Afs 49/2011–94, 19 April 2012.

137 France, Conseil d'État, 352212, 12 March 2014; Germany, Finanzgericht Niedersachsen, XII 781/93 V, 15 August 1996.

3.99 The broad concept of alienation of shares has led to judicial approaches on the matter of exit taxes under treaties. Exit taxes are based on the distinction between unrealized and realized income, according to which capital gains are taxed only when actually realized, and rely on the fact that a migrating taxpayer continues to hold assets (generally participations or immovable property) in the emigration country. Under exit taxes, taxation in the emigration country is enforced through a deemed realization event that occurs at the time of departure (i.e., when tax residency is relinquished), in spite the fact there is no actual realization of the gains that are latent on the assets.

3.100 The treaty issue related with exit taxes is whether the term 'alienation', as used in Art. 13 § 4 of the treaty includes gains arising from a deemed (as opposed to actual) disposal of assets triggered by the emigration event. So the issue is whether such a deemed realization is compatible with the capital gains article.

3.101 The prevailing judicial approach is that the exit tax charge is not limited by treaty rules in respect of emigrating individuals.[138] The emigration country is the RC until the transfer of residence and the immigration country is the RC only after that transfer, according to Art. 4 of the Model (which essentially requires that the taxpayer becomes a resident after a 183-day period).[139] This means that an exit tax is levied when the emigration country still acts as the RC of the taxpayer and the SC of the income.[140] An issue which is often at stake is the retroactivity of domestic exit taxes in respect of treaties.[141] Cases on exit taxes also cover corporate migrations[142] and sometimes corporate and individual migration are connected.[143]

3.102 A situation similar to that of companies migrating from their countries of origin occurs when a PE located in the SC transfers its assets to its head office located in another country (the RC). This situation is explicitly covered by Commentary to Art. 13 § 10, which clarifies that Art. 13 does not prevent the

138 Weizmann, Leif, 'Departure Taxation, Treaty Override? Extraterritorial Tax Law?' (1994) 34 *Eur. Tax.* 73.
139 Aumayr, Elke, 'The 183-days rule in the OECD Model Convention' in: Hohenwarter, Daniela and Metzler, Vanessa, (eds), *Taxation of Employment Income in International Tax Law* (Linde 2009).
140 Sweden, Högsta Förvaltningsdomstolen, 1 February 2016; Sweden, Regeringsrätten, 283-10, 14 December 2010.
141 The Netherlands, Hoge Raad der Nederlanden, 07/12314 – 42.701 – 43.760, 20 February 2009; Germany, Bundesfinanzhof, I B 108/97, 17 December 1997; Canada, Federal Court of Appeal, *Davis v. Her Majesty the Queen*, 15 January 1980; United States, US Tax Court, *Cecil B. Furstenberg v. Commissioner of Internal Revenue*, 26 November 1984; United States, US Tax Court, *Tedd N. Crow v. Commissioner of Internal Revenue*, 26 August 1985.
142 South Africa, Cape Town Tax Court, *The taxpayer (not disclosed) v. the Commissioner for the South African Revenue Service*, 12432, 16 November 2010; South Africa, Supreme Court of Appeal, *Tradehold Ltd. v. South African Revenue Service*, 8 May 2012.
143 The Netherlands, Gerechtshof's-Hertogenbosch 04/01756, 19 June 2008.

SCs from taxing profits arising from this transfer of assets from a PE situated in the SC, provided however that such taxation is in accordance with the business profits article.[144]

Art. 13 does not cover appreciation and revaluation of assets. The Commentary clarifies that appreciation in value is not associated with the alienation of a capital asset, that taxes on capital appreciation are covered by the treaty according to Art. 2, and that special taxes may be imposed on revaluations for accounting purposes. According to the Commentary Artt. 6, 7 and 21 address this problem adequately as the right to tax is attributed to the state of which the taxpayer who revalues is a resident, except that in the cases of immovable property or of movable property forming part of the business property of a PE.[145] **3.103**

The treatment of depreciation and devaluation of assets is not mentioned by the Commentary, and Art. 13 does not cover realized capital losses. Often domestic laws exempt foreign capital gains, thereby creating an issue for the deduction in the RC of foreign capital losses. This has led to interesting judicial decisions clarifying that capital losses are not covered by Art. 13.[146] **3.104**

Under the Model there are different types of gains which can be realized, i.e. gains from the alienation of: immovable property (Art. 13 § 1), movable property of a PE (Art. 13 § 2), ships and aircraft (Art. 13 § 3), or shares (Art. 13 § 4–5). **3.105**

Pursuant to Art. 13 § 1 gains derived by a resident from the alienation of immovable property referred to in Art. 6 and situated in the SC *may be taxed* in that SC. The Commentary notes that Art. 13 § 1, Art. 6 and Art. 22 § 1 adopt the same rule based on the situs of immovable property. When there is no provision equivalent to Art. 13 § 1 of the Model in a treaty, the SC where immovable property is situated does not have the power to tax the gains deriving from the sale thereof.[147] Art. 13 § 1 applies only to gains which a resident of the RC derives from the alienation of immovable property situated **3.106**

---

144 Commentary to Art. 13 § 10. See: The Netherlands, Gerechtshof Amsterdam, 08/00135, 15 July 2010; Germany, Bundesfinanzhof, I R 77/06, 17 July 2008; The Netherlands, Hoge Raad der Nederlanden, 36.954, 12 July 2002; Germany, Bundesfinanzhof, I R 99/08, 28 October 2009.
145 Commentary to Art. 13 § 7.
146 Denmark, Østre Landsret, 14 May 2012, B-307-10; France, Conseil d'État (351702, 12 June 2013; Germany, Bundesfinanzhof, I R 43/98, 21 October 1999.
147 Denmark, Østre Landsret, B-1386-11/ SKM 2012.468 Ø, 29 March 2012.

in the SC, but does not apply to gains derived from the alienation of immovable property situated in the RC of which the alienator is a resident.[148]

3.107 The allocation rule of Art. 13 § 2 is that gains from the alienation of movable property forming part of the business property of a PE which an enterprise of the RC has in the SC, including such gains from the alienation of such a PE (alone or with the whole enterprise), *may be taxed* in that the SC. 'Movable property' is defined as all property other than immovable property which is dealt with in Art. 13 § 1, including intangible property, such as goodwill, licences, etc.

3.108 The Commentary 2017 addresses certain abusive arrangements that relied on transparent structures which extracted income in these situations. Under Art. 13 § 2 before the Commentary 2017 the gains derived from the alienation of the movable property forming part of the business property of a PE that was situated in the SC could not be taxed in the SC when the enterprise which performed its activities in the SC was in the form of an entity or arrangement that was treated as fiscally transparent under the tax law of the SC. The Commentary provides now that the SC, under Art. 13 § 2, is allowed to tax directly the gains in the hands of the non-resident partners or members of the entity or arrangement. By contrast, where an enterprise performs its activities in the form of an entity or arrangement that a state treats as a separate taxpayer resident of one of the CSs, that state should treat the alienation of a participation in such an entity or arrangement.[149]

3.109 Art. 13 § 3 has been replaced in Model 2017 and now provides that gains that an enterprise of a CS that operates ships or aircraft in international traffic derive from the alienation of such ships or aircraft, or of movable property pertaining to the operation of such ships or aircraft, shall be taxable only in that state. So this provision refers to the state of the enterprise, while previously such gains were taxable only in the CS in which the place of effective management of the enterprise was situated. Moreover the reference to 'boats engaged in inland waterways' has been eliminated. There is no corresponding provision in the MLI. This rule is in line with Art. 8 and Art. 22 § 3 concerning respectively income and capital of international traffic enterprises.[150]

---

148 Commentary to Art. 13 § 22.
149 Commentary to Art. 13 § 26.
150 Commentary to Art. 13 § 28-2.

The Commentary clarifies the respective scope of Art. 13 § 3, Art. 13 § 2 or **3.110** Art. 13 § 5. Art. 13 § 3 applies where the enterprise that alienates the property operates itself the ships/aircrafts either for its own transportation activities or when leasing ships/aircraft on charter fully equipped, manned and supplied. By contrast, Art. 13 § 3 does not apply where the enterprise owning the ships or aircrafts does *not* operate them, for example, where the enterprise leases the property to another person, and in these cases Art. 13 § 2 or Art. 13 § 5 applies.[151]

B. Gains from the alienation of shares

Art. 13 § 1 applies to gains derived from the alienation of immovable property **3.111** situated in the SC, attributing taxing powers to the RC and the SC, while Art. 13 § 5 applies to gains from the alienation of the shares in a company attributing taxing powers *only* to the RC (i.e., the country of the seller). So one of the main problems about taxing capital gains in the SC is that assets may be vested in corporate vehicles of which shares are sold, with the result that the SC, under certain conditions, does not retain the power to tax the capital gains which may be exempt in the country of residence of the seller. This leads to a situation of double exemption.

A special problem is created by the sales of shares of companies owning **3.112** immovable property because if one looks at the formal structure of the share transaction Art. 13 § 5 should apply, while if one looks at the underlying immovable property being transferred Art. 13 § 4 should apply. Certain judicial approaches disregard the formal structure of the share transaction and look at the underlying immovable property being transferred. The traditional approach to this matter is found in a case relating to a multi-tier acquisition structure in which the court relied on the legal structure of the sale rather than on looking at the underlying assets.[152]

Art. 13 § 4 has been expanded by Model 2017. Previously pursuant to Art. 13 **3.113** § 4 gains derived by a resident of the RC from the alienation of shares deriving more than 50 per cent of their value directly or indirectly from immovable property situated in the SC could be taxed in that SC. The threshold was set at a 50 per cent participation which triggered taxation of the entire gains attributable to the shares.[153] Action 6 provided two changes with respect to Art. 13 § 4 of the 2014 version of the Model: (i) introduced a testing period

---

151   Commentary to Art. 13 § 28.1–2. See also Commentary on Art. 22 § 4.1 and 4.2.
152   France, Cour Administrative d'Appel Bordeaux 98BX0558, 9 July 2002.
153   Commentary to Art. 13 § 28.5.

for determining whether the condition on the value threshold is met; and (ii) expanded the scope of interests covered by Art. 13 § 4 to include interests comparable to shares, such as interests in a partnership or trust. Art. 13 § 4 now provides that gains derived by a resident of a CS from the alienation of shares or comparable interests, such as interests in a partnership or trust, may be taxed in the other CS if, at any time during the 365 days preceding the alienation, these shares or comparable interests derive more than 50 per cent of their value directly or indirectly from immovable property, as defined in Art. 6, situated in that other state.

3.114 Art. 9 of the MLI is quite similar but does not refer to 50 per cent of value from immovable property, rather it covers capital gains from alienation of shares or interests of entities deriving their value "principally" from immovable property. Art. 9 of the MLI in fact provides that provisions of a Covered Tax Agreement providing that gains derived by a resident of a CS from the alienation of shares or other rights of participation in an entity may be taxed in the other CS provided that these shares or rights derived more than a certain part of their value from immovable property (real property) situated in that other CS (or provided that more than a certain part of the property of the entity consists of such immovable property): a) shall apply if the relevant value threshold is met at any time during the 365 days preceding the alienation; and b) shall apply to shares or comparable interests, such as interests in a partnership or trust (to the extent that such shares or interests are not already covered) in addition to any shares or rights already covered by the provisions.

3.115 Art. 13 § 4 allows the taxation of the entire gain attributable to the shares or comparable interests to which it applies even where part of the value of these shares or comparable interests is derived from property other than immovable property located in the SC. The determination of whether shares or comparable interests derive, at any time during the 365 days preceding the alienation, more than 50 per cent of their value directly or indirectly from immovable property situated in a CS is done by comparing the value of such immovable property to the value of all the property owned by the company, entity or arrangement without taking into account debts or other liabilities (whether or not secured by mortgages on the relevant immovable property).[154]

3.116 There can be situations in which immovable property, the value of which is taken into account for the purposes of Art. 13 § 4, is alienated by the company or other entity. In this cases Art. 13 § 4 applies anyway if the shares –

---

154 Commentary to Art. 13 § 28.4 and § 28.6 clarifies that the percentage of the value of the shares that must be derived directly or indirectly from immovable property can be varied by CSs.

representing the sold immovable property – are alienated within a period of 365 days after the day when immovable property has itself been alienated. The Commentary 2017 notes that in such a case it could be inappropriate to take account of the value of that property when determining whether Art. 13 § 4 should apply to the gain on the subsequent alienation of the shares or comparable interests, because the alienation of the immovable property is taxable under Art. 13 § 1 in the state where it is situated. So the Commentary recommends an additional clause to deal with this issue.[155]

The Commentary advances some possible exclusions from the operation of Art. 13 § 4, as CSs may decide that such a rule could not apply to gains derived from certain transactions, such as: (i) the alienation of shares of companies that are listed on an approved stock exchange of one of the states, (ii) gains derived from the alienation of shares in the course of qualified corporate reorganizations, (iii) sales of shares held by pension funds and similar entities (exempt from source taxation), or (iv) qualified sales of shares in REITs.[156]   **3.117**

Art. 13 § 5 is a residual rule with respect to other paragraphs of Art. 13: the allocation rule of Art. 13 § 5 has a broad scope as it covers the gains from the alienation of any property other than that referred to in Art. 13 §§ 1–4, and provides that those gains are taxable *only* in the state of which the alienator is a resident. Art. 13 § 5 adopts the same rule as Art. 22 § 4 and this implies that for those gains there is exclusive taxation in the RC. The issue here is twofold. The first issue is whether the taxation in the RC implies that no tax is levied in the SC. The second issue is whether double exemption of capital gains can be attained when the SC does not tax because of the treaty and the RC does not tax because of domestic laws.   **3.118**

The Commentary notes in general that as capital gains are taxed neither by the RC nor by the SC, it is reasonable to pursue a *single taxation principle* (i.e., to avoid double exemption of capital gains), so that the SC has to forego the right to tax conferred on it by the domestic laws only if the RC on which the right to tax is conferred by the treaty makes use thereof.[157] This is particularly relevant with respect to sales of shares in which the combination of exclusive taxation in the RC and domestic participation   **3.119**

---

155   Commentary to Art. 13 § 26.
156   Commentary to Art. 13 § 28. See also: Nouel, Luis, 'The Tax Treaty Treatment of REITs – The Alternative Provisions Included In The Commentaries On The 2008 OECD Model' (2008) 48 *Eur. Tax.* 477.
157   Commentary to Art. 13 § 21.

exemption in the same RC can lead to double non-taxation.[158] A different outcome is found in cases in which effective double non-taxation is allowed by the treaty.[159] There is however an alternative model of taxation in which the SC has the power to levy an exit charge.[160]

3.120 The Commentary expressly acknowledges that since Art. 13 as a whole does not contain special rules for gains from the alienation of shares in a company (other than shares of a company dealt with in Art. 13 § 4), or of securities, bonds, debentures and the like, such gains are taxable only in the RC (the state of which the alienator is a resident). The characterization of securities can be rather complex.[161]

3.121 In most instances the article of the treaty about capital gains on shares attributes exclusive taxation to the country of the seller, irrespective of the structure of the transaction[162] but, in certain cases, a treaty clause attributes taxing rights also to the SC if there is a sale of a *'substantial interest'* in a company (i.e., when the vendor has a participation which exceeds a pre-defined threshold).

3.122 The 'beneficial owner' concept has been extended from the typical cases involving interest or dividends to transactions concerning the sale of shares. In these situations, the problem is whether an intermediate entity (e.g., a holding company or a trust) selling the shares of companies is in fact the beneficial owner of the capital gains.

3.123 The Commentary provides guidelines for the redemption of securities: the difference between the selling price and the par value of the shares attributed by a shareholder to the issuing company in connection with the liquidation of such company or the reduction of its paid-up capital, may be treated in the state of which the company is a resident as a distribution of accumulated profits and *not* as capital gains realized by them.[163] Judicial decisions however

---

158 Germany, Bundesfinanzhof, I R 49/09, 9 December 2010.
159 Sweden, Regeringsrätten, RÅ 2004 not. 59, 25 March 2004.
160 Sweden, Högsta förvaltningsdomstolen, 6843-10, 7 June 2011.
161 Germany, Bundesfinanzhof, I R 257/78, 19 May 1982; Canada, Tax Review Board, *Gadsen v. Her Majesty the Queen*, 25 January 1983.
162 Australia, Federal Court of Australia – Full Court, *Virgin Holdings SA v. Federal Commissioner of Taxation*, 10 October 2008; Australia, Federal Court of Australia – Full Court, *Lamesa Holdings BV v. Commissioner of Taxation*, 20 August 1997.
163 Commentary to Art. 13 § 31.

do not follow this approach[164] and generally treat redemptions under the dividends article.[165]

Art. 13 § 4 applies to capital gains derived from the alienation of shares **3.124** acquired upon the exercise of a stock option granted to an employee or member of a board of directors, while Att. 15 or 16 apply to the benefits derived from the stock option.[166]

---

164   The Netherlands, Hoge Raad der Nederlanden, 38.461, 12 December 2003.
165   Germany, Bundesfinanzhof, I R 43/98, 21 October 1999.
166   Commentary to Art. 13 § 32. See Commentary to Art. 15 §§ 12.2–12.5 and Commentary to Art. 16 § 3.1.

4

DISPUTE SETTLEMENT AND ENFORCEMENT

4.01 A foreign investor which operates in the country of destination through a PE or separate corporate vehicle (and also when there is isolated income) is often confronted with disputes involving the Tax Authorities of the CSs. This chapter focuses on the the main aspects that need to be considered in respect to dispute settlement and enforcement, first by discussing the mutual agreement procedure (MAP) (§ I), then by looking at how transfer price allocation is managed in tax treaties (§ II), and finally discussing the relevance of information in tax treaties (§ III).

I. THE MUTUAL AGREEMENT PROCEDURE

4.02 Before Model 2017, Art. 25 § 1 provided that if a person considers that the actions of one or both of the CSs result or will result for him in taxation not in accordance with the Convention, then he may, irrespective of the remedies provided by the domestic laws of those states, present his case to the CS of which the petitioner was a resident or the CS of which the petitioner was a national if the case came under § 1 of Art. 24.[1]

---

1   On the MAP before the BEPS Project: Altman, Zvi, *Dispute Resolution under Tax Treaties* (IBFD 2005); Dourado, Ana Paula and Pistone, Pasquale (eds), 'Some Critical Thoughts on the Introduction of

Art. 25 § 1 has been modified by Model 2017 in the sense that the aggrieved **4.03**
person may, irrespective of the remedies provided by the domestic law of those
states, present his case to the Competent Authority of either CS. So the
limitation that imposed the presentation of the case only to one CS has been
eliminated. The option to present his case to the Competent Authority of
either CS is to reinforce the principle that access to MAP should be as widely
available as possible and to provide flexibility. Art. 16 of the MLI contains the
same rule. The case must be presented within three years from the first
notification of the action resulting in taxation not in accordance with the
Convention.[2]

There are three types of MAP which are regulated by Art. 25 as a whole and **4.04**
which will be analysed in this chapter:

1.   type-1 (Art. 25 § 1, *adjudicative MAP*) – taxation not in accordance with
     the treaty;
2.   type-2 (Art. 25 § 3, first part, *administrative MAP*) – interpretation/
     application of the treaty;
3.   type-3 (Art. 25 § 3, second part, *legislative MAP*) – elimination of double
     taxation in cases not provided for in the treaty.

The administrative and legislative MAP belong to an expanded form of MAP
defined here as '*normative MAP*', which includes also *arbitration*.

The MAP is an alternative to domestic litigation because Art. 25 § 1 is **4.05**
available to the taxpayers affected, without depriving them of the ordinary
legal remedies: the first stage takes place exclusively in either CS, while the
second stage implies the mutual resolution of disputes through a mutual
agreement between Competent Authorities.[3] Moreover the MAP is a remedy
to misapplication of the Convention because it constitutes a special procedure

---

Arbitration in Tax Treaties' (2014) 42 *Intertax* 158; Groen, Gerrit, 'Arbitration in Bilateral Tax Treaties'
(2002) 30 *Intertax* 1; Lang, Michael and Zuger, Mario (eds), *Settlement of Disputes under Tax Treaty Law*
(Kluwer Law International 2003).

2   On the MAP in the BEPS Project: Groen, Gerrit, 'The Nature and Scope of the Mandatory Arbitration
    Provision in the OECD Multilateral Convention', (2017) 71 *Bull. Intl. Taxn.* 11; Pit, H.M., 'Arbitration
    under the OECD Multilateral Instrument: Reservations, Options and Choices', (2017) 71 *Bull. Intl. Taxn.*
    10; Arora, Hari, 'An Evaluation of the Measures in Action 14 of the Action Plan of the OECD/G20 BEPS
    Initiative Intended to Make Dispute Resolution More Effective', (2017) 71 *Bull. Intl. Taxn.* 5; Toledo Pires
    de Oliveira, Philippe, 'Action 14 of the OECD/G20 Base Erosion and Profit Shifting Initiative: Making
    Dispute Resolution More Effective – Did Action 14 "Piggyback" on the Initiative?', (2017) 71 *Bull. Intl.*
    Taxn. 1; Markham, Michelle, 'Seeking New Directions in Dispute Resolution Mechanisms: Do We Need a
    Revised Mutual Agreement Procedure?', (2016) 70 *Bull. Intl. Taxn* 82.
3   Commentary to Art. 25 § 7.

outside domestic laws set in motion solely in cases coming within Art. 25 § 1, i.e., a MAP case can be raised only if the Convention is affected.[4]

4.06 The Model/Commentary 2017 has significantly reinforced the MAP and broadened its scope. In addition to the three types of MAP listed above, the Commentary envisages that the object of Art. 25 is to promote, through MAPs, the consistent treatment of individual cases and the same interpretation and/or application of the provisions of the Convention in both states, and that domestic courts should take account of such agreements in light of the principles of international law for the interpretation of treaties, as embodied in Artt. 31 and 32 of the VCLT. Another expansion of the scope of MAP is that the application of treaty provisions has been delegated by the CSs to the Competent Authorities and the agreements reached by the Competent Authorities in these matters legally govern the application of these provisions. For example, subparagraph d) of Art. 4 § 2, provides that the Competent Authorities shall resolve by mutual agreement certain cases where an individual is a resident of both CSs under Art. 4 § 1.[5]

4.07 Further expansion of the scope of MAP are multilateral MAPs and multilateral advance pricing arrangements ('APAs'). The combination of bilateral tax conventions concluded among several states may allow the Competent Authorities of these states to resolve multilateral cases by MAP. This approach can be adopted to address allocation of profits between the PEs that an enterprise has in two different states with which the state of the enterprise has tax conventions. In these cases the Competent Authorities may have regard to considerations of equity to find an appropriate solution, for example when a number of associated enterprises of different states are involved in a series of integrated controlled transactions and there are bilateral tax conventions among the states of all the enterprises.

4.08 By contrast, APAs can determine, in advance, the transfer pricing of controlled transactions between associated enterprises of several states determining on a multilateral basis the transfer pricing for the controlled transactions. A multilateral MAP and APA may be achieved either through the negotiation of a single agreement between all the Competent Authorities of the states concerned or through the negotiation of separate, but consistent, bilateral mutual agreements.[6] Finally under the domestic laws of some countries, taxpayers are permitted to amend a previously-filed tax return to adjust

---

4   Commentary to Art. 25 § 8. See: United States, US District Court for the District of New Jersey, *Komet Inc. and Konetehdas Oy Komet v. Republic of Finland*, 1 February 2002.

5   Commentary to Art. 25 § 6.3.

6   Commentary to Art. 25 §§ 38.1–38.5 and 52.

the profits attributable to a PE to reflect an attribution of profits on the basis of Art. 7 and in these cases Competent Authorities under Art. 25 may use the MAP to reflect such adjustments.

The Model provides, in the Annex to Commentary to Art. 25, a Sample **4.09** Mutual Agreement on Arbitration. Moreover Art. 16 of the MLI improves dispute resolution through the MAP, upholding the right of every taxpayer to complain within at least three years from notification of the act giving rise to non-compliance. Art. 16 MAP applies in three cases: a) if an authority considers a complaint to be duly motivated but cannot solve the issue alone; b) in case of difficulties or doubts with respect to a treaty; or c) in cases of any other issues in relation to double taxation even outside the scope of a treaty. The implementation of any MAP is notwithstanding any national law time limits. Artt. 18–26 of the MLI regulate mandatory binding arbitration in detail: where the Competent Authorities are unable to reach an agreement concerning a case pursuant to the MAP within a period of two years, unresolved issues shall, at the request of the person presenting the case, be submitted to arbitration.

A. The adjudicative MAP

1. Cases and activation

The type-1 adjudicative MAP (Art. 25 § 1) is applied in typical treaty cases, as **4.10** well as in cases dealing with the application of transfer price rules, but certain issues are not susceptible to MAP. The treaty cases of MAP by way of example involve: attribution of profits to a PE (Art. 7 § 2); the excess part of interest and royalties (Art. 9, Art. 11 § 6, Art. 12 § 4); the determination of residence (Art. 4 § 2); the existence of a PE (Art. 5); the temporary nature of the services performed by an employee (Art. 15 § 2); the thin cap re-characterization of interest into dividends; and relief from withholding tax (procedural aspects).[7]

MAP also applies to problems of double taxation that occur in the context of **4.11** corresponding adjustments, or resulting from adjustments made to profits by reason of transfer price.[8] MAP is applicable in the absence of double taxation, if taxation is in contravention of the Convention, i.e., when taxpayer nationals of CS1 and taxpayer residents of CS2 are subjected in CS2 to discriminatory treatment under Art. 24 § 1. When a taxpayer non-resident of either CS has a PE in CS1 through which he derives income (or capital) in CS2 there is

---

7   Spain, Tribunal Supremo (Supreme Court), 2891/1998, 15 April 2003.
8   Commentary to Art. 25 § 10.

concurrent limited tax jurisdiction which is outside the scope of the Convention, as the Convention applies only to persons who are residents of one or both of the CSs and this situation can be settled by MAP.

4.12 Certain issues are not susceptible to MAP, for example, MAP can be denied for abusive transactions or serious violations, or because of constitutional constraints but the Commentary 2017 clarifies that MAP can be pursued when anti-abuse rules are applied and should be considered as a layer of dispute settlement parallel to those provided in domestic constitutional orders.[9] The mutual agreement may conflict with domestic constitutional rules preserving the principle of legality, but the Commentary observes that even domestic constitutional laws do not justify a failure to meet treaty obligations because under Art. 27 of the VCLT any justification needs to be found in the terms of the Convention itself, in accordance with accepted treaty interpretation principles.[10]

4.13 The MAP can be set in motion by a taxpayer without waiting until the taxation considered by her/him to be 'not in accordance with the Convention' has been charged against or notified to her/him. In such a case however, the taxpayer must establish that the 'actions of one or both of the CSs' *will result* in such taxation, so this taxation appears as a risk which is not merely possible but probable. For example, if a change to a CS's domestic laws results in a person being subjected to taxation not in accordance with the Convention, that person could set the MAP in motion as soon as: (i) the laws have been amended and that person has derived the relevant income; or (ii) it becomes probable that the person will derive that income. So the MAP is also activated by probable risk of double taxation, a concept which includes transfer price cases where there is substantial doubt whether the taxpayer's related party will be able to obtain a corresponding adjustment in the other CS. Art. 25 § 5 arbitration is not activated in these cases.

4.14 There is a twofold requirement for admissibility of objections as they must be presented: (i) to the Competent Authority of either CS and (ii) within three years of the 'first notification' of the action which gives rise to taxation which is not in accordance with the Convention.[11] The Commentary provides a liberal interpretation of the three-year time limit which protects administrations against late objections as it specifies that the 'first notification' should be

---

9   Commentary to Art. 25 § 26.
10 Commentary to Art. 25 § 27. See: Germany, Bundesfinanzhof, I R 111/08, 2 September 2009; Germany, Bundesfinanzhof, I R 90/08, 2 September 2009.
11 Commentary to Art. 25 § 16.

interpreted in the way most favourable to the taxpayer.[12] The time of notification varies depending on the type of situation: probable risk of double taxation; notice of assessment; self-assessment; or withholding tax.

When there is no actual taxation act but just the probable risk of double **4.15** taxation the taxpayer has the right to initiate the MAP before the three-year time limit begins.[13] In case of notice of assessment, domestic laws govern when that notice is regarded as 'given', and if there are no such rules the relevant time is the actual physical receipt or the time when the notice would normally be expected to have arrived at the relevant address.[14] If there is self-assessment the time of notification is the notification of the fact of taxation to the taxpayer, or any other circumstance that would cause a reasonably prudent person to conclude that the taxation was contrary to the Convention, such as a judicial decision. The time begins to run only when the circumstance materializes.

The Commentary 2017 suggests that where a taxpayer pays additional tax in **4.16** connection with the filing of an amended return reflecting a bona fide taxpayer-initiated adjustment, the starting point of the three-year time limit is the notice of assessment or liability resulting from the amended return, rather than the time when the additional tax was paid.[15] Finally, when the taxpayer is subject to a withholding tax the time limit begins to run from the moment when the income is paid, but if the taxpayer proves that only at a later date did he/she know that the deduction had been made, the time limit will begin from that date.[16] The three-year period continues to run *while* domestic remedies are pursued in national courts.[17]

Even if the MAP article requires that objections be presented to the Com- **4.17** petent Authorities, courts have addressed the question whether a request to initiate a MAP by way of an appeal against a tax assessment is admissible.[18] Another question that has been raised before courts is whether objections suspend domestic remedies.[19]

---

12   Commentary to Art. 25 §§ 20–21.
13   Ibid.
14   Commentary to Art. 25 § 22.
15   Commentary to Art. 25 § 23.
16   Commentary to Art. 25 § 24.
17   Commentary to Art. 25 § 25-1.
18   Austria, Verwaltungsgerichtshof, 2000/13/0031, 12 September 2001; United States, US Tax Court, *Herbert A. Filler v. Commissioner of Internal Revenue*, 27 May 1980; United States, US District Court for the District of Columbia, *Yamaha Motor Corp. USA v. United States (Internal Revenue Service)*, 19 December 1991.
19   Canada, Tax Court of Canada, *Caron v. Her Majesty the Queen*, 2 February 1998, [1998] A.C.I. 85; Austria, Verwaltungsgerichtshof, 99/15/0265, 3 August 2000.

4.18 MAP and domestic remedies may overlap because the taxpayer may use only the MAP, only domestic remedies, or both domestic remedies and MAP. Moreover when domestic remedies and MAP are pursued one of the two procedures can lead to a decision before the other. There are essentially three approaches that can be adopted in isolation or in combination by individual countries:

1. the MAP can be activated *only* after a domestic judicial decision is rendered;
2. the MAP can be activated *only if* domestic remedies are relinquished; and
3. the MAP can be activated and reached *also* before a domestic judicial decision is rendered.

(a) MAP can be activated only after a domestic judicial decision is rendered

4.19 When a country adopts a solution in which the MAP can be activated *only* after a domestic judicial decision is rendered, a conflict between a domestic judicial decision and the mutual agreement can occur.[20] In cases where a domestic judicial decision has been already issued in the CS where the MAP originated, the taxpayer may still wish to pursue the MAP and so there are two alternative doctrines: according to the former, the Competent Authorities are *not* bound by the domestic judicial decision, while according to the latter the Competent Authorities are bound by the domestic judicial decision. This outcome varies depending on domestic legal contexts.

(b) MAP can be activated only if domestic remedies are relinquished

4.20 When a country adopts a solution in which the MAP can be activated *only* if domestic remedies are relinquished, no conflict between the domestic judicial decision and the mutual agreement occurs (this solution is found, i.e., in the EU Arbitration Directive). Audit settlements often conclude a litigation without the need to reach a judicial decision: the Commentary 2017 suggests that a taxpayer should thus not be required, as part of an audit settlement, to give up the right provided by Art. 25 § 1 to present its case to a Competent Authority since this may impede the proper application of a tax treaty.[21] A variant of this approach is that the MAP *must* be activated and concluded before a domestic judicial procedure is activated *(pre-emptive MAP)*.[22]

---

20 Commentary to Art. 25 § 35.
21 Commentary to Art. 25 §§ 45.1.
22 Israel, Beit Mishpat Mehozi (District Court) Tel Aviv, *Jeteck Technologies Ltd. v. Assessing Officer Kfar Saba*, 7 April 2005.

(c)   MAP can be activated and also reached before a domestic judicial decision is rendered

When a country adopts a solution in which the MAP can be activated and also   **4.21** reached before a domestic judicial decision is rendered, a possible conflict between the domestic judicial decision and the mutual agreement can occur. The Commentary suggests that in these cases when the judicial decision is issued the arbitration process will terminate.[23] The Commentary also suggests that the Competent Authority of the CS where the MAP originated should not wait for the final adjudication, and inform the taxpayer whether it accepts a request by a taxpayer to defer acceptance of the mutual agreement until a domestic judicial decision is rendered. This should not cause time to expire before the two-year period of Art. 25 of § 5 (arbitration).[24]

The position of some states is that a MAP procedure may not be initiated by a   **4.22** taxpayer unless payment of all or a specified portion of the tax amount in dispute has been made.[25] The Commentary is in favour of the suspension of tax collection on the basis of several reasons: the payment of outstanding tax should not be a requirement to initiate the MAP if it is not a requirement before initiating domestic remedies; the requirement to pay tax prior to MAP is a cost for the taxpayer equal to the time value of the money and a cash flow burden inconsistent with the Convention's goals of eliminating barriers to cross-border trade; finally interest and penalty payments should not be imposed in a way that effectively discourages taxpayers from initiating a MAP.[26] The Commentary also suggest that states may provide that the suspension of assessment and collection procedures during the period that any MAP proceeding is pending are available under the same conditions as apply to a person pursuing a domestic administrative or judicial remedy.[27]

Changes to the Commentary to Model 2017 addressed the problem of interest   **4.23** and administrative penalties: the Competent Authorities may resolve through MAP issues related to interest and administrative penalties that give rise to difficulties or doubts as to the application of the Convention and adopt flexible approaches to provide relief from interest accessory to the tax liability that is the object of a mutual agreement procedure request.[28]

---

23   Commentary to Art. 25 §§ 79.1.
24   Commentary to Art. 25 § 34.
25   Commentary to Art. 25 § 46. Canada, Tax Court of Canada, *Caron v. Her Majesty the Queen*, 2 February 1998.
26   Commentary to Art. 25 §§ 47–48.
27   Commentary to Art. 25 § 47-1.
28   Commentary to Art. 25 §§ 49-1 and 49-3.

2. MAP procedure and implementation

4.24 Art. 25 § 2 sets out the basic MAP procedure and provides that the Competent Authority of the CS where the MAP originated shall endeavour, if the objection appears to it to be justified and if it is not itself able to arrive at a satisfactory solution, to resolve the case by mutual agreement with the Competent Authority of the other CS, with a view to the avoidance of 'taxation not in accordance with the Convention'. Any agreement reached shall be implemented in spite of any time limits in the domestic laws of the CSs.

4.25 Essentially there are two stages to the MAP procedure: the first stage involves dealings between the taxpayer and the CS where the MAP originated, while the second stage involves dealings between the CSs.

4.26 The first stage of the MAP procedure establishes, on the one hand, the right of the taxpayer to apply, and, on the other hand, certain duties of the Competent Authorities. The taxpayer has the right to apply to the Competent Authority of either CS.[29] Correspondingly the Competent Authority is under an obligation to consider whether the objection is *justified*, and, if it appears to be justified, to *take action*. The Commentary specifies that the objection is justified when it is reasonable to believe that there will be, in either of the CSs, taxation not in accordance with the Convention.[30] If the Competent Authority considers that the taxation complained of is due wholly or in part to a measure taken in the taxpayer's CS, the resolution must be reached unilaterally by the requested Competent Authority without resort to MAP through an adjustment or allowing such reliefs as appear to be justified.[31]

4.27 The Competent Authorities have a duty to negotiate, but do not have a duty to resolve the dispute, so that stage 2 opens with an approach to the Competent Authority of the other state by the Competent Authority to which the taxpayer has applied, but there is no duty to reach a decision.[32] The requirement in Art. 25 § 2 that the Competent Authority 'shall endeavour' to resolve the case by mutual agreement with the Competent Authority of the other CS means that the Competent Authorities are obliged to seek to resolve the case in a fair and objective manner, on its merits, in accordance with the

---

29 Commentary to Art. 25 § 31.
30 Commentary to Art. 25 § 31.1. Spain, Tribunal Supremo (Supreme Court), 2891/1998, 15 April 2003.
31 Commentary to Art. 25 § 32.
32 Commentary to Art. 25 §§ 36–37. See: Germany, Bundesfinanzhof, VII R 16/78, 12 February 1979.

terms of the Convention and applicable principles of international law on the interpretation of treaties.[33]

In seeking a mutual agreement, Competent Authorities must first determine **4.28** their position in the light of the rules of their respective taxation laws and Convention and subsidiarily have regard to considerations of equity.

The Competent Authority has a duty to activate the procedure, not the local **4.29** offices.[34] Competent Authorities should: notify taxpayers as soon as possible of their intention to make a transfer price adjustment, as well as communicate with each other and publicize domestic rules, guidelines and procedures concerning MAP.[35] Taxpayers should be given every reasonable opportunity to present the relevant facts and arguments. Formalities should be kept to a minimum and mutual agreement cases should be settled on their merits and not by reference to any balance of the results in other cases.

The fact that a mutual agreement is reached by the Competent Authorities **4.30** creates a set of legal issues concerning the implementation of such an instrument within the domestic laws of the CSs.[36] The Commentary takes the view that the mutual agreement is binding because the last sentence of Art. 25 § 2 provides that any agreement reached shall be implemented in spite of any time limits in the domestic laws of the CSs,[37] and suggests that subsequent unexpected changes that alter the fundamental basis of a mutual agreement should be considered as requiring revision of the agreement.[38]

The issue whether the mutual agreement is binding has been addressed by **4.31** national courts. There are essentially two views: according to the former the mutual agreement is binding, according to the latter it is not binding.[39] This position is generally complemented by the view that the mutual agreement prevails over administrative decisions.[40] National courts have sometimes taken

---

33 Commentary to Art. 25 § 5.1.
34 Austria, Verwaltungsgerichtshof, 99/15/0265, 3 August 2000.
35 Commentary to Art. 25 § 40–41.
36 Avery Jones, John F., 'The Relationship Between the Mutual Agreement Procedure and Internal Law', (1999) 8 *EC Tax Review* 4; Skaar, Arvid Aage, 'The Legal Nature of Mutual Agreements under Tax Treaties', (1992) 26 *Tax Notes Int.* 1441.
37 Commentary to Art. 25 § 29.1.
38 Commentary to Art. 25 § 29.2.
39 Norway, Høyesterett (Supreme Court), 878/2001, 5 June 2002, *Rt.*, 2002, 718; Belgium, Hof van Beroep Gent, 5 December 2000.
40 Austria, Verwaltungsgerichtshof, 99/15/0265, 3 August 2000.

the position that the mutual agreement is not binding, generally on the basis of constitutional domestic constraints.[41]

4.32 Another issue which arose at national judicial level was whether the treaty, as interpreted by the courts, prevails over a conflicting interpretation of the mutual agreement. Generally, courts rely on their interpretation of the treaty to override the mutual agreement. The issue has been addressed in Belgium in a series of cases concerning the treatment of income of the so-called 'active partners'.[42]

4.33 The Commentary observes that the implementation of a mutual agreement should normally be made subject to the acceptance of such mutual agreement by the taxpayer, and the taxpayer's withdrawal from domestic remedies.[43] These two requirements however are not always met. A problematic situation is one in which the mutual agreement is issued while domestic remedies by the involved taxpayer are still pending: the Commentary suggests that Competent Authorities or courts should accept a request by a taxpayer to defer acceptance of mutual agreement until domestic remedies have ended.[44]

B. Expanded forms of MAP: normative MAP and arbitration

4.34 Type-1 adjudicative MAP under Art. 25 § 1 is a procedure which does not ensure a form of binding dispute settlement. The administrative and legislative MAP under Art. 25 § 3 (type-2 and 3 'normative MAP') expands the protection of tax treaty dispute settlement, while Art. 25 § 5 arbitration ensures a binding solution (if accepted by all parties).

4.35 Type-2 MAP addresses general and practical difficulties in the interpretation or application of the Convention (Art. 25 § 3 first sentence). *General difficulties* concern a category of taxpayers, even if they have arisen in connection with an individual case, while *practical difficulties* are those which could impair or impede the normal operation of the Convention, for example, the relief from tax deducted from dividends, interest and royalties. Typical cases of the type 2 MAP complete or clarify the definition of a term, settle difficulties that may emerge from the new system of taxation, determine conditions for

---

41 Germany, Bundesfinanzhof, I R 111/08, 2 September 2009. Germany, Bundesfinanzhof, I R 90/08, 2 September 2009; United States, US Court of Appeals for the Federal Circuit, *Xerox Corp. v. United States*, 6 December 1994.

42 Belgium, Hof van Beroep, G 02/6, 28 February 2002.

43 Commentary to Art. 25 § 45.

44 Commentary to Art. 25 § 42.

re-characterization of interest as dividends under thin cap rules,[45] and have a binding effect on administrative agencies.

Under Art. 25 § 3 first sentence the Competent Authorities may also resolve a case presented under Art. 25 § 3 with the Competent Authority of any third state if taxation on income or on capital in that third state is likely to affect or be affected by the resolution of the case.[46] Mutual agreements rendered in connection with these difficulties go beyond the individual application of the treaty to a specific situation and provide evidence of country practices.[47]   **4.36**

Finally, on the basis of Art. 25 § 3 last sentence Competent Authorities may also consult together for the elimination of double taxation: this is type-3 MAP, which is aimed at elimination of double taxation in cases not provided for in the Convention. For example, the situation of a resident of a third country with PEs in both CSs creates double taxation which should be addressed by the MAP. In that situation the Competent Authorities of the CSs agree to apply their respective domestic tax laws and provide relief from double taxation of the profits of such PEs. Mutual agreements resulting from type-3 MAP tend to have a normative outcome because they take the form of an agreed regulation that covers sets of situations not originally covered by the treaty. Art. 25 § 3 last sentence does not, however, allow the CSs to eliminate double taxation where the provision of such relief would contravene their respective domestic laws or is not authorised by the provisions of other applicable tax treaties.[48]   **4.37**

Art. 25 § 4 provides that the Competent Authorities of the CSs may communicate with each other directly, including through a joint commission consisting of themselves or their representatives, for the purpose of reaching an agreement in the sense of the preceding paragraphs. The Commentary provides broad guidelines about consultations, direct communication, means of communication, joint commission for communication, guarantees to tax-payers, the right to make representations, and the right to be assisted by counsel.   **4.38**

Art. 25 § 5 introducing arbitration was established in the Model in 2014 and aimed at ensuring a binding treaty-level solution of disputes. The Model 2017 has amended § 5 of Art. 25. The difference from the previous paragraph is   **4.39**

---

45 Commentary to Art. 25 § 51.
46 Commentary to Art. 25 § 55.2.
47 Germany, Bundesfinanzhof, I R 111/08, 2 September 2009. Germany, Bundesfinanzhof, I R 90/08, 2 September 2009.
48 Commentary to Art. 25 § 55.1.

that the period of two years after which the arbitration procedure is activated – instead of starting from the presentation of the case to the Competent Authority of the other CS – starts now from the date when all the information required by the Competent Authorities in order to address the case has been provided to both Competent Authorities.

4.40 More precisely the text of Art. 25 § 5 is the following:

> Where,
>
>> a) under paragraph 1, a person has presented a case to the Competent Authority of a CS on the basis that the actions of one or both of the CSs have resulted for that person in taxation not in accordance with the provisions of this Convention, and
>> b) the Competent Authorities are unable to reach an agreement to resolve that case pursuant to paragraph 2 within two years from the presentation of the case to the Competent Authority of the other CS date when all the information required by the Competent Authorities in order to address the case has been provided to both Competent Authorities,
>
> any unresolved issues arising from the case shall be submitted to arbitration if the person so requests in writing. These unresolved issues shall not, however, be submitted to arbitration if a decision on these issues has already been rendered by a court or administrative tribunal of either state. Unless a person directly affected by the case does not accept the mutual agreement that implements the arbitration decision, that decision shall be binding on both CSs and shall be implemented notwithstanding any time limits in the domestic laws of these states. The Competent Authorities of the CSs shall by mutual agreement settle the mode of application of this paragraph.

4.41 So Art. 25 § 5 provides now that *unresolved issues* about which the Competent Authorities were unable to reach an agreement under Art. 25 § 2 within two years, are solved through an arbitration process at the request of the person who presented the case. These *'unresolved issues'* are those which prevent the conclusion of a mutual agreement and only those can be submitted to arbitration.

4.42 The Commentary makes it clear that the arbitration is an extension of the MAP that deals with unresolved issues, and not an alternative measure to the MAP. If the Competent Authorities have reached a mutual agreement that does not leave any unresolved issues, then there cannot be arbitration. By contrast, if the mutual agreement leaves some unresolved issues, then only these unresolved issues can be brought to arbitration.

4.43 Under Art. 25 § 5, the resolution of the case as a whole continues to be reached through the MAP, while the resolution of a particular issue, which is preventing the mutual agreement, is handled through an arbitration process.

This distinguishes the arbitration established by Art. 25 § 5 from other commercial or government-private party arbitration where the jurisdiction of the arbitral panel extends to resolving the whole case.

If a MAP has not been previously activated, no arbitration can be reached: the **4.44** taxpayer is able to request arbitration of unresolved issues in all cases dealt with under the MAP, but where the MAP is not available, Art. 25 § 5 is not applicable. In some states, Art. 25 § 5 cannot be introduced in the treaties because constitutional barriers prevent arbitrators from deciding tax issues, or access to Art. 25 § 5 is restricted to cases involving factual or PE issues or transfer price.

Pursuant to Art. 25 § 5 a person, who has presented a case to a Competent **4.45** Authority of a CS (Art. 25 § 1) on the basis that the actions of one or both of the CSs have resulted for that person in taxation not in accordance with the Convention, may request that any unresolved issues arising from the case be submitted to arbitration. This request may be made at any time after a period of two years that begins when all the information required by the Competent Authorities in order to address the case has been provided to both Competent Authorities (not, as before, from the date when the case was presented to the Competent Authority). Recourse to arbitration is not automatic; the person who presented the case may prefer to wait beyond the end of the two-year period or not to pursue the case. The Commentary suggests that the two-year period will be suspended when the MAP itself is suspended, for example, where the MAP case concerns issues that are pending before a court or administrative tribunal and a CS.[49] The two-year period starts when all the information required by the Competent Authorities has been provided. The sample mutual agreement included in the Annex of the Commentary suggests a process that is similar to the one used in Part VI of the MLI.

The Commentary 2017 emphasizes the last statement of Art. 25, which **4.46** provides that the Competent Authorities of the CSs shall by mutual agreement settle the mode of application of Art. 25 § 1. This requires the Competent Authorities to agree on the mode of application of that process so that most of the procedural aspects of the process are determined in an agreement between the Competent Authorities based on the sample 'mutual agreement on arbitration' included in the Annex, or by a Convention based on the example provided for by Part VI of the MLI.[50]

---

49 Commentary to Art. 25 § 70.2.
50 Commentary to Art. 25 §§ 65.1 and 85.

4.47   A case is not considered to have been resolved as long as there is *at least one issue* on which the Competent Authorities disagree. The two Competent Authorities cannot deny a request for arbitration if there are still unresolved issues. By contrast, the two Competent Authorities can deny a request for arbitration if there are no unresolved issues. In practice if the Competent Authorities agree on all issues, they can prevent arbitration by deciding all those issues.

4.48   A case is considered to have been presented to the Competent Authority, if sufficient information has been presented to that Competent Authority to allow it to decide whether the objection underlying the case appears to be justified. The arbitration process is available where the person considers that taxation not in accordance with the Convention has already/actually resulted from the actions of one or both of the CSs, while it is not available where it is argued that such taxation will eventually result from such actions.

4.49   The decisions reached in the arbitration are reflected in the mutual agreement that is presented to the taxpayer and to persons directly affected by the decision. The purpose of Art. 25 § 5 is to allow the Competent Authorities to reach a conclusion on the unresolved issues that prevent a mutual agreement from being reached. When that conclusion is achieved though the aid of arbitration, the essential character of the mutual agreement remains the same.

4.50   The unresolved issues cannot be submitted to arbitration if a decision on these issues has already been rendered by a court or administrative tribunal of either state. Unless a person directly affected by the case does not accept the mutual agreement that implements the arbitration decision, that decision shall be binding on both CSs and shall be implemented notwithstanding any time limits in the domestic laws of these states. The Competent Authorities of the CSs by mutual agreement settle the mode of application of this § 1.

4.51   The arbitration decision is only binding with respect to the specific issues submitted to arbitration. Some states may wish to allow the Competent Authorities to depart from the arbitration decision, provided that they can agree on a different solution. Competent Authorities of CSs shall by mutual agreement settle the mode of application of Art. 25 § 5 through an exchange of diplomatic notes.

II. TRANSFER PRICE IN TAX TREATIES

Cross-border controlled transactions among enterprises under common own- **4.52** ership or control are often manipulated through transfer pricing techniques to distort taxable income or by deducting excess costs in high-tax jurisdictions and shifting those costs as profits to low-tax jurisdictions. When these cross-border controlled transactions occur among enterprises under common ownership or control that are resident in two CSs linked by a tax treaty, or when these transactions occur between the head office in CS1 and a PE in CS2, there are treaty transfer price issues.

To address this problem Actions 8, 9, and 10 of the BEPS Project – building **4.53** on the established OECD approach – are aimed at ensuring that transfer pricing outcomes are in line with value creation, but have not lead directly to change of the Model. Treaty transfer price issues are traditionally addressed by attribution rules correlative and adjustments for business profits (Art. 7 §§ 2–3), and by rules about the use of arm's length for associated enterprises (Art. 9).

A. Attribution rules for business profits

Art. 7 § 2 establishes attribution rules based on the separate enterprise fiction **4.54** under which profits are attributed to a PE on an arm's length basis, and Art. 7 § 3 provides a mechanism of correlative adjustments which leads to the elimination of double taxation if the RC and the SC agree on the allocation, or if a binding arbitration is in place.

Art. 7 § 2 applies with respect to dealings between the PE and other parts of **4.55** the enterprise to determine the amount of the profits attributable to the PE and is based on the separate enterprise fiction. More specifically this rule provides that for the purposes of Art. 7 and Arts. 23A–23B, the profits that are attributable in each CS to the PE referred to in Art. 7 § 1 are the profits it might be expected to make, in particular in its dealings with other parts of the enterprise, if it were a separate and independent enterprise engaged in the same/similar activities under the same/similar conditions, taking into account the functions performed, assets used and risks assumed by the enterprise through the PE and through the other parts of the enterprise.

Art. 7 § 2 relies on the so-called 'separate enterprise fiction' according to **4.56** which a PE is a separate enterprise that is independent from the rest of the enterprise of which it is a part, a fiction that rests on the arm's length principle (see Commentary to Art. 9 § 1). Thus the Commentary remarks that profits can be attributed to a PE even though the enterprise as a whole has never made profits for tax/accounting purposes, and also specifies that Art. 7 § 2 does not seek to allocate overall profits of the whole enterprise to a PE and its other parts but simply requires that the profits attributable to a PE be determined as if it were a separate enterprise.[51] How profits are attributable to the PE is related to the business model adopted by a transnational firm.[52]

4.57 The Commentary covers branch-subsidiary equal treatment and observes that the separate and independent enterprise fiction mandated by Art. 7 § 2 should not be restricted to the application of Artt. 7, 23A and 23B, but should also extend to the interpretation/application of other articles of Convention, to ensure that PEs are treated in the same way as subsidiaries.[53] With regard to the equal treatment issue of deduction of expenses for the purposes of Art. 24 § 4 the Commentary notes that PEs must be accorded the same right as resident enterprises to deduct trading expenses that are, in general, deducted from taxable profits. Such deductions should be allowed without any restrictions other than those also imposed on resident enterprises.

4.58 The separate enterprise fiction should lead to the elimination of double taxation through a two-step attribution based on functional analysis and the arm's length approach: the RC must eliminate double taxation on profits properly attributable to PE (Art. 23A or 23B), 'if the SC (state where PE is located) attempts to tax profits that are not attributable to PE under Art. 7, this may result in double taxation of profits that should properly be taxed only in the RC (state of enterprise)'.[54]

4.59 The two-step attribution of profits to a PE under Art. 7 § 2 follows from the calculation of profits (or losses) from all its activities, including transactions with independent enterprises, transactions with associated enterprises (with direct application of OECD transfer price Guidelines), and dealings with other parts of the enterprise.[55]

4.60 Step 1 of the attribution of profits involves a functional analysis that leads to several objectives:

1. attribution to PEs, of rights and obligations arising out of transactions between the enterprise of which PE is a part and separate enterprises;

---

51 Commentary to Art. 7 § 17. In general: Commentary to Art. 25 § 16.
52 Spain, Tribunal Supremo, 1626/2008, 12 January 2012.
53 Commentary to Art. 7 § 33.
54 Commentary to Art. 7 § 18.
55 Commentary to Art. 7 § 20.

2. identification of significant people functions relevant to attribution of *economic ownership of assets* and attribution of economic ownership of assets to PE;
3. identification of significant people functions relevant to *assumption of risks* and attribution of risks to PE;
4. identification of *other functions* of PE;
5. recognition and determination of nature of those dealings between PE and other parts of same enterprise and attribution of capital based on assets and risks attributed to PE.[56]

Step 2 of the attribution of profits then implies that transactions with associated enterprises attributed to PE are priced in accordance with the guidance of OECD transfer price guidelines which are applied by analogy to dealings between the PE and other parts of the enterprise of which it is a part. So the pricing based on an arm's length includes standard *comparability analysis* (characteristics of property or services, economic circumstances and business strategies) and application of the guidelines' transfer price methods.[57] Proper documentation and recourse to the 2010 Report is advised so that taxpayers can demonstrate clearly that it would be appropriate to recognize dealing because this may substantially reduce potential for controversies.[58] **4.61**

The Commentary discusses the effects of the separate enterprise fiction essentially in four headings: the fact that transfer price allocation leads to adjustments in the SC; the relevance of Art. 7 § 2 for the purposes of double taxation relief in the RC; the recognition that the separate enterprise fiction does not create notional income; and that different amounts of attributable profits may emerge as a result of domestic laws of the CSs. **4.62**

There is a twofold effect of Art. 7 § 2. First, transfer price allocation in the framework suggested by the Commentary leads to adjustments in the SC, so *if* the price between the head office and PE exceeds the arm's length price, *then* Art. 7 § 2 authorizes the SC to adjust profits attributable to PE to reflect the arm's length price.[59] Second, Art. 7 § 2 applies not only for purposes of determining profits of the SC but also for application of Artt. 23A and 23B by the RC which must determine profits attributable to PE in order to provide relief from double taxation.[60] **4.63**

---

56 Commentary to Art. 7 § 21.
57 Commentary to Art. 7 § 22.
58 Commentary to Art. 7 §§ 23, 25–26.
59 Commentary to Art. 7 § 24.
60 Commentary to Art. 7 § 27.

4.64 The separate enterprise fiction may lead to profits being attributed to the PE, but may never create notional income.[61] For example the circumstances of a particular case may justify considering that economic ownership of a building used by the PE should be attributed to head office, and in such a case Art. 7 § 2 could require deduction of a notional rent in determining the profits of the PE, but that fiction could not be interpreted as creating income from immovable property in the SC (Art. 6).[62]

4.65 The separate enterprise fiction determines only profits (and allegedly not expenses) that are attributable to a PE: 'once the profits that are attributable to a PE have been determined in accordance with § 2 of Art. 7, it is for the domestic laws of each CS to determine whether and how such profits should be taxed as long as there is conformity with the requirements of Art. 7 § 2' and 'conditions for deductibility of expenses are a matter to be determined by domestic laws, subject to provisions of [the] Convention and, in particular, § 3 of Art. 24 (see § 33 and 34 below)'.[63] The Commentary states, for example, that domestic laws which deny the deduction of expenses not incurred exclusively for the benefit of the PE are in violation of Art. 7 § 2, while domestic law rules that prevent the deduction of certain categories of expenses (e.g., entertainment expenses) are not in violation of Art. 7 § 2.

4.66 The Commentary acknowledges that the separate enterprise fiction based on arm's length may lead to different amounts as a result of domestic laws,[64] and this is a fatal problem of the suggested approach: if binding arbitration is not available then the amount of taxable income in the SC for taxation and in the RC for FTC can differ.[65]

4.67 New Art. 7 § § 2–3 replaced previous §§ 3–5. Art. 7 § 3 on deduction of expenses provided that in determining the profits of a PE, there should be allowed, as deductions, expenses incurred for purposes of PE, including executive and general administrative expenses so incurred, whether in the state in which the PE is situated or elsewhere. Previous Art. 7 § 3 limited the deduction of expenses that directly or indirectly benefited the PE, such as general and administrative expenses (allocated to a PE on a cost-basis). Current Art. 7 § 2 allows only the deduction of an arm's length charge for

---

61   Commentary to Art. 7 § 28-1.
62   Commentary to Art. 7 § 28-2.
63   Commentary to Art. 7 § 30.
64   Commentary to Art. 7 § 31.
65   Commentary to Art. 7 § 32.

these dealings, but recognizes also that all relevant expenses of the enterprise, wherever incurred, be taken into account.[66]

The previous Art. 7 § 4 provided that attribution of profits to a PE was to be done on the basis of an apportionment of the total profits of the enterprise to its various parts. That provision was eliminated because it was difficult to ensure that the result of its application was in accordance with the arm's length principle, for example when manufacturing and selling units were involved.[67]   **4.68**

The previous Art. 7 § 5 provided that 'no profits shall be attributed to a PE by reason of mere purchase by that PE of goods or merchandise for enterprise'. The previous Art. 7 § 5 also provided that profits to be attributed to PE were to be 'determined by the same method year by year unless there is good and sufficient reason to the contrary'. The new approach does not allow for application of such fundamentally different methods and therefore avoids the need for such a provision.   **4.69**

B.   Correlative adjustments of business profits

The Commentary focuses on different aspects of correlative adjustments in respect of the combination of Artt. 7 and 23A/23B in the situation in which the adjustments lead to the same or a different result in the RC and the SC.[68] Art. 7 § 3 establishes a correlative adjustments mechanism aimed at addressing the mismatches that can result from the application of the domestic laws of the CSs and which relies on a combined application of the attribution rule (Art. 7) and the relief rule (Artt. and 23A or 23B). So while Art. 7 restricts the taxing rights of the SC in which the PE is situated, Artt. 23A–23B oblige the RC to provide relief from double taxation and ensures that there is no unrelieved double taxation of profits properly attributable to the PE. The Commentary notes, correctly, that double taxation is avoided when the taxpayer determines profits attributable to the PE in the same manner in the RC and the SC in accordance with the Art. 7 § 2 attribution, because there is the same result for the purposes of Artt. 7 and 23A or 23B (see, however, § 66). For example, if the same arm's length price has been used in both states, then double taxation related to that dealing is eliminated under Artt. 23A or 23B.   **4.70**

---

66   Commentary to Art. 7 §§ 38–43.
67   France, Conseil d'État, 70906, 15 May 1992.
68   Commentary to Art. 7 § 44–52.

4.71 By contrast, double taxation is not avoided when there are mismatches in the RC and the SC because CSs do not reach agreement. The Commentary cites the example of different approaches for determining, on the basis of attribution of 'free' capital to a PE, interest expenses attributable to that PE. In most cases there is no need for adjustments, but it is difficult to reconcile this position with current national audit practices. The Commentary also notes that other remedies are available such as the MAP under Art. 25 or domestic dispute resolution, but the fact is that these mechanisms do not necessarily prevent mismatches (unless binding arbitration is pursued).

4.72 In theory the only solution to prevent double taxation would be to enforce the adjustments mechanism of Art. 7 § 3 through binding arbitration. The Commentary 2017, in light of the fact that binding arbitration recommended by Art. 25 § 5 is a practice that is not adopted by many countries, advances important solutions. First, it notes that under the domestic laws of some countries, taxpayers are permitted to amend a previously-filed tax return to adjust the profits attributable to a PE to reflect an attribution of profits on the basis of Art. 7: in these cases Competent Authorities under Art. 25 may accordingly use the MAP, to reflect domestic adjustments. Second, the Commentary recommends that CSs introduce a provision limiting the length of time during which an adjustment may be made pursuant to Art. 7 § 2 to prevent mismatches over time.[69]

4.73 The adjustment mechanism works as follows: *if* the taxpayer has not determined profits attributable to PE in conformity with Art. 7 § 2, *then* each state is entitled to make adjustments to ensure conformity with Art. 7 § 2. *If* one state makes an adjustment in conformity with Art. 7 § 2, *then* the other state makes a reciprocal adjustment, so that double taxation is prevented through the combined application of Art. 7 § 2, and of Art. 23A or 23B.[70] So the initial adjustment of either the SC or the RC leads to a secondary spontaneous adjustment by respectively the RC or the SC.

4.74 Art. 7 § 3 does not specify the method by which a corresponding adjustment is to be made. The initial adjustment could be made by the SC in which the PE is situated, but the adjustment could also be granted in the RC through adjustment to exemption or FTC under Artt. 23A and 23B. Moreover, if the initial adjustment is made by the RC where the parent company is situated, the correlative adjustment could be made by the SC in which the PE is situated by re-opening assessment, or by reducing the taxable income of PE by

---

69 Commentary to Art. 7 §§ 59.1 and 62.
70 Commentary to Art. 7 §§ 50 and 65.

an appropriate amount. Art. 7 § 3 leaves open the question of whether there is a time limitation for a state to make an appropriate adjustment to profits attributable to a PE following an upward revision of these profits in the other state.[71]

Art. 7 § 3 shares the main features of Art. 9 § 2 because it applies reciprocally **4.75** *only if* initial adjustment has been made either by the SC where the PE is situated or by the RC. However a corresponding adjustment is *not* automatically to be made under Art. 7 § 3 simply because the profits attributed to the PE have been adjusted by one of the CSs. Regardless of which state makes the initial adjustment, the other state is obliged to make an appropriate corresponding adjustment only if it considers that the adjusted profits correctly reflect what the profits would have been if the PE's dealings had been transactions at arm's length. So the other state is committed to make such a corresponding adjustment only if it considers that the initial adjustment is justified both in principle and as regards the amount.[72]

The domestic laws of the SC where the PE is located may not allow the SC to **4.76** make an adjustment, or the SC may have no incentive to make the adjustment. The result is that the two CSs may adopt different interpretations of Art. 7 § 2. For example, *if* the price of the same dealing is determined as 90 in the SC and 110 in the RC, *then* the profits of 20 may be subject to double taxation.[73] Art. 7 § 3 addresses that situation: *if* an adjustment has been made by the RC in conformity with Art. 7 § 2, *then* a corresponding adjustment must be made in the SC on profits that are taxed in both states. The Commentary provides alternative versions of Art. 7 § 3 providing a binding MAP.[74] It is only a binding MAP that makes correlative adjustment work to prevent double taxation/exemption.

Art. 17 §§ 1–2 of the MLI adopts the same approach, as it requires a CS to **4.77** make adjustments to the profits of a taxpayer if the other CS makes an at arm's length pricing adjustment to the profits of a taxpayer in the first CS. This means that any increase or decrease in that other CS would be mirrored by a corresponding adjustment. This provision essentially matches Art. 7 §§ 2 and 3 of the Model. In fact Art. 17 § 1 MLI provides that where a CS includes in the profits of an enterprise of that CS – and taxes accordingly – profits on which an enterprise of the other CS has been charged to tax in that other CS and the profits so included are profits which would have

---

71 Commentary to Art. 7 §§ 61–62.
72 Commentary to Art. 7 § 58-1.
73 Commentary to Art. 7 § 56.
74 Commentary to Art. 7 § 68.

accrued to the enterprise of the first-mentioned CS if the conditions made between the two enterprises had been those which would have been made between independent enterprises, then that other CS *shall make* an appropriate adjustment to the amount of the tax charged therein on those profits. In determining such adjustment, due regard shall be had to the other provisions of the Covered Tax Agreement and the Competent Authorities of the CSs shall if necessary consult each other. Art. 17 § 2 MLI shall apply in place of or in the absence of a provision that requires a CS to make an appropriate adjustment.

4.78 There is an exact scope of Art. 7 § 3 adjustments, as Art. 7 § 3 only applies with respect to differences in determining profits attributed to a PE that result in the same part of the profits being attributed to different parts of the enterprise. Expenses are deductible, which is a matter of domestic laws as long as there is conformity with Art. 7 § 2.[75] Art. 7 § 3 affects the computation of exemption or credit under Artt. 23A or 23B only to provide double taxation relief, which would otherwise be unavailable. Therefore Art. 7 § 3 does not apply if the profits of the PE have been fully exempted by the SC or if the tax paid in the SC has been fully credited against the RC's tax under the domestic laws of the RC. Moreover the secondary adjustment affects only double taxation relief but does not affect the application of other articles of the Convention.[76]

C. Arm's length for associated enterprises

4.79 Art. 9 § 1 provides that *if* an enterprise of a CS participates directly or indirectly in the management, control or capital of an enterprise of the other CS, *or* the same persons participate directly or indirectly in the management, control or capital of an enterprise of a CS, and in either case conditions are made/imposed between the two enterprises in their commercial/financial relations which differ from those which would be made between independent enterprises, *then* any profits which would, but for those conditions, have accrued to one of the enterprises, but, by reason of those conditions, have not so accrued, may be included in the profits of that enterprise and taxed accordingly.

4.80 The OECD has created extensive transfer pricing ('TP') guidelines aimed at the application of the arm's length standard which are technically outside the Commentary. As a result, in this matter national courts tend to apply those

---

75   Commentary to Art. 7 § 66.
76   Commentary to Art. 7 § 65.

guidelines rather than the Commentary, which is in fact quite short and summarized. The Commentary makes explicit reference to this new body of comments and guidelines and points out that the conditions for the application of Art. 9 are set out in the report entitled *Transfer Price Guidelines for Multinational Enterprises and Tax Administrations* ('OECD TP Report' or 'Guidelines') which is periodically updated to reflect the progress of the work of the CFA in this area. That report represents internationally agreed principles and provides guidelines for the application of the arm's length principle of which Art. 9 is the authoritative statement.[77] These Guidelines are now complemented by Actions 8–10 of the BEPS Project.

As a result, on the one hand, judicial decisions about the Commentary as such **4.81** are quite limited, while, on the other hand, a massive body of administrative guidelines, rulings and settlements has been developed at national level. This section of the chapter therefore will be limited to a summarized analysis of judicial decisions explicitly relating to Art. 9 and will cover the use of the OECD TP Report, applications of Art. 9 based on domestic laws, judicial reflections on the concept of arm's length, the hierarchy of TP tests, procedural aspects in the application of TP guidelines, TP and thin cap rules as well as the relationship between Art. 9 and other treaty articles.[78]

It is worth mentioning here that the traditional judicial debate about the use of **4.82** the Commentary in respect of the application of treaty provisions, in the area of TP has effectively shifted to a debate about the use of the OECD TP Report, rather than the application of the Commentary itself.

The predominant judicial position is that the OECD TP Report is relevant. **4.83** For example, cases acknowledge that the TP methods suggested by the OECD TP Report may be applied domestically.[79] As a further example, with regard to intra-group loan agreements, courts explicitly refer to the OECD TP Report in determining the arm's length value and determining that the evaluation of contractual terms of the transaction is part of the functional

---

77 Commentary to Art. 9 § 1. The literature on transfer price is massive, for an introduction see: King, Elizabeth, *Transfer Pricing and Corporate Taxation* (Springer 2009); Schön, Wolfgang and Konrad, Kai A., (eds), *Fundamentals of International Transfer Pricing in Law and Economics* (Springer 2012); Boos, Monica, *International Transfer Pricing. The Valuation of Intangible Assets* (Kluwer Law International 2003); Brauner, Yariv, 'Value in the Eye of the Beholder: The Valuation of Intangibles for Transfer Pricing Purposes' (2008) 28 *Tax Law Rev.* 79; IFA, Transfer Pricing and Intangibles (2007) 92a *Cahiers Droit Fisc. Int'l*; Markham, Michelle, *The Transfer Pricing of Intangibles* (Kluwer Law International 2005); Brauner, Yariv, 'Cost Sharing and the Acrobatics of Arm's Length Taxation' (2010) 38 *Intertax* 554.

78 See: Erasmus-Koen, Monica, 'Art. 9 of the OECD Model Convention' in: Anuschka Bakker (ed), *Transfer Pricing and Business Restructurings* (IBFD 2009).

79 Australia, Administrative Appeals Tribunal, *Roche Products Pty Ltd. v. Commissioner of Taxation*, 22 July 2008.

analysis suggested by the OECD.[80] In certain cases courts explicitly endorsed the Guidelines as soft law.[81] Other cases affirm that the OECD TP Report provides explanations of the problems but is not binding.[82] Although the judicial position is that the OECD TP Report is relevant, there are instances of an opposite judicial position.[83]

4.84 Domestic laws have evolved either by making a general reference to the OECD TP Report, or by explicitly acknowledging that the OECD TP Report is evidence of a policy process. This attitude has led to diversified applications of domestic laws loosely based on Art. 9 either through administrative guidelines or soft law. It is impossible here to provide a full account of these domestic applications, so a very concise review of judicial positions is presented. In certain situations the OECD guidelines fill the gaps in domestic laws.[84] In other situations courts simply refer to domestic TP rules which in general are similar to Art. 9 in adopting the arm's length principle, as occurred for example in a US case in which the court referred to Section 482 IRC in adjudicating transfer pricing cases.[85] What happens is that in many instances the domestic TP provisions lead to diversified applications which depend on the (often complex) circumstances of the case at hand.[86] The Commentary provides a summarized description of the arm's length concept[87] and courts have acknowledged that this general concept takes the form of a hierarchy of tests.[88]

4.85 The fact that the very broad principle provided for by Art. 9 has led to diversified applications of domestic laws implies that procedural aspects are relevant and often considered by national courts. The Commentary explicitly addresses the question whether Art. 9 prevents the application of domestic procedural rules and makes the point that in some cases the application of domestic laws may result in adjustment to profits at variance with the

---

80   Argentina, Tribunal Fiscal de la Nación 20.972-I, 15 August 2007.
81   Italy, Corte Suprema di Cassazione, 22023, 22 June 2006.
82   Sweden, Regeringsrätten ,117-1989, 22 October 1991.
83   Australia, Federal Court of Australia – Full Court, *SNF (Australia) Pty Ltd. v. Commissioner of Taxation of the Commonwealth of Australia*, (2010) 79 ATR 193.
84   The Netherlands, Hoge Raad der Nederlanden, 36.446, 28 June 2002.
85   United States, US Tax Court, *Ciba-Geigy Corp. v. Commissioner of Internal Revenue*, 1 August 1985; United States, US Court of Appeals for the Fifth Circuit, *Compaq Computer Corp. and Subsidiaries v. Commissioner of Internal Revenue*, 28 December 2001; Netherlands, Gerechtshof Den Haag (, 87/84 M III, 13 June 1984.
86   United States, US Tax Court, *DHL Corp. and Subsidiaries v. Commissioner of Internal Revenue*, 30 December 1998; France, Conseil d'État, 55543, 2 November 1987.
87   Commentary to Art. 9 § 2.
88   Canada, Tax Court of Canada, *Alberta Printed Circuits Ltd. v. Her Majesty the Queen*, 29 April 2010, Canada, Supreme Court of Canada, *GlaxoSmithKline Inc. v. Her Majesty the Queen*, 18 October 2012.

principles of Art. 9.[89] In respect of the burden of proof and disclosure of information the Commentary notes that almost all member countries consider that additional TP information requirements or the reversal of the burden of proof imposed by TP rules do not constitute discrimination within the meaning of Art. 24. In line with this indication national courts have developed local procedural solutions: for example, courts have held that the burden of proof is generally on the taxpayer who must substantiate all information stated in his tax return, but in TP disputes the burden of proof shifts to the tax authorities.[90] Courts often view Art. 9 as a broad anti-avoidance clause to be implemented through domestic laws,[91] in accordance with a traditional concept that has been now superseded by the mass of OECD principles and guidelines which indicate that Art. 9 is a structural rule.[92]

The Commentary recognizes that Art. 9 plays an important role in the **4.86** application of thin cap rules in so far as it constitutes a standard for determining the proper amount of debt on the basis of market conditions.[93] The Commentary also takes the position that Art. 9 does not prevent the application of national thin cap rules in so far as their effect is to assimilate the profits of the borrower to an amount corresponding to the profits which would have accrued in an arm's length situation.[94]

Art. 9 is indirectly connected to Art. 11 § 6 and to Art. 12 § 4 which **4.87** respectively apply the arm's length rule to interest and royalties when certain requirements are met. The Commentary clarifies that *if* by reason of a '*special relationship*' between the payer and the beneficial owner or between the payer, the beneficial owner and some other person, the amount of the interest or royalties paid exceeds the arm's length amount, then Artt. 11 or 12 respectively apply only to interest or royalties paid in excess of the arm's length amount.[95] A special relationship also covers relationships by blood or marriage and the community of interests as distinct from the legal relationship giving rise to the payment of the interest.[96] In spite of these clarifications national

---

89 Commentary to Art. 9 § 4.
90 Czech Republic, Nejvyšší Správní Soud, 1 Afs 99/2012-52, 13 March 2013.
91 Malaysia, Commissioners for Her Majesty's Revenue and Customs, PKR 421 (Kuala Lumpur), 10 August 1987.
92 France, Conseil d'État, 34430 – 36880, 14 March 1984.
93 Commentary to Art. 9 § 3. See: Canada, Tax Court of Canada, *Specialty Manufacturing Ltd. v. Her Majesty the Queen*, 25 August 1997.
94 Commentary to Art. 9 §.
95 Commentary to Art. 11 §§ 32–33. and Commentary to Art. 12 §§ 22–24.
96 Commentary to Art. 12 §§ 34, and §§ 22–24, adopts the same concept in respect to royalties.

courts have focused on whether the existence of such a special relationship could be demonstrated by reference to domestic transfer pricing rules.[97]

4.88 The Commentary suggests that the category of income in which excess-interest and excess-royalties are classified should be determined on a case-by-case basis.[98] Art. 11 § 6 allows the adjustment of the rate at which interest is charged (with the consequence that the excess amount is disallowed as a deduction for the payer of the excess-interest), but does not allow re-characterization of the loan as a contribution to equity capital. If respective domestic laws oblige the two CSs to apply different articles of the Convention for the purpose of taxing the excess, it is necessary to resort to the MAP.[99]

4.89 Art. 9 § 2 regulates broadly the primary and secondary adjustments that should result from the application of TP rules in a bilateral treaty situation. Art. 9 § 2 provides that where a CS includes in the profits of an enterprise of that state – and taxes accordingly – profits on which an enterprise of the other CS has been charged tax in that other state and the profits so included are profits which would have accrued to the enterprise of the first-mentioned state *if* the conditions made between the two enterprises had been those which would have been made between independent enterprises, *then* that other state *shall make* an appropriate adjustment to the amount of the tax charged therein on those profits. In determining such adjustment, due regard shall be had to the other provisions of the Convention and the Competent Authorities of the CSs shall if necessary consult each other.

4.90 As primary and secondary adjustments may lead to disputes between the parties concerned over the amount and character of the appropriate adjustment, the MAP provided for under Art. 25 is an appropriate procedure to be pursued particularly in its binding form.[100]

4.91 The Commentary notes that the re-writing of transactions between associated enterprises on the basis of arm's length may give rise to economic double taxation, in so far as an enterprise of state A whose profits are revised upwards is taxed on an amount of profit which has already been taxed in the hands of its associated enterprise in state B. So the concept of a primary adjustment advanced by the Commentary is that in these circumstances, state B should

---

97   Czech Republic, Nejvyšší Správní Soud, 2 Afs 42/2008-62, 30 April 2008.
98   Commentary to Art. 11 § 35; Commentary to Art. 12 § 25.
99   Commentary to Art. 11 § 36, deleted in Commentary 2017. See: Czech Republic, Nejvyšší Správní Soud 2Afs 108/2004-106, 10 February 2005.
100 Commentary to Art. 9 § 11.

make an appropriate adjustment to relieve the double taxation.[101] The Commentary 2017, in light of the fact that binding arbitration recommended by Art. 25 § 5 is a practice that is not adopted by many countries, notes that under the domestic laws of some countries, taxpayers are permitted to amend a previously-filed tax return to adjust the profits attributable to a PE to reflect an attribution of profits on the basis of Art. 7: in these cases the Competent Authorities under Art. 25 may accordingly use MAP, to reflect domestic adjustments.[102]

Art. 11 § 6 provides that where, by reason of a special-relationship between **4.92** the payer and the beneficial owner or between both of them and some other person, the amount of the interest, having regard to the debt-claim for which it is paid, exceeds the amount which would have been agreed upon by the payer and the beneficial owner in the absence of such a relationship, the provisions of Art. 11 shall apply only to the last-mentioned amount. In such cases, the excess-payment shall remain taxable according to the laws of each CS, due regard being had to the other provisions of the Convention.

Art. 12 § 4 similarly provides that where, by reason of a special relationship **4.93** between the payer and the beneficial owner or between both of them and some other person, the amount of the royalties, having regard to the use, right or information for which they are paid, exceeds the amount which would have been agreed upon by the payer and the beneficial owner in the absence of such a relationship, the provisions of Art. 12 shall apply only to the last-mentioned amount. In such case, the excess payment shall remain taxable according to the laws of each CS, due regard being had to the other provisions of the Convention. So Art. 9 is indirectly connected to Art. 12 § 4 which applies the arm's length rule to royalties when certain requirements are met.[103]

III. TAX TREATIES AND INFORMATION

A. Exchange of information

'Tax information' can be defined as 'knowledge communicated or received **4.94** concerning taxpayers' particular facts or circumstances': the information adds new data to that already known, cannot be predicted and resolves uncertainty, so it clearly has economic value. More specifically tax information allows

---

101 Commentary to Art. 9 § 5.
102 Commentary to Art. 9 § 6.1.
103 Commentary to Art. 12 §§ 22–24.

agents (tax authorities) to make choices that yield higher expected payoffs/ utility than they would obtain from choices made in the absence of information.[104] Tax information should be understood in the context of the interdependent tax strategies of the RC and the SC. The RC has the predominant strategy in so far as it extends its tax jurisdiction to the foreign income (sourced in the SC) of its residents, and the taxes paid in the SC are fully credited against the taxes paid in the RC.[105]

4.95 However, taxpayers may under-report (or not report) in the RC their income produced in the SC. This opportunistic behaviour is, at least in part, determined, on the one hand, by the fact that the RC cannot enforce its extraterritorial legislative tax claims directly in the territory of the SC, and, on the other hand, by the fact that the SCs may offer low or no taxation to non-residents investing in that country and not cooperate with the RC in respect of enforcement of claims by the RC. The result is that the high mobility of passive or financial income leads to an obfuscation of relevant tax information through bank secrecy and other forms of confidentiality pursued by un-cooperative SCs.

4.96 RCs, in order to enforce their tax legislation, need the cooperation of the SCs to obtain information about income produced by their residents in those countries.[106] So residence taxation operates correctly as long as the RCs are actually capable of acquiring information from the SCs about income produced in those countries, and one of main concerns of OECD countries is the tax evasion realized by resident taxpayers not reporting or underreporting their income produced abroad. As a result, the strategic interests of the high-tax RCs clashes with the strategic interests of the low-tax SCs, labelled by high-tax RCs as 'un-cooperative behaviour'. Thus, a CS essentially needs information from the other CS, which it is obliged to provide if certain requirements are met. So in this chapter the usual terminology referring to the RC and the SC will change to the Requesting-CS (usually the RC) and the Requested-CS (usually the SC).

---

104   Commentary to Art. 26 §§ 1–4.2.
105   See in general: Dean, Steven, 'The Incomplete Global Market for Tax Information' (2007) 49 *Boston College Law Rev.* 605; Anamourlis, Tony and Nethercott, Les, 'An Overview of Exchange Agreements and Bank Secrecy' (2009) 63 *Bull. Intl. Tax.* 616; Gangemi, Bruno, 'International Mutual Assistance Through Exchange of Information, IFA General Report' (1990) 75b *Cahiers Droit Fisc. Intl.*; IFA, 'Exchange of Information Cross-Border Cooperation between Tax Authorities' (2013) 98b *Cahiers Droit Fisc. Intl*; Oberson, Xavier, 'The OECD Model Agreement on Exchange of Information – A Shift to the Applicant State' (2003) 57 *Bull. Intl. Tax.* 16; Owens, Jeffrey, 'Moving Towards Better Transparency and Exchange of Information on Tax Matters' (2009) 63 *Bull. Intl. Tax.* 557; Ruchelman, Stanley and Shapiro, Susan, 'Exchange of Information' (2002) 30 *Intertax* 408.
106   Germany, Bundesfinanzhof, I B 35/05, 13 January 2006.

Art. 26 addresses the fundamental problems in the exchange of information: **4.97** what kind of information should be exchanged (§ 1); how this information should be treated when effectively transmitted (§ 2); what are the limitations to the exchange of information (§ 3); what kind of information-gathering measures should be undertaken to collect the requested information (§ 4); and the general principle that bank secrecy is not a limitation to the exchange of information, except in particular cases (§ 5).

Art. 26 of the Model is now complemented by a Model Tax Information **4.98** Exchange Agreement ('TIEA') and together they are evidence of the emergence of new standards for the exchange of information which can be summarized as follows: (i) the existence of mechanisms for exchange of information upon request, where such information is 'foreseeably relevant'; (ii) the absence of restrictions on such exchanges, such as bank secrecy or other domestic tax interest requirements; (iii) the availability of reliable information (in particular bank, ownership, identity and accounting information); and (iv) the respect for the taxpayer's rights and strict confidentiality rules for the information exchanged. The latest development is the building-up of the network for tax transparency at an international level. The Global Forum currently includes many member countries on an equal footing and is conducting a peer-review process.[107]

The exchange of information is now subject to a set of rules that were **4.99** previously missing in international tax law: (i) international treaties, either bilateral or multilateral, specifically regulating mutual assistance between the CSs and based on the Model TIEA; (ii) provisions governing the exchange of information embedded in bilateral treaties (Art. 26); (iii) rules regulating exchange of information within regional contexts, such as the EU rules; and (iv) unilateral instruments enacted by individual countries with extra-territorial effect (such as U.S. FATCA).

1. Concept of tax information and scope of the exchange

Art. 26 § 1 provides that the Competent Authorities of the CSs shall **4.100** exchange such information as is foreseeably relevant for carrying out the

---

107 On the OECD campaign: OECD, *Countering Offshore Tax Evasion* (OECD 2009); OECD, *Improving Access to Bank Information for Tax Purposes, the 2007 Progress Report* (OECD 2007); OECD, *Keeping it Safe – The OECD Guide on the Protection of Confidentiality of Information Exchanged for Tax Purposes* (OECD 2012); OECD, *Manual on the Implementation of Exchange of Information for Tax Purposes* (OECD 2006); OECD, *Promoting Transparency and Exchange of Information for Tax Purposes* (OECD 2010); OECD, *Report Progress in Fighting Offshore Tax Evasion, but Says More Efforts Are Needed* (OECD 2007); OECD, *Tax Co-operation 2009: Towards a Level Playing Field* (OECD 2009); OECD, *Tax Co-operation: Towards a Level Playing Field* (OECD 2006); OECD, *Tax Co-operation: Towards a Level Playing Field* (OECD 2007).

provisions of the Convention or for the administration or enforcement of the domestic laws concerning taxes of every kind and descriptions imposed on behalf of the CSs, or of their political subdivisions or local authorities, in so far as the taxation thereunder is in accordance with the Convention.

4.101 The Competent Authorities shall exchange such information as is 'foreseeably relevant' (as opposed to 'necessary', as provided for by the Model of 1992) to secure the correct application of 'the Convention or of the domestic laws of the CSs concerning taxes of every kind and description imposed in these states' (as opposed to 'taxes covered by the Convention', as provided for by the Model of 1992).[108] The Commentary does not specifically define what is 'foreseeably relevant' information but national courts have made clarifications.[109]

4.102 Another issue that has been addressed by the courts is whether a spontaneous exchange of information (i.e., the transmission of information to a CS which spontaneously activates, without any request by the other CS) was allowed under the exchange of information article of the treaty.[110] While the current attitude is clearly in favour of a broad approach to the information that is deemed to be 'foreseeably relevant' under the previous wording of Art. 26 § 1 some courts had taken a narrow approach.[111]

4.103 The Commentary clarifies that so-called 'fishing expeditions' are excluded from the scope of Art. 26 and that the standard of 'foreseeable relevance' is intended to provide for exchange of information for the widest possible extent.[112] The exclusion of fishing expeditions does not bar the Competent Authorities from exchanging other sensitive information related to tax administration and compliance, for example, risk analysis techniques or tax avoidance or evasion schemes because information covered by Art. 26 § 1 is not limited to taxpayer-specific information.[113]

4.104 Before 2000, Art. 26 § 1 only authorized the exchange of information in relation to the taxes covered by the Convention (Art. 2), but the 2005 amendment to Art. 26 § 1 authorizes exchange of information concerning any

---

108 Commentary to Art. 26 § 5.1.
109 Singapore, High Court, *BJY & Ors v. Comptroller of Income Tax*, 13 September 2013; Germany, Bundesfinanzhof, I R 79/07, 29 April 2008.
110 Germany, Bundesfinanzhof, I B 218/04, 10 May 2005; Germany, Finanzgericht Nordrhein-Westfalen, 4 V 5580/04 S, 10 January 2005.
111 Germany, Finanzgericht Hamburg, Hamburg, 30 September 2004.
112 Commentary to Art. 26 § 5. See: United States, US District Court for the Southern District of New York, *Luis A. Fernandez-Marinelli v. United States*, 29 November 1995.
113 Commentary to Art. 26 § 5.1.

tax imposed on behalf of the CSs.[114] By contrast, the exchange of information does not imply additional assistance by the Requested-CS.[115] Exchange of information concerning custom duties finds its legal basis in other international instruments not governed by Art. 26.[116]

The information which is exchanged may be relevant only for the implemen-   **4.105** tation of domestic laws or only for the implementation of treaties, but in most cases it is relevant for both domestic laws and treaties. Information is for the application of treaties when for example the information is about the amount of royalties transmitted; whether the recipient of royalties is a resident of the RC and the beneficial owner of the royalties; the allocation of profits between associated enterprises; the application of MAP; or is a combined application of Artt. 15 and 23A.[117]

Information that is relevant only for the implementation of domestic laws for   **4.106** example is about the price for transactions or VAT input tax credits, and information concerning a third country,[118] but a restrictive approach has been sometimes adopted according to which the exchanged information must only pertain to the treaties.[119]

Information can be exchanged on request (i.e., with a special case in mind),   **4.107** automatically (i.e., information about categories of income in the SC are transmitted to the RC), or spontaneously (i.e., a CS acquires information which it supposes to be of interest to the other CS).[120] The Requesting-CS needs to receive information in a particular form to satisfy its evidentiary legal requirements about depositions of witnesses or authenticated copies of original records. On the other hand, the Requested-CS may decline to provide the information in the specific form requested if it is not known or permitted under its domestic laws, but it must nevertheless provide the information in some other form.[121]

---

114   Commentary to Art. 26 §§ 5.3 and 10.1.

115   Switzerland, Bundesgericht/Tribunal fédéral, No. 101 Ib 160, 16 May 1975.

116   Commentary to Art. 26 § 5.2.

117   Commentary to Art. 26 § 6–7.

118   Austria, Verwaltungsgerichtshof, 93/15/0047, 24 April 1997; Canada, Federal Court, *Pacific Network Services Ltd. v. Minister of National Revenue*, 8 November 2002.

119   Belgium, Hof van Cassatie/Court de Cassation, RC035G4, 16 May 2003; Germany, Finanzgericht Bayern, 5 V 2356/99, 14 July 1999; Germany, Bundesfinanzhof, I R 306/82, 23 July 1986.

120   Germany, Finanzgericht Bayern, 5 V 2356/99, 14 July 1999; Germany, Bundesfinanzhof, I B 72/87, 20 January 1988; Germany, Bundesfinanzhof, I R 306/82, 23 July 1986; Germany, Bundesfinanzhof, I B 35/05, 13 January 2006; Italy, Corte Suprema di Cassazione, 3981, 3 April 2000; Italy, Corte Suprema di Cassazione, 3254, 20 March 2000; United States, US Tax Court, *Alan B. Karme v. Commissioner of Internal Revenue*, 24 March 1980.

121   Commentary to Art. 26 § 10.2-1.

4.108 There should be no prejudice to the general rules and legal provisions governing the rights of defendants and witnesses in judicial proceedings, in particular in light of the fact that the exchange of information for criminal tax matters can also be based on bilateral or multilateral treaties on mutual legal assistance.[122] Information that existed prior to the entry into force of a treaty is covered by the exchange of information article of the treaty, as long as the assistance with respect to this information is provided after the treaty has entered into force and the exchange of information article of that treaty has become effective.[123]

4.109 Art. 26 § 2 deals with the actual treatment by the Requesting-CS of the information obtained from the Requested-CS. Art. 26 § 2 provides that any information received under Art 26 § 1 by the Requesting-CS shall be treated as secret in the same manner as information obtained under the domestic laws of that Requesting-CS and shall be disclosed only to persons or authorities (including courts and administrative bodies) concerned with the assessment/ collection of, the enforcement or prosecution in respect of, the determination of appeals in relation to, the taxes referred to in Art. 26 § 1, or the oversight of the above. Such persons or authorities shall use the information only for such purposes and may disclose the information in public court proceedings or in judicial decisions.

4.110 The reciprocal assistance between tax administrations is feasible only if each administration is assured that other administration will treat the received information with proper confidence. Therefore, the confidentiality rules of Art. 26 § 2 apply to all types of information received under the exchange of information article of the treaty. A foremost concern is the maintenance of secrecy in the Requesting-CS, a matter of domestic law: communicated information should be treated as secret in the Requesting-CS in the same manner as information obtained under the domestic laws of that state and the

---

122 Commentary to Art. 26 § 10.3-2. See: United States, US District Court for Northern District of Illinois, *Gilbert Wolf v. United States*, 21 December 1984, 601 F. Supp. 435; United States, US Tax Court, *Midwest Generator Company v. Commissioner of Internal Revenue*, 17 February 1988; United States, Supreme Court, *United States v. Powell*, 23 November 1964; United States, US Court of Appeals for the Tenth Circuit, *Salomon Juan Marcos Villarreal v. United States*, 22 April 2013; United States, US District Court for the Western District of Texas, *Bull D S.A. de C.V. v. United States*, 5 January 2007; United States, US District Court for the Southern District of California, *Paul N. Hiley, PNH Financial Inc. v. United States*, 2 October 2007; United States, US Court of Appeals for the Fifth Circuit, *Zbigniew Emilian Mazurek v. United States*, 7 November 2001; United States, US District Court for the Central District of California, *Lidas Inc., David Chelala, Liliane Chelala v. United States*, 5 February 1999; United States, US District Court for the Central District of California, *Yeong Yae Yun v. United States*, 13 November 2000.

123 Commentary to Art. 26 § 10.3. See: United States, US District Court for the Southern District of Texas, *Julio Roberto Zarate Barquero v. United States*, 15 June 1993.

sanctions for the violation of secrecy in the Requesting-CS are governed by the administrative and penal laws of that state.[124]

The information obtained may be disclosed to persons and authorities **4.111** involved in assessment or collection of, enforcement/prosecution in respect of, determination of appeals in relation to, taxes with respect to which information may be exchanged under Art. 26 § 1.[125] The information obtained may also be disclosed to the assessed taxpayer and his proxy, to the witnesses, to governmental or judicial authorities, and to oversight bodies (i.e., authorities that supervise tax administration and enforcement authorities).[126] Information, once used in public court proceedings or in court decisions, can be quoted from the court files or decisions for other purposes even as possible evidence.[127]

Limitations to internal disclosure are not directly listed by Art. 26 § 2, but **4.112** can be implied from the list of internal disclosures allowed by Art. 26 § 2. In the first place, there can be no disclosure of exchanged information to persons outside Art. 26 § 2, regardless of domestic information disclosure laws such as freedom of information or other legislation that allows greater access to governmental documents. In addition, information received by the Requesting-CS may not be disclosed to a third country unless an express provision in the treaty between the CSs allows such disclosures.

The position of the courts, in the light of domestic laws, is that taxpayers do **4.113** not generally have a right to access information received from foreign tax authorities.[128] Moreover the Requesting-CS may not use information for non-tax purposes and therefore must resort to specific means to collect such information (a treaty concerning judicial assistance in case of a non-tax crime).[129] Tax authorities in the Requesting-CS can however share with other law enforcement agencies and judicial authorities in that CS tax information on high priority matters (i.e., to combat money laundering, corruption, terrorism financing).

---

124 Commentary to Art. 26 § 11-2.
125 Commentary to Art. 26 § 12.
126 United States, US District Court for Northern District of Illinois, *Gilbert Wolf v. United States*, 21 December 1984, 601 F. Supp. 435; France, Conseil d'État, 311808, 26 January 2011.
127 Commentary to Art. 26 § 13. See: Italy, Corte Suprema di Cassazione, 3254, 20 March 2000; Italy, Corte Suprema di Cassazione, 3981, 3 April 2000.
128 New Zealand, Court of Appeal, *ER Squibb and Sons v. Commissioner of Inland Revenue*, 2 October 1992; United States, US District Court for the District of Arizona, *Aloe Vera of America, Inc. et al. v. United States*, 21 September 2000.
129 Commentary to Art. 26 § 12.3-1. See: Canada, Federal Court, *Montreal Aluminium Processing Inc. and Albert Klein v. Her Majesty the Queen*, 4 July 1991.

2. Limitations to the exchange of information

4.114 Full reciprocity should always operate in the exchange of information, because each CS has an interest in cooperating to obtain similar cooperation in the future; and the Commentary points out that Art. 26 is generally based on full reciprocity unless indicated otherwise.[130]

4.115 The fact is that very often there are asymmetries in the interests of the Requesting-CS versus the Requested-CS. For example, the Requesting-CS to obtain information 'free rides' on the administrative capabilities of the Requested-CS simply because it is not capable of obtaining that information acting alone. By contrast, the Requested-CS may very well have an interest in not sustaining the cost of carrying out administrative activities in favour of the Requesting-CS. In many cases the Requested-CS even has an interest in withdrawing the relevant information on the basis of local concerns.

4.116 Art. 26 § 3 regulates this tension between the respective interests of the Requesting-CS and the Requested-CS establishing two types of refusal by the Requested-CS to transfer the requested information: first, a refusal to provide the requested information that implies the violation of domestic laws or administrative practices of the Requested-CS (Art. 26 § 5 a) and b); and second, a refusal to provide the requested information that would imply the violation of secrecy rules or public order (Art. 26 § 5 c)).

3. Violation of domestic laws or administrative practices of the Requested-CS

4.117 Art. 26 § 3 provides that in no case shall Art. 26 §§ 1 and 2 be construed so as to impose on the CS the obligation: a) to carry out administrative measures at variance with the laws and administrative practice of the Requesting-CS or the Requested-CS; and b) to supply information which is not obtainable under the laws or in the normal course of the administration of the Requesting-CS or the Requested-CS. The Requested-CS must not go beyond its domestic laws except for bank secrecy.[131] Moreover, if asymmetries in information systems of the CSs limit the exchange of information, the Commentary advises to broaden the scope of the exchange of information.

4.118 When this concept of reciprocity is applied to the relationship of the Requesting-CS versus the Requested-CS a few guidelines emerge. First, the Requesting-CS cannot take advantage of the information system of the Requested-CS if it is wider than its own system. This is what in fact occurs in

---

130 Commentary to Art. 26 § 18.1.
131 Commentary to Art. 26 § 15. See: New Zealand, Court of Appeal, *Avowal Administrative Attorneys Ltd. and Others v. District Court at North Shore and the Commissioner of Inland Revenue*, 11 May 2010.

the exchange of information in which the Requesting-CS relies on the better positioning of the Requested-CS about the transactions carried out by the taxpayer in its own territory. Second, the requested information must be obtainable in the normal course of administration by the Requested-CS, on condition that tax authorities of the Requesting-CS would make similar investigations or examinations for their own purposes.[132]

Third, the Requested-CS may refuse information if the request implies that it **4.119** must carry out administrative measures not permitted under its own domestic laws or to supply items of information that are not obtainable under its own domestic laws.[133] Fourth, the Requested-CS may refuse to provide information only if the Requesting-CS would be precluded by law from obtaining or providing the information, or if the Requesting-CS's administrative practices result in a lack of reciprocity (i.e., failure to provide sufficient administrative resources).[134]

The violation of domestic laws or administrative practice as a ground for not **4.120** providing information can be in respect of notification procedures in the Requested-CS; the Commentary takes the position that notification procedures should not be applied in a manner that frustrates the efforts of the Requesting-CS or unduly delays the effective exchange of information.[135] Procedural problems as a ground for denying requested information have been discussed in several US cases concerning IRS summonses instrumental to the collection of requested information.[136]

There are situations in which only one CS provides a certain procedure, and **4.121** this may be invoked by the other CS as a reason to withdraw the requested information. For example, a certain ruling procedure may be admitted only in the Requested-CS, but not in the Requesting-CS, so that the Requested-CS can decline if the requested information is not obtainable under domestic laws or in course of administrative practice of the Requesting-CS. By contrast, the

---

132 Commentary to Art. 26 § 16–17.
133 United States, US Supreme Court, *United States v. LaSalle National Bank*, 19 June 1978; United States, US District Court for the Southern District of New York, *A.L. Burbank & Co. Ltd. v. United States*, 1 August 1974; United States, US District Court for the Southern District of New York, *Lincoln First Bank v. United States*, 14 February 1980; United States, US District Court for the Eastern District of Louisiana, *Zbigniew Emilian Mazurek v. United States*, 19 September 2000; United States, US District Court for the Southern District of New York, *Gabriel Azouz v. United States (Internal Revenue Service)*, 13 December 1999.
134 United States, US District Court for the Southern District of New York, *A.L. Burbank & Co. Ltd. v. United States*, 1 August 1974.
135 Belgium, Court d'Appel Liège, 0255/0461, 20 March 2002.
136 United States, Supreme Court, *United States v. Powell*, 23 November 1964.

Requested-CS cannot decline if the absence of a ruling regime in the Requesting-CS is based on a reciprocity argument.[137]

4.122 Another example is the privilege against self-incrimination, a rule which forbids the government from compelling any person to give testimonial evidence that would likely incriminate him or her during a subsequent criminal case: the Requested-CS may decline to provide information if under similar circumstances the Requesting-CS would have been precluded by its own self-incrimination rules from obtaining information. In practice, however, the privilege against self-incrimination has little impact because it cannot be claimed by taxpayers in tax assessment procedures not at risk of criminal prosecution.[138]

4. *Violation of secrecy rules or public order*

4.123 Art. 26 § 3 c) provides that in no case shall Art. 26 §§ 1 and 2 be construed so as to impose on the Requesting-CS or the Requested-CS the obligation to supply information which would disclose any trade, business, industrial, commercial or professional secret or trade process, or information the disclosure of which would be contrary to public policy (order public).

4.124 The Commentary adopts a narrow sense of 'secret' as a limitation and observes that the application of secrecy rules must take account of confidentiality rules and then discusses the actual limitations established by Art. 26 § 3 c) (no exchange of information if trade or business secrets of private entities or vital interests of the state are involved). In particular, secrets mentioned in Art. 26 § 3 c) should not be taken in too wide a sense. Before invoking this provision, a CS should carefully weigh if the interests of the taxpayer really justify its application. It is clear that too wide an interpretation would in many cases render ineffective the exchange of information provided for in the Convention.[139] This approach is shared by national courts.[140]

4.125 The application of the secrecy rules must take account of the confidentiality rules: the Requested-CS may decide to supply the information if the taxpayer involved does not suffer any adverse non-tax consequences from the transfer of information. These non-tax adverse consequences are often prevented by the

---

137 Commentary to Art. 26 § 15.1.
138 Commentary to Art. 26 § 15.2.
139 Commentary to Art. 26 § 19. For a judicial application of this indication: Singapore, Singapore High Court, *Comptroller of Income Tax v. BJX*, 2013, SGHC 145.
140 Germany, Finanzgericht Nordrhein-Westfalen, 4 V 5580/04 S, 10 January 2005; Germany, Bundesfinanzhof I R 306/82, 23 July 1986.

confidentiality rules which ensure that information can only be used for tax purposes by public entities.[141]

The language of Art. 26 § 5 c) is clear in providing that there can be no **4.126** exchange of information if trade or business secrets are involved, but the potentially broad scope of this limitation is eroded by current approaches that reduce the ambit of protected trade or business secrets. First, the Commentary points out that in most tax cases the exchange of information involves no trade or business secrets.[142] Second, the Commentary and national courts take the position that financial information constitutes a trade or business secret only in certain limited cases such as in the disclosure of a proprietary formula.[143] This approach is reinforced by the language of Art. 26 § 5 dealing with bank secrecy and by national cases enforcing such provision of the Model.

The Requested-CS may decline to disclose information relating to confiden- **4.127** tial communications between attorneys (attorney privilege), and their clients to the extent that communications are protected from disclosure under domestic laws.[144] But the scope of protection under attorney privilege should be narrowly defined: no protection should be given to documents delivered to an attorney to shield them from disclosure of the identity of a person not protected as a confidential communication, and communications between attorneys are not confidential if they act as nominee shareholders, trustees, settlors, company directors or under a power of attorney.[145]

The Commentary also adopts a narrow sense of 'vital interests of the state' **4.128** (i.e., public order) as a limitation to exchange of information and points out that such a limitation is relevant in extreme cases, such as tax investigation in the Requesting-CS motivated by political, racial, or religious persecution, or information held by secret services.[146]

5. Information-gathering measures and bank secrecy

Art. 26 § 4 provides that if information is requested by the Requesting-CS in **4.129** accordance with Art. 26, the Requested-CS shall carry out its information-gathering measures to obtain the requested information, even though that

---

141 Germany, Bundesfinanzhof, I B 35/05, 13 January 2006.
142 Commentary to Art. 26 § 19.2.
143 Singapore, High Court, *BJY & Ors v. Comptroller of Income Tax*, 13 September 2013.
144 Commentary to Art. 26 § 19.3-1.
145 Commentary to Art. 26 § 19.3-2, § 19.4.
146 Commentary to Art. 26 § 19.5. See: Germany, Finanzgericht Nordrhein-Westfalen, 4 V 5580/04 S, 10 January 2005.

Requested-CS may not need such information for its own tax purposes. The term 'information-gathering measures' used by Art. 26 § 4 includes laws and administrative or judicial procedures that enable the requesting CS to obtain and provide the requested information irrespective of the interests of the Requested-CS.[147]

4.130 The Requested-CS cannot invoke Art. 26 § 3, arguing that under its domestic laws it can only supply information in which it has an interest for its own tax purposes. So in practice the Requested-CS must exert the same information-gathering capabilities it would exert in a domestic situation.[148]

4.131 Art. 26 § 4 also provides that the obligation of the Requested-CS to use its information-gathering measures to obtain the requested information is subject to the limitations of Art. 26 § 3, but in no case shall such limitations be construed to permit the Requested-CS to decline to supply information solely because it has no domestic interest in the information. The Commentary clarifies that lack of interest by the Requested-CS does not operate as a derogation of the duty of the use information-gathering measures.[149]

4.132 Indeed, in many instances the Requested-CS even has an interest in not providing the information, particularly when that information regards financial transactions of taxpayers covered by bank secrecy. So the approach adopted by the Commentary, that information must be provided even if not needed by the Requested-CS, is reinforced by the language of Art. 26 § 5 dealing with bank secrecy and by national cases enforcing such provision of the Model. Before 2005 this obligation of the Requested-CS although not expressly stated in Art. 26 was evidenced by country practices.[150]

4.133 Art. 26 § 5 provides that in no case shall Art. 26 § 3 be construed as permitting the Requested-CS to decline to supply information solely because the information is held by a bank, other financial institution, nominee or person acting in an agency or a fiduciary capacity or because it relates to ownership interests in a person. The Commentary makes it clear that under Art. 25 § 5 bank secrecy is not a reason to refuse information. Moreover, the limitations of Art. 26 § 3 cannot be used to prevent the exchange of information held by banks, other financial institutions, nominees, and agents

---

147   Commentary to Art. 26, § 19.7.
148   Commentary to Art. 26, § 19.8. See: Germany, Bundesfinanzhof, VII R 16/78, 12 February 1979; Canada, Federal Court, *Montreal Aluminium Processing Inc. and Albert Klein v. Her Majesty the Queen*, 4 July 1991.
149   Commentary to Art. 26, § 19.7.
150   Commentary to Art. 26 § 19.6.

and fiduciaries.[151] Art. 26 § 5 overrides Art. 26 § 3, because Art. 26 § 3 would otherwise permit a requested CS to decline to supply information on grounds of bank secrecy. National courts have actually anticipated these OECD policies.[152]

The Commentary clarifies that under Art. 26 § 5 the Requested-CS may **4.134** invoke Art. 26 § 3 limitations only if *not* related to bank secrecy. So Art. 26 § 5 does not preclude the Requested-CS from invoking Art. 26 § 3 to refuse to supply information held by a bank, or a person acting in an agency or fiduciary capacity, *but* the refusal must be based on reasons unrelated to the person's status as a bank, or fiduciary.[153] For example, there is a duty of exchange of information when a legal representative acts in an agency capacity, but attorney privilege may provide a possible basis for declining to supply the information.[154]

There is also a duty of exchange of information when company X owns **4.135** company Y in the RC, both companies are incorporated under the laws of the RC, and the SC conducts a tax examination of the business operations of company Y in the SC requesting from the RC ownership information of any person in company Y's chain of ownership. There is a duty of exchange of information when an individual A in the RC maintains a bank account with Bank B in the SC and the RC makes a request to the SC for all bank account income and asset information held by Bank B in order to determine whether there were deposits of untaxed earned income.[155]

The Requested-CS cannot decline to supply information solely because the **4.136** information is held by persons acting in an agency or fiduciary capacity, arguing that under the domestic laws of the Requested-CS the information held by a fiduciary is treated as a 'professional secret'.[156] The Requested-CS shall not decline to supply information solely because it relates to an ownership interest in a person, including companies and partnerships, foundations or similar organizational structures. Moreover, information requests cannot be

---

151 Commentary to Art. 26 § 19.11. See in general: Rust, Alexander and Fort, Eric, (eds), *Exchange of Information and Bank Secrecy* (Wolters Kluwer 2012).
152 Singapore, High Court, *BJY & Ors v. Comptroller of Income Tax*, 13 September 2013.
153 Commentary to Art. 26 § 19.14-1.
154 Commentary to Art. 26 § 19.14-2a.
155 Commentary to Art. 26 § 19.15. See: Switzerland, Bundesgericht/Tribunal fédéral, A-5390/2013, 8 January 2014.
156 Commentary to Art. 26 § 19.12-1.; Commentary to Art. 26 § 19.1.

declined merely because domestic laws treat ownership information as a trade or other secret.[157]

B. Assistance in the collection of taxes

4.137 States should be able decide whether and to what extent assistance in collection of taxes should be provided to another state under a treaty.[158] So while Art. 27 provides for comprehensive collection assistance, some states may prefer to provide a more limited type of collection assistance.[159] Unlike the exchange of information under Art. 26, there are no specific standards advocated at OECD level in this matter.

4.138 Art. 27 provides a model of extensive assistance in the collection of taxes along the following lines: scope of reciprocal assistance in collection (§ 1); definition of Revenue-claim by the Requesting-CS for collection in the Requested-CS (§ 2); acceptance of Revenue-claim by the Requested-CS (§ 3); procedure for conservancy measures (§ 4); time limits and priority for Revenue-claims (§ 5); proceedings on Revenue-claims (§ 6); cessation of Revenue-claims (§ 7); and limitations to assistance (§ 8).

4.139 Art. 27 § 1 provides that the CSs shall lend assistance to each other in the collection of Revenue-claims. This assistance is not restricted by Artt. 1 and 2. The Competent Authorities of the CSs may by mutual agreement settle the mode of application of Art. 27. Under Art. 27 a CS is obliged to assist the other state in the collection of taxes owed to it, provided that the requirements of Art. 27 are met.[160] So when collection of taxes is involved, the assistance is not restricted to resident or non-resident persons of the CSs.[161]

4.140 The documentation that should accompany a request for collection of taxes by the Requesting-CS is a declaration that the Revenue-claim is enforceable and an official translation of the documentation in the language of the Requested-CS.[162]

---

157   Commentary to Art. 26 § 19.3. See: Switzerland, Bundesgericht/Tribunal fédéral, A-6053/2010, 10 January 2011.
158   Commentary to Art. 27 § 1.
159   Commentary to Art. 27 § 2.
160   Italy, Corte Suprema di Cassazione, 760, 17 January 2006; Canada, Federal Court, *Chua v. Her Majesty the Queen*, 6 November 2000.
161   Commentary to Art. 27 § 4.
162   Commentary to Art. 27 § 7.

The costs of the Requested-CS in satisfying a request made under Art. 27 **4.141**
§§ 3 or 4 are charged to the debtor but it is necessary to determine which state
will bear any costs that cannot be recovered from that person. Collection costs
can be ordinary or extraordinary costs. Ordinary costs are those directly and
normally related to the collection, i.e., those expected in normal domestic
collection proceedings and will not be reimbursed by that other state. Extraordinary costs are those that exceed ordinary costs and are borne by the
Requesting-CS, unless otherwise agreed bilaterally. When a CS anticipates
that extraordinary costs may be incurred, it informs the other CS and indicates
the estimated amount of such costs so that the other state may decide whether
such costs should be incurred.[163]

Practical issues of the assistance in collection include limits of time, exchange **4.142**
rates when a Revenue-claim is collected in another currency; how should any
amount collected pursuant to a request under Art. 27 § 3 be remitted to the
Requesting-CS. These issues can be regulated by the CSs through MAP or
otherwise.[164]

Art. 27 § 2 defines the term 'Revenue-claim' for purposes of Art. 27. A **4.143**
'Revenue-claim' includes taxes, interest, penalties, costs of collection and costs
of conservancy. The Revenue-claim can include any type of taxes,[165] but some
states may prefer to limit the application of Art. 27 to taxes that are covered by
the Convention under Art. 2.[166] If the request concerns a tax that does not
exist in the Requested-CS, the Requested-CS follows the procedure applicable to a claim for a tax of its own which is similar to that of the
Requesting-CS or any other appropriate procedure. Some states may wish to
limit the types of tax to which Art. 27 will apply or to clarify the scope of
application of these provisions by including in the definition a detailed list of
the taxes.[167]

Art. 27 § 3 provides that when a Revenue-claim of a CS is enforceable under **4.144**
the laws of that state and is owed by a person who, at that time, cannot,
under the laws of that state, prevent its collection, that Revenue-claim shall,
at the request of the Competent Authority of that state (the Requesting-
CS), be accepted for purposes of collection by the Competent Authority of

---

163 Commentary to Art. 27 § 8.
164 Commentary to Art. 27 § 9.
165 Commentary to Art. 27 § 26.
166 Commentary to Art. 27 § 11.
167 Commentary to Art. 27 § 12. See: Commentary to Art. 27 § 14. For a judicial application of this indication:
     United Kingdom, Court of Appeal of England and Wales (Civil Division), *HMRC and Anr v. Ben Nevis
     Holdings Ltd.* [2013] EWCA Civ 578, [2013] STC 1579; Canada, Federal Court, *Chua v. Her Majesty the
     Queen*, 6 November 2000.

the other CS (the Requested-CS). That Revenue-claim shall be collected by the Requested-CS in accordance with its laws applicable to the enforcement/ collection of its own taxes as if the Revenue-claim were a Revenue-claim of that Requested-CS. In essence a Revenue-claim 'finally owed' by a person resident in the Requesting-CS must be accepted by the Requested-CS if certain conditions are met, and is then collected by the Requested-CS.

4.145 The Revenue-claim has to be enforceable under the laws of the Requesting-CS and be owed by a person who, at that time, cannot, under the law of that state, prevent its collection. This will be the case where the Requesting-CS has the right, under its domestic laws, to collect the Revenue-claim and the person owing the amount has no administrative or judicial rights to prevent such a collection.[168]

4.146 A Revenue-claim can be collected even though there is still a right to appeal to an administrative body or a court as regards the validity or the amount of the claim. If, however, the domestic laws of the Requested-CS do not allow it to collect its own Revenue-claims when appeals are still pending, then Art. 27 § 3 does not authorize it to do so.[169]

4.147 States may wish to allow collection assistance where a Revenue-claim may be collected in the Requesting-CS notwithstanding the existence of appeal rights even though the Requested-CS's own laws prevent collection in that case can modify the treaty with alternative wording.[170]

4.148 If the requirements of Art. 27 are met, then the Requested-CS has a duty of acceptance of the request made by the Requesting-CS and of pursuing the collection under its domestic laws. Except with respect to time limits and priority (see Art. 27 § 5), the Requested-CS is obliged to collect the Revenue-claim of the Requesting-CS as though it were the Requested-CS's own Revenue-claim even if, at the time, it has no need to undertake collection actions related to that taxpayer for its own purposes.

4.149 Art. 27 § 3 limits the collection assistance to claims with respect to which no further appeal rights exist if, under the Requested-CS's domestic laws,

---

168 Commentary to Art. 27 § 15.
169 Commentary to Art. 27 § 16.
170 Commentary to Art. 27 § 16-1. See: Belgium, Rechtbank van Eerste Aanleg Kortrijk, 1984–10–29, 29 October 1984.

collection of that states own Revenue-claims are not permitted as long as such rights still exist.[171]

Art. 27 § 4 provides that when a Revenue-claim of the Requesting-CS is a **4.150** claim in respect of which that Requesting-CS may, under its laws, take conservancy measures to ensure its collection, that Revenue-claim shall, at the request of the Competent Authority of that Requesting-CS, be accepted for purposes of taking conservancy measures by the Competent Authority of the Requested-CS.

The Requested-CS shall take conservancy measures in respect of that **4.151** Revenue-claim in accordance with its laws as if the Revenue-claim were a Revenue-claim of the Requested-CS even if, at the time when such measures are applied, the Revenue-claim is not enforceable in the Requesting-CS or is owed by a person who has a right to prevent its collection.

Art. 27 § 4 enables the Requesting-CS to request the Requested-CS to take **4.152** measures of conservancy even where it cannot yet ask for assistance in collection, i.e., when the Revenue-claim is not yet enforceable or when the debtor still has the right to prevent its collection. For example, there can be a request for the seizure of assets before final judgment to guarantee that these assets will still be available when collection can eventually take place.[172] States that consider that it is not appropriate to take measures of conservancy in respect of taxes owed to another state may decide not to include Art. 27 § 4 in their treaties or to restrict its scope.[173]

A request for measures of conservancy cannot be made unless the **4.153** Requesting-CS can itself take such measures with respect to the related Revenue-claim (see the Commentary to § 8). In making a request for measures of conservancy the Requesting-CS should indicate what stage in the process of assessment or collection has been reached. The Requested-CS will then have to consider whether in such a case its own laws and administrative practice permit it to take measures of conservancy.[174]

Art. 27 § 5 provides that, notwithstanding Art. 27 §§ 3 and 4, a Revenue- **4.154** claim accepted by the Requested-CS for purposes of Art 27 §§ 3 or 4 shall

---

171 Commentary to Art. 27 § 17. See: Germany, Bundesfinanzhof, VII B 154/07, 27 February 2008; United States, US District Court for the Northern District of Ohio, *Quincy A. Miller v. United States (Internal Revenue Service)*, 11 July.
172 Commentary to Art. 27 § 20.
173 Commentary to Art. 27 § 19.
174 Commentary to Art. 27 § 21.

not, in that Requested-CS, be subject to the time limits or accorded any priority applicable to a Revenue-claim under the laws of that Requested-CS by reason of its nature as such. In addition, a Revenue-claim accepted by the Requested-CS for the purposes of Art. 27 §§ 3 or 4 shall not, in that Requested-CS, have any priority applicable to that Revenue-claim under the laws of the Requesting-CS.

4.155   So according to Art. 27 § 5 the time-limits of the Requested-CS do not apply to a Revenue-claim made by the Requesting-CS.[175] Moreover the rules of the Requested-CS that prioritize its own Revenue-claims over the claims of other creditors do not apply to a Revenue-claim when a request for assistance is activated by the Requesting-CS.[176]

4.156   Thus, as long as a Revenue-claim can still be enforced or collected (Art 27 § 3) or gives rise to conservancy-measures (Art 27 § 4) in the Requesting-CS, no objection based on the time limits or priorities under the laws of the Requested-CS may be made in the Requested-CS.[177] The Commentary, however, notes that Art. 27 § 5 does not prevent the application of general rules concerning time limits or priorities which would apply to all debts (i.e., rules giving priority to a claim by reason of that claim having arisen or having been registered before another one).[178]

4.157   Art. 27 § 6 provides that proceedings with respect to the existence, validity or the amount of a Revenue-claim of a CS shall not be brought before the courts or administrative bodies of the other CS. The main purpose of this rule is to prevent administrative or judicial bodies of the Requested-CS from being asked to decide matters which concern whether an amount is owed under the domestic laws of the Requesting-CS.[179]

4.158   Art. 27 § 7 provides that when a Revenue-claim or a conservancy measure ceases to be enforceable after a request has been made by the Requesting-CS to the Requested-CS, then the Requesting-CS must promptly notify the Requested-CS of this change of situation.[180] Art. 27 § 7 includes two provisions: one for the cessation of Revenue-claims as such (lett. a), and one for the cessation of conservancy measures to ensure collection of Revenue-claims (lett. b).

---

175   Commentary to Art. 27 § 22.
176   Commentary to Art. 27 § 25.
177   Commentary to Art. 27 § 23.
178   Commentary to Art. 27 § 27.
179   Commentary to Art. 27 § 28. See: Italy, Corte Suprema di Cassazione, 760, 17 January 2006.
180   Commentary to Art. 27 § 29.

The Requested-CS can then refuse to provide assistance in the cases referred **4.159** to in Art. 27 § 8.[181]

In particular the Requested-CS can refuse:

1. to carry out administrative measures at variance with the laws and administrative practice of the Requested-CS or of the Requesting-CS;
2. to carry out measures which would be contrary to public policy (order public);
3. to provide assistance if the Requesting-CS has not pursued all reasonable conservancy or collection measures, as the case may be, available under its laws or administrative practice;
4. to provide assistance in those cases where the administrative burden for the Requested-CS is clearly disproportionate to the benefit to be derived by the Requesting-CS.

The fact that Art. 27 does not impose on the Requested-CS administrative **4.160** measures at variance with the laws and administrative practice of that or of the other CS means that if the Requesting-CS has no domestic power to take measures of conservancy, the Requested-CS can decline to take such measures on behalf of the Requesting-CS. Similarly, if the seizure of assets to satisfy a Revenue-claim is not permitted in the Requested-CS, that CS is not obliged to seize assets when providing assistance in collection under Art. 27.[182] Art. 27 does not require the Requested-CS to provide assistance in those cases where the administrative burden for that Requested-CS is clearly disproportionate to the benefit to be derived by the Requesting-CS. This implies for example, that the Requested-CS can refrain from providing assistance if it considers that the taxes with respect to which assistance is requested are imposed contrary to generally accepted taxation principles.[183]

---

181 Commentary to Art. 27 §§ 30–31.
182 Commentary to Art. 27 § 32.
183 Commentary to Art. 27 § 37.

INDEX